MY JOURNEY THROUGH TIME

A SPIRITUAL MEMOIR OF LIFE, DEATH, AND REBIRTH

by

DENA MERRIAM

Distributed by SCB Distributors

FIRST EDITION
ISBN: 1979438250
ISBN 13: 9781979438254

Interior Layout and Design: Vick Singh
Editing by PARVATIMARKUS.COM
Photo of Dena Merriam by David Katzive

"All of what you experience will pass away when you die, Thema, and your life will seem to you then as only a dream. Am I sitting here with you now? Do we exist? At some point our meeting will become just a dream to you, one you may not even remember. But nonetheless it has a reality that will never die. The fact that you and I are here together will always be, because what comes into being can never die, only transform. Our meeting exists outside of time, which continually flows like a river, ever changing, but there are those things that exist beyond time. One day you will know this."

DEDICATION

This book is dedicated to my guru Paramahansa Yogananda and the great gurus of my lineage, through whom all knowledge and spiritual growth has come; to my earthly father, who provided me with much needed support and encouragement; and to the Divine Mother, who sustains all life, guides our journey, and welcomes us home.

Contents

PART IV

EARLY 15TH CENTURY INDIA

PART V

LATE 15TH CENTURY PERSIA

PART VI

16TH CENTURY JAPAN

PART VII

17TH CENTURY INDIA

PART VIII

BETWEEN BIRTHS

Introduction

This is the story of how certain events in my life led to an awakening of memories of previous births, and how those memories provided insight and a deeper understanding of the work I was to do in the world and the complex interplay of *karma*. It is also a testament to the effect of meditation on my life. That is not to say that other meditators have experiences similar to the ones I describe in this book, for each one's path is unique. I marvel at the great diversity of spiritual experiences as each one of us unfolds our individual romance with the Divine.

I began meditating at the young age of 20, when meditation was not common in the United States, and I took very much to heart my guru's instructions to develop a regular and committed meditation practice. Over the years I found an intuitive faculty developing, a way of *knowing* that surpasses the rational, logical mind.

I remember once in those early years being awakened at my house in the middle of the night by a large crash, as if the roof was falling in. I jumped up with a start and went around the house checking for any signs of damage. Everything was fine, but the next morning I heard on the news that a roof had crashed down on a building in a neighboring town. How was I to experience the sound of a roof falling so far away? Similarly, I once had a conversation with a colleague who was describing her work with a prominent man from the museum world, when I suddenly blurted out that he was having an affair. She was startled and, confirming it, asked how I had found out. I had never met this man and knew nothing about him except this one fact that had come into my consciousness. How did I know this?

Most people have had such experiences, but often we pay little mind to how we know certain things. The intuitive faculty is present in everyone, but we are not taught to cultivate it. Consistent, deep meditation can develop this faculty and give us access to a vast store of knowledge that we can't otherwise access.

The process of remembering

The process by which I have come to see and know my previous births has been the same every time, but it is hard to describe. There is always a trigger, an awakening factor—a person, place, or event—that is followed by a magnetic pull inside, a deep interiorization of my consciousness to the extent that I am cut off from the exterior world. In such a state, I hear conversations and see interactions that I normally would not be able to witness. It is as if I am sucked into a storehouse where these visual images are kept, and once they are released I find myself in a movie, completely identified with the personality through whose eyes everything is being revealed. The perspective is deeply personal as I am seeing events and people through the lens of my memory.

I have wondered, at times, if the memories I am accessing are indeed mine, or whether I am drawing from a large collective pool and tapping into another person's memory bank. I have learned to accept them as mine only through my intuitive faculty, which I trust as a guiding force in my life, and by seeing how the thought patterns and themes of the past life are similar to the ones I am now living. I have never taken what I have seen at face value, but have always inquired deeper into the truth of what has been revealed.

My guru was very cautious about delving into the past and thus I have adopted this cautious approach: accept what has been given, which has always been for some teaching, but never press further for that which has not been revealed.

As it has become known among my circle of friends and acquaintances that I have seen such things, many have approached me for insight into their past lives, but in every case I have drawn a blank. It has not been given to me to peer into the privacy of another's past, only my own. That makes perfect sense, for these experiences are not given for any purpose other than to gain greater self-knowledge and understanding of why we are here. They are not to be taken lightly, and they are not for the purpose of satisfying curiosity. There are many fanciful books about reincarnation and it is hard to discern which are based in spiritual truth. It is for this reason that I share my experiences with more than a little trepidation.

Reincarnation

Recent studies conducted by the Pew Research Center show that acceptance of reincarnation has grown tremendously among the American public in the last few years. Once relegated to the belief systems of the Eastern religions, reincarnation is now accepted by many people who belong to the Abrahamic faiths. Similarly, karma has become a widely embraced concept that is becoming part of everyday parlance. Yet, these systems are very complex and difficult to understand.

Even now with the openness to these spiritual concepts, it takes some courage to talk openly about one's memories of past births. Partly this is because it is difficult to distinguish between truth and fantasy, even among those who accept the reality of reincarnation. How do we know that what we are seeing and experiencing is real? This is the case with many spiritual experiences and a challenge faced by spiritual practitioners of all faiths. In the end, it is only we who can determine the reality of our own experiences.

The Abrahamic traditions teach that we have only one life, although the mystics of these traditions (Islamic Sufis, Jewish Kabbalists, and Christian mystics) teach otherwise. The *dharma* traditions, such as Hinduism and Buddhism, teach that we keep reincarnating until we are free from all karmic ties. Both are true.

How can that be?

It is a matter of identity. If you identify with your personality, it is true that this personality will only experience itself once, although it will exist eternally in your memory bank. All the conditions that have made me Dena will only exist this one time. When the body of Dena stops breathing, this personality will be seen as a dream—thought forms stored in the memory bank of the higher "me"—which can be accessed when needed. The learning will be carried over to the next personality formation.

If you identify with the higher Self, the Atman, the part that keeps reincarnating, you know yourself to be continually adopting new personalities in the journey of awakening. So the question of the ages is *Who am I?* Through meditation, the identity shifts from the personality to the higher Self, and therefore I identify with all the personalities I have taken on . . . and with none of them. I go beyond personality, beyond the limitations that life's conditions create for one particular episode in the ongoing journey toward full awakening.

I share with you my own personal journey through time—through life, death, and rebirth—in the hope that it can help you, the reader, to access the elements of your own journey so you find and fulfill the deeper purpose of your present life.

Karma

When we are born, we begin anew, with all possibilities open to us. We come released from the memories of the past, temporarily freed of the hurts and sorrows, the attachments and clinging, the pain of separation. All of these are left behind, the curtain closed. Why do we not remember who we were before? Surely our birth is not the beginning and our death is not the ending. I, too, used to wonder why this forgetting, but my experiences have taught me that there is benefit in putting memories to sleep, clearing the slate so we can make fresh choices. There is no real purpose in prying open a door to our past that is meant to be left shut. Curiosity often leads people to seek to re-open the past, but such curiosity brings no true advancement on the upward path.

There are, however, exceptions to this routine forgetting. There are those memories that filter through, that refuse to be put to rest. Most people have some experience of this, especially in childhood when past inclinations are strongest. In time, whatever is needed to be known will reveal itself. There comes a point in our evolution when we will know all that came before and also see the foundation being laid for what is to come.

So much of life is a playing out of the thoughts, desires, and actions that were initiated in times past: the people we meet, the loves that tug at us, the wealth or poverty that comes, betrayals, broken ties. All of these are the result of thoughts or actions that began long ago, regardless of whether or not we are aware of their origin.

Since I first began my spiritual path in this life, I have been interested in the workings of karma—the universal law that bears the fruit of what we have sown. Karma is action and reaction, the law of gravity applied to thought and deed, the seemingly unbending law of cause and effect. What goes up, comes down; the energies we send out return in some manner at some time. I have wondered how this works and how we can neutralize these karmic returns so that we are not in bondage to the past. But this interest is not what led to the curtain lifting for me.

My current life

I was born with the door to my past only half closed, and from an early age memories haunted me. I remember my birth, coming out into the glaring light and seeing forms in a half-hypnotic state. The first presence that I felt was my father's. It was his arms that cradled me, and there was comfort in that physical closeness that eased the tremendous discomfort in finding myself confined once again to a physical form.

I was born into a secular Jewish family to parents who clung to Jewish culture and identity, more from an historical than spiritual perspective. From childhood, I loved Mother Mary and would pray to her at night. In my early years, I developed a passion for ballet, and as I grew older I would find myself dancing in my dreams, performing way beyond the physical capabilities I had in this life. In elementary school I began to study French and was soon dreaming in French. It became the language of my interior life.

As I grew into my teens, I became an avid reader, falling in love with Russian novels. I was fascinated by 19th century Russia. Then as my political life began to awaken and my father took me to Washington for the marches against the war in Vietnam, and as I participated in the civil rights movement, I became a Marxist.

I went off to college just outside Cambridge, Massachusetts, and within a few weeks met a man, a junior at Harvard University, who would become my husband by the end of my freshman year in college.

My political interests were soon replaced by a driving quest for the spiritual. It was the age of hippies and flower children, and there was a tremendous sense of freedom and discovery. During my second year at college, my husband and I went to hear a talk by a Harvard professor, Richard Alpert, who had just returned from India, where he had been transformed into Baba Ram Dass. Shortly after that talk, a friend of ours handed us a book, *Autobiography of a Yogi* by Paramahansa Yogananda. My husband and I were both hooked from the moment we saw his face on the cover. We shared the book, each reading a chapter at a time. That was the beginning of my spiritual journey this time around. We both recognized Yogananda as our guru. Yogananda had left his physical form in 1952, but he had created an organization to continue his teachings. We applied to the Self-Realization Fellowship to study the meditation techniques and I began what was to become a lifelong practice of meditation.

At first we were saddened that Yogananda was no longer in the body and, at the behest of friends, we went from teacher to teacher. But each time we sat before another master, Yogananda's form came before us and we knew that our relationship was a dictate from the past. In the body or not, Yogananda was the chosen one for us. As a result, we were spared much grief. Many of the teachers who came to the west at that time and in the years to follow did not appear to be of the same stature as my guru. Too many succumbed to the lure of sex and money and to the commercialization of the sacred teachings.

My husband was accepted at medical school in New York, so we moved to the city. Soon after, I had a son and then another. The half-closed curtain was already fluttering open and memories were beginning to stir, but had not yet come awake. When my husband finished medical school and began his academic medical career, we began looking for a house in a community with a good school system. I had money from my parents to buy a house, but every house my husband fell in love with, they vetoed. He wanted an old farmhouse; they wanted a well-kept suburban home for the kids and me. Finally, after much looking, we were shown a beautiful old country concert hall that had been turned into a residence. Its grand living room had a domed ceiling, two stories high. It had been built in the 1920s for concerts, and the main room seated two hundred people for performances. The second floor, built on the periphery of the living room, had been added in the 1950s when it had been converted into a home.

As soon as I saw the house, I knew it was the one. My husband didn't really like it, but my parents approved and so we purchased it. The only condition my mother set was that I never put a picture of my guru over the fireplace in the grand room. I agreed and have abided by her request to this day. However, that did not stop me from turning the grand room into a meditation hall, with photos of my guru and our lineage of masters everywhere else in the room.

My meditation practice was a source of contention between my mother and me. Meditation was not commonly practiced in the U.S. in the early 1970s when I began, and putting up images of gurus was strictly against Jewish law. Yet my guru was such a strong presence for me that I wanted his photo everywhere I set my eyes and so they surrounded me, much to my mother's dismay.

The house had beautiful moldings and other elegant qualities, but oddly enough what struck me most was the black-and-white checkerboard pattern on the second floor landing, at the top of the wide staircase. It was made out of cheap linoleum, not marble, but I would find myself staring at that checkerboard floor for no reason. In Marcel Proust's book, *A la recherche du temps perdu* (*Remembrance of Things Past*), a madeleine is the trigger—a simple cookie had the power to revive the memories of the past. There is often a trigger, something that awakens that which is dormant. For me, the white-and-black checkerboard of the second floor landing was the first awakening factor.

A year after we moved into the house, my marriage began to fall apart. I had been focused on raising my two sons, 8 and 4-½ years old at the time. As my marriage was dissolving, my husband advised me to move back into an apartment in the city, but I was determined to hold onto the house no matter what that entailed. I was surprised at my determination to cling to the house. The very thought of leaving it created great anxiety and pain, and I decided I would hold onto it at all costs.

I went to work for my father as a freelance writer. My father had started a public relations firm in the 1940s after the war, and it had become one of the largest privately held PR firms in the country. I commuted an hour to the city in order to hold onto a house that was way beyond my means to maintain, but that held great personal significance for me.

My life was busy in the years following my divorce—in and out of relationships, raising children, commuting and fulfilling my job responsibilities, meditation, spiritual readings, and listening to tapes by spiritual teachers of my guru's line—and through it all I was growing in understanding. During difficult periods I devoted myself to meditation and clung to my guru. He was my raft, and his presence was enough to keep me going.

I had been taught not to look for the rewards of meditation effort, but to keep on with the practice, knowing that one day there would be a breakthrough and one's whole perception of life would change. My guru used to say that the path to God is not a circus; therefore, don't look for extraordinary experiences, which are not the real measure of spiritual growth. I found this to be true. For me, the benefits of meditation were greater patience and self-containment, less emotionality, more balance, and the cultivation of an interior life that brought with it the recognition that true happiness is not found in the external world. In the process I was becoming a person at peace with myself, more content and, yes, more filled with joy. Meditation was so much a part of my life that I couldn't do without it. During these years as a single working mother, my motto was "keep on keeping on." I was not seeking or expecting any extraordinary experiences.

Then the dreams came and everything changed. Come along with me now to a remembrance of the lives I have recovered, including their significance to the life I lead now.

PART I

EARLY 20ᵀᴴ CENTURY RUSSIA

Just as the embodied soul continuously passes from childhood to youth to old age, similarly, at the time of death, the soul passes into another body. The wise are not deluded by this.

—Bhagavad Gita 2:13

As we live through thousands of dreams in our present life, so is our present life only one of many thousands of such lives which we enter from the other more real life... and then return after death.

Our life is but one of the dreams of that more real life, and so it is endlessly, until the very last one, the very real life of God.

—Count Leo Tolstoy

Chapter 1

A few years after I moved into my house and was separated from my husband, I began to dream of a very grand house. There are different types of dreams. Most are of a subconscious nature, a melding of thoughts and fears, mixing together people and events from our everyday lives, which often reveal feelings that we push beneath the surface of our consciousness. Some dreams are of a symbolic nature and convey a message. They tell us something about ourselves and can provide guidance, even be an indication of some future event. And then there are those dreams that are really visions. They are of a superconscious nature, lifting us to a higher place where we can see reality more clearly. Over the years I had many such dreams or visions where my guru appeared to me and transmitted an important message or teaching.

For over ten years, the dreams of this grand house continued. They were always of the same place, and they left behind a trail of sadness and disquietude when I awoke, as well as a sense of longing. Longing for what, I couldn't say. I only knew that the house was very familiar and upon waking I felt a sense of loss. I would say to myself, "I was there again, there in that house." I never told anybody. What could I say? I go to a certain house at night in my dreams? What would that mean to anyone? So I kept these dreams to myself.

Sometimes, in the dream, I would be walking through rooms that were empty of people. The furniture would be covered as if we were closing up the house. The house was so large I would get lost walking through the rooms. I could see the circular driveway where carriages were parked, and sometimes old-fashioned cars. It was a white house built of wood, surrounded by lots of pine trees, with no other house in sight. When I tried to understand where this was, I would find myself at a dead end. I could go no further.

During those years life was full of distractions—children growing up, the challenges of divorce and single parenthood, relationships found and lost, the ups and downs of work, the struggle to maintain a large house on a modest income. I took great comfort and a sense of security in my suburban house with its expansive yard and gardens. In the years after my divorce I struggled to hold onto it, barely making ends meet at the end of each month. This kept me fully engaged, and I would put aside the dream until the next time it arose. The more I dreamt of the other house, the more I clung to the one in which I now lived.

I was working as a writer, but my father knew that I needed more money and so he encouraged me to get involved in the management of the business, along with my two sisters and brother, who were all working there. I had little interest in the business side of the company. After my divorce, I had gotten a Master's Degree in sacred literature at Columbia University and embarked on the study of comparative religion, drawn to finding the unity that underlies all the religious traditions. I loved the study, but I could not support my children that way. My father knew my interest was in spiritual matters, but he also had a very practical side.

One day my father called me to his office. "I want you to join the company's Executive Committee," he said.

Half-heartedly I asked, "What does the Executive Committee involve? The boys still need me at home." My sons were in their early and mid-teens, and I was still working part-time.

"You should be involved in the management of the company finances. The writing work you are doing is good. Keep doing that. But gradually you need to do more if you are to make more money."

"You know I am not very good with finance. That has never been my interest."

"You have very good instincts though," he insisted in a firm voice. I knew not to contradict my father when he took that tone.

My father and I had a very special tie. He had wanted to be an artist when he was young, and then he dreamed of becoming a writer, but his wife, my mother, vetoed both options and sent him into the business world. So he started a business that was a bridge to the arts. He was one of the early people to see the role of corporate support for the arts. Over time he began to enjoy it, and the company enabled him to stay involved in the arts. Later he built a name for himself as a photographer of sculpture and that became his passion. So he sympathized greatly with my personal interest in spiritual matters, which was my version of his artistic interest, and he supported me in every way he could.

"I've hired a consultant who can work with you on management issues. He is joining the Executive Committee as well. I've known Jay for some time. He sits on many boards and is extremely bright. You will find him interesting. I want you to spend time with him. He will guide you."

I smiled. I knew that this consultant would also be a counsel for him. He said, "He'll be at the next Executive Committee meeting in two weeks."

It was the hour just before dawn. I was not sleeping or dreaming, and yet I wasn't awake. The quality of the light and the full awareness of my mind let me know I was experiencing a vision. I saw a child, not more than four years old, with blond curly locks flowing down her back. She was clothed in a dress that fell halfway between her knees and her ankles, not fully covering the lace-up boots on her feet. It looked like a dress from the early years of the 20th century. I heard a voice say, "You have wanted to know who you were in your previous birth. This is you." The voice was without gender and came from deep inside me. I asked, "Where is it?" and in response I heard the word, "Russia."

I knocked on the office door. A strong, low voice called, "Come in." I hesitated. Why did my heart flutter? Again I heard, "Come in." Calming my heart, I opened the door and saw him sitting behind the desk, phone in hand.

"Denashka," Jay greeted me with a warm smile. "Sit down. I'll be off in a few minutes." He continued his phone conversation . . . in Russian. We had met a few hours earlier at the Executive Committee meeting, but I had not been mentally present. My mind was absorbed in the vision I had experienced a week earlier. Since that time, I could think of nothing else. Jay saw that I was distracted. I assumed that my nervousness was due to the fact that I was struggling to hide my mental absence. How could I focus on anything else, let alone finance! I sat patiently in a chair opposite his desk as he continued his phone call.

How odd, I thought, that he addressed me with an affectionate Russian ending to my name, and how strange that he was speaking on the phone in Russian. After a few minutes, he ended his call and greeted me again.

"Was that Russian you were speaking?" I asked.

He nodded and changed the subject. "Your father wants me to work with you on management issues. "

"I know." I tried to muster up some interest.

"Did you go over the P&L statements that were distributed?"

I was at a loss. I had just put the papers inside a folder without looking at them. "I haven't had a chance yet," I replied.

He must have suspected that I was not familiar with these spreadsheets, so he clarified: "You need to review the profit-and-loss statements for each group to see where the losses are. We are going to have to make some cuts. Come, let's go over them." He took out the spreadsheets and led me through the statements.

My mind was racing. Why did he address me as he did? I waited until he was finished before asking, "How is it that you speak Russian?"

He said, "I have business there." He abruptly packed up his briefcase and added, "I'll be in the office again at the end of the week. Let's get together then."

Jay was a very bright African-American businessman about my age who had formed a special relationship with my father. Just as I had left Judaism for Hinduism, he had come from a Christian background yet felt most keenly drawn to Judaism. A rather large man, tall and broad, he had dark penetrating eyes and a deep voice. His face was round and full, and there was always a cheerful twinkle in his eyes. He was an engaging man, but there was something mysterious about him. One would never know exactly when he would show up or where to find him. It was also difficult to find out what his business was, except that he was a consultant. My father had great confidence in his intellectual and management abilities. For me, there was something else that I couldn't put my finger on. I was attracted to him, no doubt, but it was a subtle attraction, a familiarity that was in odd contrast to the emotional distance he kept.

One day not long after Jay arrived, our relationship took a turn. His door was the only one in the office that was always kept closed, whether he was in there or not. I knocked and entered after hearing his low "come in." He greeted me with "Denashka," as he always did, but then he began to speak to me fully in Russian. I looked at him blankly, not understanding a word, yet something resonated deep inside.

My vision of myself as a small child in Russia had not awakened any memories of that time. Intuitively I knew what I had seen was true.

Without a doubt I knew myself to be that child, but I knew no more of the story. I had a natural curiosity, but I had never really been obsessed about knowing the details. I was too busy living this life. But from the moment Jay started speaking to me in Russian, something shifted. It didn't matter that I didn't understand him. What mattered was that he was speaking to me in Russian as if I should understand.

It is said that every act and every thought that has ever emerged from any being is recorded and stored in the ethers, in what is often referred to as the Akashic Records. Nothing is lost or gone, only hidden from sight. Masters are able to access these records. We, too, have that ability as we develop spiritually.

That night I was driving back home from my office in the city, about halfway through the one-hour trip. The sound of Jay speaking to me in Russian was going through my mind. Although I didn't understand the words, I was reflecting on the feelings the sounds had evoked—feelings of sadness, which I didn't understand but couldn't shake. Locked in this sadness and confused by it, I suddenly saw her. She arose in my mind's eye and I saw her as clearly as if she were standing before me in physical form. Her gentle violet eyes were filled with love, the darkness of her hair a vivid contrast to her pale white skin. Her hair was pulled up and wrapped around the back of her head with bits of wave falling to the side. Her waist was very slender. Papa took great pride in Mama's slender waist, even after bearing three children. She was dressed according to the fashion of the early 1900s. She was beautiful and, at the sight of her, the bond between us re-ignited. In that moment, all the pain of separation burst forth and I couldn't contain myself. Tears came pouring out. I could barely see the road ahead. I steered the car off the road onto an emergency lane. As the tears flew from my eyes, I lay my head on the steering wheel and I was back in Russia.

"Mama," I cried. "Mama!" I was a child crying for my lost mother. "*Je t'aime, je t'aime,*" I cried out over and over, speaking to her spontaneously in French. She smiled and called, "*Sonya, ma cherie.* "When my tears subsided, I asked "*Ou est tu?*" But she just smiled and faded away.

I remained thus for about thirty minutes and then continued the drive home. My mother was gone again, but I had found her. She had come to me and somehow I knew I would not lose her again.

When I reached home, my two teenage children were waiting for dinner. My mind was in another world, but I had to care for this one.

They were eager to talk about the day at school, but I couldn't get the image of my Russian mother out of my mind. This was the beginning of learning to be simultaneously in two worlds, two time periods. I made dinner and spoke to my children about the day's happenings, while at the same time I was speaking to my mother in some other part of the universe. I had no idea where she was now, but there was not a shadow of a doubt that this was the Russian mother I had once loved so much. And there was no doubt that we had found each other; she could feel my love and know the thoughts I directed towards her, and I could feel the boundless love she was sending me. I heard her call my name throughout the next days. "Sonya, Sonya." And the memories began to return.

Over weeks and months the pieces came together. Often in meditation I would witness scenes and hear bits of conversations as if I were watching a film, but these experiences could come at any time— during work, in a meeting, making dinner for my children, in the bath, while driving. Day after day scenes from my past birth unfolded.

* * *

"Sonya, hurry, change for dinner. Papa will be here soon." My mother seemed particularly anxious this day. I had been late returning from ballet; we had been rehearsing for a performance, and it was the first time I was to perform in public. I was both thrilled and nervous. "Hurry, hurry," mama said, practically pushing me up the stairs. "I don't want papa to see you like this."

I quickly changed into a fine dress. Papa was very formal and expected all three of us children to be dressed properly for dinner. I felt the tension as soon as Papa arrived. His sternness was not unusual, but tonight he seemed particularly brusque and sharp with mama. As we sat around the dinner table he asked each of us to say something about our day. We knew we only had time for a few sentences. I couldn't contain myself and mentioned the rehearsal, although I should have known better. Papa didn't approve of my dancing. As soon as the words came out of my mouth, I regretted them. He looked sternly at mama.

"Marie, you know she is not to be in any public performance. I have made myself clear on this matter. Why do you encourage her?"

"We will discuss this later," she replied quietly, as she continued to eat her dinner.

"There is nothing to discuss," he said firmly. "You have allowed this to go too far. I told you long ago that you are permitting her to foster false hopes." He turned to me. "Sonya, dancing in public is not befitting a young woman of your station. I have told you this repeatedly. No more of this dancing. You are getting too old now and must put your mind elsewhere."

"But dear, she is not even twelve. Let her have the rest of her childhood," exclaimed Mama in my defense.

"Papa," I blurted out. "You and Mama love ballet. You are a patron . . ." My voice choked.

"To be a patron is one thing. You may also be a patron when you get older. But no daughter of mine will be seen on stage. This is final. I see that I must speak to the director of the school myself since your mother seems unwilling to do so."

Without asking to be excused, I got up from the table and ran from the room. How could he do this to me? I knew my ballet master would have to abide by Papa's wishes, as he was one of the main patrons of the ballet, but how humiliating for me.

"Sonya, come back here. You have not been excused," he called sternly. But I was already up the stairs.

"Excuse me, but I can't bear to see her so upset," my mother said as she rose to come after me.

"Marie, you coddle her. It is high time she realize what is expected of her in life."

"She is still a child."

Once in my room, I slammed the door and sank to the floor. I couldn't imagine how I could live without dancing. When I was dancing, the world faded away. Everything disappeared as I melted into the music. I became the notes as they pulsated through my body. It was the music, not I, that lifted my limbs. I had no control whatsoever. I surrendered to the music and my body moved as lightly as a wisp of a cloud. Dancing was not a thing I chose to do. It was something I was compelled to do and my greatest joy. It was the only time I felt free. How could he take that from me? I wouldn't let him. I would run away!

My mother entered and quietly took me in her arms. "Don't fret, *ma cherie*," she said gently in her melodic voice. "He is burdened right now with many concerns. We will find a way. I promise you."

"But how?" I sobbed. "He won't let me go to ballet class anymore."

"Then I will get a dance tutor for you until you are older and can assert yourself. I won't let him take this away from you. You must trust me."

My mother knew that I was talented and had a chance to join the Mariinsky Theater. She knew it was what mattered most to me, but it would take long hours of practice. It would have to come before all else. Papa had consistently fought this, but something had pushed him over the edge. Perhaps it was the realization that I could perform on stage that made him decide to intervene and cut short my dreams of dancing.

My earliest memories were of tension between my parents. My father was an aristocrat. A relative to the tsar through his mother's lineage, he worked in the finance ministry of the government. Cold and distant, he was mostly concerned with appearances. My mother was from a wealthy middle-class French family. They had met while Papa had been on assignment in Paris and he had fallen in love with her great beauty. His mother strongly disapproved of their marriage, but he defied her, the only time he ever did. She never quite got over it. My grandmother had great ambitions and wanted her son to marry up, not down. Over time the differences between my parents became more apparent, even to us children. I remember being constantly surprised at my mother's faithful love and acquiescence to my father. She had left her home and country for him, and even though she never felt fully at ease in Russia and was never fully accepted by his family, she never mentioned this. But we knew and understood the unspoken fact of our family. It was most apparent during our weekly visits to Grandmama, Papa's mother, on Sundays for afternoon tea. We kept up this family ritual as long as she was alive, whether Papa was with us or away traveling.

Grandmama inspired fear. She rarely smiled and always wore a stern expression, giving the impression that she disapproved of something you said or did. I never heard her speak a kind word to Mama. To the contrary, she was always critical of Mama for failing to dress us properly, or failing to teach us the proper thing to say when greeting one of her friends, or some other custom. Mama took her criticism gracefully, calmly acquiescing with a nod or apology.

My memory of Grandmama is of her wearing a black lace dress that trailed along the floor, with a high collar that covered her fragile neck. Her grey hair was tied up tightly on top of her head. She was very thin, with prominent facial lines. She was always decked out in heavy jewels that were the pride of her family. In her living room, where we had our tea, we sat before a large painting of Catherine the Great, one of her ancestors, as she never failed to remind us. She had become very bitter after losing her husband early in life. Papa on occasion alluded to her family struggles over property and position, so he was quite sympathetic to her and made many excuses for her cold demeanor.

I had no love for Grandmama, but I respected her and sat as still as could be when in her company. Anna, my younger sister by two years, was fidgety by nature but managed to contain herself. Andrei, younger by six years, had the most difficulty sitting still, and this caused Grandmama's repeated criticism of Mama. Papa would often intervene and ask Mama to take Andrei into another room so he could have a quiet conversation with his mother. How Anna and I would envy Andrei's chance to escape the rigidity of those Sunday teas! All of us, except Papa, sighed in relief when it was time to depart. Once back in our carriage, the knot in my stomach would begin to unwind.

Later, I realized that the tension surrounding those visits was tied to Grandmama's mistreatment of Mama. I could not defend poor Mama, but I could not bear to see her chastised in front of us all, as if we would love her any less. We dared not think what would happen if we got on the bad side of Grandmama! She controlled much of the family wealth and had many powerful connections. This, Mama once told me, was why Papa was so attentive to her. As a child I paid no mind to the many intrigues that took place within the extended family, but I was aware that there were powerful struggles and enmities.

Mama's family was simpler, perhaps because they were far away and we hardly saw them. I knew little of Mama's parents as she rarely spoke of them. She seemed most fond of her maternal grandmother and told stories that she had heard from her, often with a sigh of sadness. But when mama's mother died, she took up an interest in the occult and began to attend séances. That became my introduction to spiritual life. I remember going to a séance with my mother when I was around eight or nine years old. My mother donned a thick veil so as not to be recognized. The room was crowded with people when we entered. We stood in the rear of the room and waited for everyone to leave before my mother approached the woman leading the séance. When we were alone with her, Mama lifted her veil and introduced herself. She asked that this visit be kept confidential. The medium nodded, knowing how unwise it would be for rumors to spread. Mama said she wanted to contact her mother.

The process started. A spirit came, but it wasn't my grandmother. After some time another spirit came. Mama seemed to be deeply moved. Her eyes were tearing. She took out her handkerchief and dabbed the corners of her eyes. I didn't follow what was being said. I was too busy looking around at all the strange things in the room: crystal balls, strange drawings of beings that looked like angels, and many books. The books intrigued me, but I dared not leave Mama's side. She was engrossed in conversation with the spirit who had come. After it was over and we were on our way home, I asked her if it really had been her mother.

"I believe so," she said. "I do believe in this, *ma cherie*, but we mustn't say anything to Papa. You know that." I nodded, knowing only too well the things that had to be kept from him.

Mama came from a Catholic family, but she had accepted the Russian Orthodox religion when she married my father. Religion was not important to my father, but he always followed what was expected, especially during the holidays. Mama had a deeply religious, or I should say spiritual side. She loved Mother Mary. I remember her taking me into a Catholic Church, heavily veiled, and sitting in front of a statue of Mary. During my childhood I saw Mama engage in other questionable practices to help her make contact with the spirit world. She dared not confide in anyone except me, lest word get back to Papa, so I learned early on to accept the existence of a spiritual but very private world.

After the explosion with Papa over my dancing, I kept a greater distance from him. I was not permitted to attend the Mariinsky School any longer, and I could not participate in the public performance for which I had been rehearsing. Heartbroken, I couldn't forgive him, despite his many attempts to reach out to me. Finally, Mama reached a compromise with him. She was allowed to employ a dance tutor for me if I did well in all my other subjects. She convinced him that dancing was more for my personal well-being, for building confidence, than for any professional training. He accepted this, but reminded me quite often that I had no future in ballet. When I quietly protested to Mama, she would wisely advise: "Accept this for now. None of us know what the future holds. At least he allows you to continue training. When you are older, it will be easier to exert your will." I followed her advice and kept quiet, learning to be grateful for the small battles she won for me.

It was summer and we were preparing to leave for our *dacha*, our house in the country. Summers were the happiest times as there was much more freedom in the country. Papa would come only on the weekends and so there was less formality in the house. In my early childhood, we used to take a carriage to the country. Even after Papa had gotten a motorcar, we continued to use carriages in the country, as it took Mama some coaxing to get over her distrust of the new vehicles.

The large white wooden house came into view. As a child it seemed enormous. I could hardly find my way from one end to the other. As I grew older, it no longer seemed as expansive, but it was still a large house, with many sitting rooms and more bedrooms than we had use for. The entryway was large, with a semi-circular staircase on one side. At the top landing was a black-and-white checkerboard marble hallway. When I was younger, my sister Anna and I used to hop from one color stone to the next, trying to see who could make it all the way down the long hall without touching the opposite color. I was too old for this game now, but as soon as we arrived Anna and Andrei raced up the stairs to begin the stepping race.

"There is a surprise for you, Sonya," my mother whispered quietly to me. "In the yellow parlor at the far end of the hall." Her whole face lit up with her smile. I hurried to see what was awaiting me in the parlor. As I got close, I heard music. My heart leapt, still wondering what it could be. Opening the door, I gasped in joy. Mama had turned the parlor into a dance studio, with a new floor, a full-length ballet barre, and my ballet master and the pianist were there!

Mama was close behind me. "But Papa . . ." I asked. "What will he say?"

"He won't be here much this summer, and he rarely comes to this part of the house. We need not rush to tell him," she looked at me tenderly.

"Oh, Mama," I hugged her tightly. She was a master at trying to fulfill my every desire. The only sadness I had in leaving St. Petersburg was leaving behind my dancing for the summer. Now that would not be necessary. I realized what a brave step Mama had taken in defying Papa's wishes, and I loved her more dearly for it. Once he found out, she would be severely scolded for sure, but perhaps we could get through the summer without him knowing.

"Now you can rehearse to your heart's content, *ma cherie*," she said as she caressed my hair. And that is exactly what I did.

Mama had a Jewish tailor. She was very loyal to Joseph, despite Papa's objections. Mama defended him saying he was one of the best tailors in the city. Mama had a cousin in Paris who would send her drawings of the latest fashions, before they even arrived in St. Petersburg. Mama would send for fabrics from France and Italy and have Joseph make her dresses to match the drawings. She was among the most fashionably-dressed women in the city. Papa was proud of this, although he attributed it more to Mama's creativity than to Joseph's talent.

One day Joseph arrived for a final fitting of a new dress he was making for Mama. It was green velvet and of intricate design, with many folds, bows, and bits of lace tucked into the fabric at various places. Mama looked beautiful. I sat with them in Mama's sitting room and watched as he pulled and tucked the dress around her slender waist. Suddenly Mama stopped him.

"Something is not right with you today, Joseph. What is it? You have hardly spoken since you arrived."

"Nothing, Madam," he replied as he reached down for more pins.

"No, Joseph, I see it in your face. Tell me." Mama pulled away so that he could not continue with his work.

He was quiet for a few minutes. Mama added, "It is one of your children, isn't it?"

"How did you know?" He looked up in surprise. Mama was a bit clairvoyant and often surprised people with her surmises. "It is my youngest, Sarah. She has taken ill and none of the medicines we have applied seem to be working."

"Have you called a physician?" Joseph shook his head. "Go home now, Joseph," Mama said. "I will change and come immediately with my physician. My intuition tells me this could be serious. Do not delay. I will follow." Joseph left and Mama changed into her street clothes. I stayed with her, overcome with curiosity.

"Mama, how old is Sarah?

"About Anna's age, I think. She has always been frail since birth."

"Will she die?" I asked meekly.

"My God, I hope not! Joseph is very attached to her."

"I want to go with you," I said. I had never been to Joseph's house and didn't know why I was asking.

"No, *ma cherie*. This is not for you. Papa would be very angry," she looked at my pleading eyes.

"But I really want to go," I insisted. I could see her battling different emotions— knowledge of Papa's response and the desire to appease me.

After a few minutes, she said, "Oh, alright. You may come but you must be quiet about this. Hurry and get ready." I ran to my room and looked around. What could I bring her? I grabbed a doll that Mama had brought me many years earlier from Paris. I had outgrown any interest in dolls long ago, but kept this one because it was from Paris.

Mama had sent for her private physician, who arrived as we were ready to leave. We drove in silence through the streets of St. Petersburg, leaving behind my neighborhood. As we entered Joseph's neighborhood, Mama took my hand and said, "It is good for you to see this, *ma cherie*. You have never been to this side of the city before. Don't be afraid. The people here are good people, just like us. There is nothing to be afraid of."

It wasn't that I was afraid. It was just that I had never seen such run-down houses and people dressed so shabbily, and young children playing in the streets without any grownups around. We never left our home unaccompanied. How strange to see children in the streets alone. I didn't ask any questions; I just stared.

The carriage stopped. "We are here," Mama said, as she and her physician stepped down. She saw my hesitation and said, "You may stay in the carriage and wait if you prefer." I shook my head and stepped down also, trailing close behind her.

When we entered the house, Mama's physician indicated that the two of us were to wait in the kitchen while he examined the child. Joseph took him into Sarah's room while Mama and I sat with Joseph's wife and their other children. She was preparing the evening meal and three of her daughters were helping. The kitchen seemed quite in turmoil. Pots for cooking were spread throughout the kitchen, and everyone was busy doing some chore. There was no place to sit so Mama and I waited by the door until one the boys brought us two chairs. I was amazed to see how everyone was working together without complaining. Mama seemed not to notice. She had brought some cakes for the family and handed them to Joseph's wife, who thanked her profusely. Mama tried unsuccessfully to make conversation, but Joseph's wife only blushed and curtseyed. It was very awkward. I kept my eyes on the floor so as not to notice the girls peeking up from their work to stare at me.

They seemed a happy family, so different from the atmosphere of our home. When we entered everyone had been chatting with such informality, but as we sat there and waited, their voices quieted to a whisper. I watched as the boys set the table. There seemed to be no servants in the house. *They eat in the kitchen*, I thought to myself in amazement. Ironically, although the family seemed to have so little, I almost envied the intimacy of their family life.

The physician finally emerged with Joseph. Mama went over and spoke with them. I couldn't hear exactly what they were saying, but it was something to do with the hospital and cost. Finally it was time to leave. When we got outside to the carriage, I realized I had not given my doll to Sarah and so ran back to the house. Joseph was still at the door.

"Can you give this to Sarah?" I asked meekly, handing him the doll.

"Thank you, Sonya. That is very kind. Sarah will appreciate this beautiful doll."

I ran back to the carriage. Mama and the physician spoke in hushed tones on the way home. My mind was elsewhere so I didn't pay much mind. I was thinking about Joseph's family and what it must be like to live in such simple surroundings. But when I heard them mention hospital, my ears perked up. I heard Mama say she would bear the cost and the physician responded, "You are very generous and I am not at all surprised by your offer." Mama was anxious, I could tell, and I dared not ask what would happen to poor little Sarah.

We were late for dinner and Papa was not pleased. He asked Mama where we had been. Mama just replied that we had been to see the tailor Joseph without saying anything about the sick child. He became very irritable. "You took Sonya there?" he asked in disbelief. "How could you have taken her to that neighborhood? It was irresponsible of you to put her in such danger."

Mama didn't answer. After dinner, Papa and Mama withdrew to the drawing room and I sat outside the door to listen. I heard Papa raise his voice. Mama quietly held her own. Papa said something in a low tone, which I couldn't hear, and Mama chastised him in a stern voice and called him anti-Semitic. Then she began to cry. After that Papa's tone became gentler. It was rare for Mama to cry. I didn't know whether to stay on my perch by the door or to leave. A few minutes later, I heard the doorknob turn and I ran upstairs to my room.

That night I lay awake thinking about what I had seen and heard that day. It was not the first time Mama had accused Papa of being anti-Semitic. She had explained to me what the word meant. She said Papa didn't like the Jewish people, but she explained that was because he didn't know any. Her maternal grandmother had been Jewish, she told me, and so she felt differently. She had loved this grandmother almost as much as she loved her mother. When I asked her if Papa knew about her grandmother, she looked away and shook her head. Then I understood that was another one of Mama's secrets that she shared only with me. It was a great responsibility for a young child to be the holder of her mother's secrets.

Sarah died a few weeks later. I remember seeing Mama dressed in black, heavily veiled, preparing to go to the funeral.

"I want to go with you," I said.

"You know Papa will be furious," she replied.

"I don't care." By this time my Grandmama had died and there had been a very solemn funeral held in one of the large Orthodox churches, with many members of the extended family attending. I felt very badly that Sarah had died and wanted to show that I cared.

"Well, her sisters and brothers will be glad to see you," Mama said, relenting. "But you must wear a veil and say nothing of this, even to Anna and Andrei. Can you keep it quiet?" I nodded.

The funeral was a very simple affair, held in a Jewish cemetery, with only the family around and a few of their neighbors. It was the first time I attended any Jewish ceremony and I liked the simplicity, the informality of it. We didn't stay long, but in the short time that we were there I saw Mama pray. Later I asked her about it.

"I was praying to Mother Mary that she receive little Sarah."

"But she is Jewish," I said in amazement.

Mama laughed and patted my head. "*Ma cherie*, the Mother receives us all, Christian or not. And she doesn't care where we pray—in a simple Jewish graveyard or a grand Orthodox church. It is the heart that matters, not the place."

Chapter 2

I t was the spring of 1917. There were disturbances in the city, so Papa sent us all to the countryside early this year. He didn't come. I didn't understand or care much about political matters, but I knew that something was amiss. Papa was not himself; he had been very distracted throughout the winter. Some days he barely paid any attention to our childish misbehaving, but at other times he would lash out over nothing. We didn't know quite what to expect, so we tiptoed around the house, trying not to be noticed by him. As the season wore on, his condition grew worse. He hardly went to the Ministry anymore and would sit around the house, trying to look busy.

When I asked Mama what was wrong, she replied that he was worried about the political and financial situation of the country, but that everything would be fine as soon as the war was over. But the war dragged on. The Germans were invincible, or so it seemed. But that was far away and our lives continued as before, with some shortage of goods but no real hardship, at least for us. For others, it was different. When we were out, we often encountered street protests and had to change our route. Driving in a motorcar became risky.

One evening, an angry mob surrounded our motorcar. I had been out with Mama and Andrei. Papa had instructed us always to be home before dark, but Mama had errands to do and it grew late. The people surrounding our car were holding signs and shouting. Andrei became very frightened and began to cry. Mama held him close, remaining calm, and instructed the driver to drive slowly so as not to hurt anyone. As the crowd pressed against our motorcar and Andrei's cries grew louder, I saw Mama close her eyes. I could see through the evening shadows that she was praying. Holding tight to Mama's hand, I stared at the scene around me. As darkness fell, I also grew scared, but my fear was tinged with sadness. Why were they so angry? They didn't know us, or did they?

Did our motorcar give us away? What was happening to my beautiful city, its once mellow light overcast by threatening clouds? Once everyone seemed to have their place, busy with their own lives, but now everything seemed mixed up. It was all so confusing. Was it the war that created this tension, a war that nobody wanted as Mama often said, or was there a deeper cause?

Mama had little respect for the Tsar and his German wife. Increasingly I heard her telling Papa that they would bring us to the brink of disaster. Papa had no response. Earlier he would have objected and defended them, but no more. Words seemed to have abandoned him and his face wore the look of defeat.

I was fourteen, too young to understand what it meant when the structure of a society fell apart, but old enough to feel the anxiety and pain of dissolution. We made it home safely that night, but the next day Papa sent us to the countryside. Our tutors came with us so our studies would not be interrupted. Papa insisted on staying home, in case he was needed at the Ministry. As we left, I could see the worried look on Mama's face.

"I will be fine, Marie. You take care of the children," Papa said in a subdued voice. For the first time I felt very sorry to leave Papa alone. In the past we had often gone ahead to the country, but now things were different. I had been estranged from Papa these last few years, ever since he made such a fuss over my dancing, but that all seemed unimportant now. I knew we had to support him and I reached out to hug him. He held me tightly and I could feel the tension in his body.

"Papa, when will you come?"

"Soon," he said. "I hope very soon."

Those last few months at our country house were not very joyous ones. Mama did her best to be cheerful and to keep us busy, but there was a tension in the air that followed us even to the beautiful countryside. Papa came every now and then to visit, but his condition seemed to grow worse and Mama worried about his health.

One day Papa showed up at our country home unexpectedly. I was practicing with my ballet master in the studio Mama had built for me. I had finished a difficult series of steps when I heard loud clapping. I looked up and saw Papa standing at the door, the first time he had actually entered the studio. My mouth dropped open. I didn't know what to expect. Would he chastise me or, worse, scold Mama? But instead he hugged me.

"Look at what your mother has done for you. This is a wonderful studio, better even than the Mariinsky. I am so glad. And your dancing is ... I am so proud of you ..." His voice faltered. I looked at him in surprise, wondering if his mental condition had grown worse. Had he forgotten how much he had protested my dancing? And was he not angry that Mama had created this professional studio for me? He seemed no longer to care.

Later I told Mama what he had said. She smiled and replied, "He has other things on his mind these days. Perhaps now he can put this into perspective. Considering all the troubles in the country, he should not be worrying about your dancing."

"I suppose that is good," I said. Or maybe not, I thought. Perhaps it is a sign of how bad things are becoming.

Papa tried to be cheerful during that visit, but he couldn't fool us. The night before he was to leave, he told Mama over dinner that she should begin to pack up the country house. "But the summer is not over," Mama replied in surprise.

Papa was silent for a few minutes, and then said in a quiet voice, "I have been advised that we should leave Russia, and time is of the essence now."

Mama looked shaken. "Leave Russia?" she asked in a trembling voice. "Where will we go?"

"I am making plans," he replied quietly.

"Have things gotten so bad?" she asked, her eyes tearing. He nodded. "When do we have to leave?"

"It's a matter of weeks, maybe days. The sooner you come back to St. Petersburg, the better. We will decide after that."

Neither Andrei nor Anna nor I said a word. We sat looking at our parents as they decided our fate. I tried to finish my dinner, but had lost my appetite. I saw that Anna and Andrei were also uninterested in the food before us. We knew this was a serious conversation, and all three of us knew not to speak or to trouble our parents in any way.

Mama said, "I will need three days to get the house ready, at least three days."

Papa nodded. "If you can be ready that quickly, then I will wait and not return to the city tomorrow."

"I would prefer that you stay here with us," said Mama gently, putting her hand on top of his. There was a sad look in her eyes. "There is so much to do to pack up the house and say goodbye; it won't be easy. We have to provide for all the staff. What will we say?"

"Nothing need be said. They will understand. Everyone knows what is coming. The political situation will resolve itself and perhaps in a year we will be back."

"A year," Mama said quietly. "That is a long time to be away."

Everything seemed to end that night. Our tutors were sent back to the city the next day. Mama was busy packing up clothes, covering the furniture, and putting away valuables to close up the house. Anna and Andrei didn't seem to understand the full import of what was happening and so they spent much of the next few days in one game or another. But I understood that we were leaving and there was great uncertainty as to when we would return. I found myself walking through the house from one end to the other, as if to implant in my memory every inch of the place that I considered to be my dearest home, a place where my happiest childhood days had been spent, the house that had given me so much freedom, where I could escape into my world of music.

Papa sat in the library those days and waited, hardly speaking. If one asked him a question, he would answer and then fall silent. Most of the responsibility fell on Mama, as she went through his files and papers, destroying some things, packing others.

Then there were their quiet conversations in the evenings as they discussed the future, the timetable, and where we would go. I could not hear what they were saying, but I could see Papa drifting further and further away from us and Mama becoming more and more attentive to him; she took on her shoulders the burden of what was happening to our family. It seemed that she had to make the decisions now and there was a newfound resolve in her manner.

I cannot describe those last hours at the house, or the moment when I had to say a final goodbye. It was as much the uncertainty as the separation that tore at my heart. I sat that last morning in my ballet studio, not rehearsing, just saying goodbye to it. I did not know what the future held for me. In the past, dancing had been my refuge, soothing away all the discomfort I found in my family surroundings, enabling me to create my own world of beauty, ease, and freedom. But that world was retreating. There was an anxiety and tension in the house far beyond anything we had experienced before, and even dancing could not help me escape.

Papa's frailty put us all on edge. We were used to relying on him, the rock of the family, for everything. Although a rigid and distant figure, there was comfort in his certainty of belief, in his sticking to tradition and the boundaries imposed by society. Anna and I may have resented this, but our rebellion against him and all he represented did not detract from our unacknowledged recognition of the security he provided. This became all the more apparent now. In the confusion of those last days, I looked sorrowfully at the sad figure my father had become and all my anger toward him fled. I saw how much he had given us. It was only then that I was able to find my love for him.

On that last day at the house, all was set, the motorcars packed, the family waiting by the cars, but I could not stop myself from running back for one last goodbye.

"Sonya," my mother called in a sterner voice than was her custom as she held my arm to restrain me.

"Let her go," said my father in his weakened voice. "She loves this house more than any of us. Let her say goodbye."

Freeing myself from my mother's grip, I raced into the house, up the stairs and into my ballet studio. There I sank to the floor and let the tears flow. I didn't know why I was crying, except I had a terrible feeling in the pit of my stomach. Suddenly I felt my father's arms around me. He didn't say a word as he held me to his chest and patted my head. We sat there for quite some time and, when my sobs subsided, he lifted me to my feet and led me back down the stairs to the waiting motorcar.

As soon as we were back in St. Petersburg, we began preparing for our departure. It was impossible to speak with Papa now as he had become so withdrawn, spending all day in the library, pouring over books; he put some in one pile, some in another. Mama told us we were going to spend a few months with Papa's Aunt Katya, who lived in Bucharest. Her daughter, Papa's cousin, was to accompany us, along with several of the servants, including our Nana.

"Papa and I will come later," Mama explained.

"What do you mean? You are not coming with us?" I asked in an alarmed voice. This was not the plan.

Mama looked away and didn't respond. She seemed to be struggling for words. Then she said very carefully, "Sonya, *ma cherie*, I need you to be very strong now. You are the oldest and must look after Anna and Andrei until we . . ."her voice broke off, "until we are able to leave here." After collecting herself she added, "Papa cannot leave just now, and I cannot abandon him. I hope that we can follow in a few weeks, as soon as his mind is settled."

"What do you mean, you hope . . .?" my voice began to crack.

"We will follow," she said with resolve. "We will come to Bucharest in a short time. It will only be a matter of a few weeks, *ma cherie*." She took my hands in hers and said with forced cheerfulness, "We are not going away forever, just until this political transition takes place and the protest dies down. It will all work out. It must, for everyone's sake."

It was the night before our departure. Mama came to say goodnight and asked me to pick out what I was going to wear the next day for the train ride. I picked out a dress. Mama took it out of my closet, looked at the lining and then put it back, muttering to herself that it wouldn't do. She selected another one. "Would you wear this one?" she asked, examining the petticoat." I nodded. I was filled with anxiety and really didn't care what I wore.

She took the dress and withdrew into her sitting room. I couldn't sleep and later made my way into her room. I found her sewing something into the hem of my dress. The family jewels were laid out in front of her. She was so absorbed in what she was doing that she didn't hear me enter the room. I sat quietly beside her and watched as she picked up a bracelet and laid it inside part of the hem and began to sew.

"What are you doing, Mama?" I asked in a trembling voice. The imminent separation from her cast a long shadow over my heart, which no amount of comforting from her could shake.

"Oh, you startled me, Sonya," she exclaimed, nearly jumping out of her chair. "I didn't hear you come in." She put down my dress and took both of my hands in hers. Her velvety eyes held mine. She looked at me steadily, speaking in a soft and controlled voice, "*Ma cherie*, listen to me carefully. I am sewing into your dress our most precious family jewels. If for some reason we are unable to return to Russia for a while, we will have money to begin a new life. They are very valuable. Some have been handed down to your Grandmama from her Grandmama. Listen to me, nobody, but nobody can know about this. You must not speak of this to anyone. You must keep them hidden until I can reach Budapest."

"Not Aunt Katya . . ."

"No. Not Aunt Katya. Not Anna, or Andrei, or even Nana. Nobody. Do you understand me?" I nodded. Her voice, although quiet, was very firm. I had never seen her so serious. "This is a secret between you and me. Nobody else can know, nobody at all. These jewels are very precious and they will allow us to survive outside of Russia if we need to. The times are very uncertain and we cannot trust anyone. Look at what I have done." She showed me where she had sewn them and told me what each one was. "I have only Grandmama's ruby necklace left to do. It is very big and the most expensive and precious of them all. I must find a place in your petticoat where it won't bulge." She laid out the necklace to show me. "In all there will be thirty pieces of jewelry. I will try to bring the rest when I come." Mama sighed and then said, "You mustn't let anyone wash the dress or petticoat until you have taken out the jewels. If I don't arrive in a fortnight, take them out and hide them in a closet, under a floorboard or some such place where nobody can get to them. You must keep guard over them until I can get there. I am counting on you, Sonya. Our future will depend on these."

"But Mama," I protested, "why can't you bring the jewels when you come? Why must I carry them?" I was terrified at the thought of such a huge responsibility. How could I keep them hidden in the event that Mama's travel was delayed?

"Nobody will think to check a child. We don't know under what conditions we will be able to leave. No, they are safer with you, *ma cherie*. The sooner they get out of Russia, the better. Besides I will have other precious things to carry."

I sat silently as she went back to her sewing, trying to fit Grandmama's elaborate necklace into the hem of my undergarment. "Will you really come in a fortnight?" I asked in a trembling voice, overtaken by some foreboding.

She put down her sewing and held me close to her. "We will be there very soon, *ma cherie*. Haven't I always kept my word to you?"

"You have," I replied in a choked voice as I clung to her chest.

"Now go get some sleep. You have a big day tomorrow."

As I started for the door, she called me back. She took off the locket from her neck and put it on me. "All of the jewels are from Papa's family. This is all I have from mine. My mother gave it to me when I left France to protect me. I have kept it all these years, and now I give it to you, to protect you, Andrei, and Anna until I can reach you."

I touched the locket. I knew it was very precious to Mama.

"There is a picture of Mother Mary inside," she said. "Look at it whenever you feel sad or afraid and she will comfort you. I feel much better knowing you will have this."

How many times in the years to come would I grasp that locket in my hands? It was to become my lifeline, not to Mother Mary but to my own Mama.

Papa didn't leave the house anymore, so he didn't come to the train station. We said goodbye to him in the library. He was not a hugging man, but this day he pulled me to his chest and held me there. He did the same to Anna and Andrei. Then he turned back to his books without a word.

Mama came with us. The drive to the station was chaotic. There were so many people in the street that day. The streets were lined with men who appeared to be guards, but they weren't the typical officers. Mama tried to distract us and kept chatting on about what to expect at Aunt Katya's. When we arrived at the station, it took some time to locate our cousin. But there she was, flustered and eager to embark. Mama handed her a letter and some gifts for Aunt Katya, along with our travel papers. She entered the train to help us get settled in our cabin, then it was time to say goodbye. I didn't want to let go of her hand. She gathered us all into her arms and said, "Now I know at least you will be safe, *ma cheries*."

"Please come," Anna pleaded at the last moment. "Don't stay here."

Andrei clung to her and started to cry. Nana tried to pull him away but he wouldn't let go.

"Children, the train is ready to depart. I must get off." As Andrei's cries grew louder, she seemed paralyzed. "Sonya," Mama called to me firmly. "I need you to take charge." I had no time to think of my own sorrow as I took my crying brother into my arms. Tears welled in my eyes as I watched her pull herself away and back out of our cabin. I stood by the window with my distraught brother and Anna by my side. We watched her as she waved with her handkerchief and then began to dab her eyes.

The whistle blew, the train pulled away, and we watched our dear mama become smaller and smaller until she was just a speck on the horizon.

* * *

"Denashka," Jay called me gently. "We are waiting for your vote. Do you vote for this acquisition?"

I looked at him blankly, my mind far away, waving goodbye to Mama. He saw that I was not paying attention.

"We are all in favor of the acquisition," my father said. "We are just waiting for your vote."

"The acquisition?" I asked faintly, struggling to bring myself back into the present. I looked around at my siblings and father and the others who were part of the Executive Committee. Then I remembered that we were discussing the purchase of a firm whose environmental policies I didn't agree with. I would not vote for it, but I knew that my father thought the acquisition was necessary to help one of our offices. It was difficult for me to go against my father, but I had strong environmental principles. "I abstain," I said.

"Alright," my father said. "I know how you feel, but everyone else has agreed so we will move forward. It is a good financial move for us, and we will make sure you are comfortable with their clients going forward."

I nodded, eager to end the meeting so I could be alone and go back into the past. For weeks now I had been reliving my early years in Russia, and I couldn't free myself from them. Over and over I relived these scenes from the past, feeling myself as the aspiring dancer and then as the child separated from her parents, heading into an unknown world. Try as I might, I couldn't remember what happened after that. My memories stopped on the train that day we parted from my mother.

Were we reunited a few weeks later, as she said we would be, or did my life take a different turn? I tried to spend more time in meditation, thinking this would release the memories stored in the subconscious mind. Bits of memories would come back to me, sometimes at the oddest times; I would remember a scene from childhood and would rush off to be alone. Then the tears would come. I couldn't explain the emotions stirred by these memories, but they were strong.

In some ways it was like watching a movie. I would see the scenes unfold, but I was totally identified with the heroine. I knew that I was that young girl Sonya, and I recognized in her some of my own early traits. As a young girl, I had been obsessed with ballet; as I grew older, people often mistook me for a dancer by the way I stood. When the great ballet companies came to the city, I went with my parents night after night, never getting enough. Sometimes I went to my room, put on ballet music, and danced and danced, drifting into my own world.

"Earth to Mom, Earth to Mom." My younger son tugged at me. "Mom, what are you thinking about?" I was sitting by the window, blankly staring out.

"Sorry," I replied. "What is it?"

"I'm hungry. What's for dinner?"

"I guess it is that time." I pulled myself back to the present, although my mind was back in Russia, at the train station, living again that last farewell. The love I felt for Mama was still with me. He continued to tug at me. "Okay, okay," I smiled at him and got up to prepare dinner.

I was living in two different time periods and, although there were difficult moments, I learned to manage the two realities. I could stay focused on the demands of the present while my mind was far away. The most challenging part was that there was nobody to confide in, nobody with whom I could share the experience. When I tried to speak about it, the whole thing sounded so strange that I simply kept quiet. I questioned whether or not I was imagining the whole thing, or had wandered into deep water and lost my grip on reality. I told myself, "I am a single mom, holding a good job, managing quite well. No, I am not losing my mind." I could attend to all the details of my life and that of my children. No, I was not crazy. I was having an experience that perhaps many others had, but of which few spoke. Perhaps my memories were more vivid, that was all.

In the months since Jay had been working with the company, we had become close. Although I felt there was a romantic possibility, this potential did not develop. We were both divorced with children, but whenever I inquired into his personal life, a cool distance came between us and he changed the subject. Our link was the company but, more than that, it was Russia. He was my connection to the past, yet I had not uncovered who he had been to me. Jay traveled extensively; I never knew when he would show up at the office. Whenever he was there and called me, I went running in the hope that he would awaken more memories.

It was comforting to hear him address me in Russian and, although I didn't understand my connection to him, I knew there was one. Jay did not have a mystical nature, and there was no way I could share with him what I was going through. He was much like my father—practical, culturally identified with the Jewish tradition, and very much the businessman. It was very odd that I felt this attraction for him. All of the men I had been attracted to after my divorce were involved in spiritual matters, mostly drawn to the Hindu tradition. So this attraction made no sense unless it was a remnant from the past.

Everyday affairs kept me well occupied until, one day several months later, I found myself again in the past.

Chapter 3

I t was with heavy heart that we arrived in Bucharest. My father's relative was at the train station to greet us. An elderly woman, Aunt Katya was the youngest sister of my Grandmama. She left Russia in her youth when she was married off to a Romanian prince. She was the closest relative we had who was living outside of Russia, which is why we were sent to her. She had visited us in St. Petersburg many times, so she was familiar to us, but her home was not. Bucharest was a stark contrast to the city I called home. It had none of the elegance, but also none of the protests, no mobs crowding around our motorcar, and that was a welcome relief.

After we arrived at the house, Andrei, Anna, and I huddled together by the door, unused to being without our parents.

"Come in, children," said Aunt Katya in a cool but welcoming voice. "This will be your home, at least until your Papa arrives."

"When will that be?" asked Andrei.

"As soon as possible, I am sure," she replied. We were shown to our rooms.

Aunt Katya observed many of the formalities we were accustomed to under Papa's watchful eye. Dinner was a formal affair that required us to be properly dressed. We knew not to speak until we were spoken to, so meals passed with little conversation. Aunt Katya's husband had died, but her son and his wife lived with her. They were a solemn, childless couple, and there was little joy in the house. We tiptoed around, staying mostly together, counting the days as they crept by. One week, two weeks, three weeks . . . and no word of Mama or Papa.

One day I overheard Aunt Katya's son telling her that the transitional government in Russia had fallen and the Bolsheviks had taken over.

"This does not bode well," she said. My heart froze, and the thought passed through my mind that this might have delayed Mama and Papa's departure. Aunt Katya caught sight of me. "I am sure your parents are safe," she said, "but this will make it more difficult to return to Russia anytime soon."

The thought that my parents might not be safe had not occurred to me before. My only concern was the speed with which they were able to leave Russia, not that they might be in any danger. "Safe?" I quickly inquired. "Could they be in danger?"

"No, no, of course not," she replied hastily. I caught the brief glance that passed between Aunt Katya and her son. Somehow her words were not convincing. I surmised that there was more to the situation than I was being told.

Weeks passed, then months, and still no word of Papa and Mama. We resumed our lessons with tutors Aunt Katya found for us, according to Mama's instructions. My unease increased with the passing time. I found a corner in my closet to hide the dress into which Mama had sewn the jewels, telling Nana that it had been soiled and I had thrown it away. One day Aunt Katya called us to her. We hurried to her sitting room, expecting some word from Russia, but our excitement was cut short when we saw the serious expression on her face.

"Children," she said slowly. "I have tried every means to get word of your parents, to no avail. Either they have gone into hiding, or . . ." She fell quiet.

My eyes shot open wide. "Or what?"

"It is possible," she continued slowly, "that your Papa has been put in prison."

"Prison!" I exclaimed. "For what?"

"For no reason, my dear, except his association with the Tsarist regime."

"And Mama?"

"We don't know. In any case it means you will remain here with me for a while. We will keep trying to get word of them, but it is getting increasingly difficult." Then she said, "I am sure at some point they will be able to get away and join us. But it may be longer than any of us realized."

"But we must find them!" I exclaimed, unwilling to accept the fact that they were missing. "There must be more that we can do. We have other relatives in Russia. What has happened to them? Aunt Olga for instance . . ." I was thinking of Papa's older sister. She and Papa were not on good terms, but surely she would know something of his whereabouts.

Aunt Katy's son intervened. "Do you think we have not done everything in our power to try to get word of them?" he asked in an annoyed tone.

"Hush," Aunt Katya said firmly to him. "It is understandable that the children are upset." Turning to me she continued. "We had heard that Olga was in Germany but we have been unable to find her. Sonya, we will keep trying to reach your parents. I can assure you that we will do everything in our power."

When we were alone, Anna burst into tears. "I am not staying here. I hate it," she cried.

"I want to go home," cried Andrei, adding his tears to hers.

"What choice do we have?" I asked them, holding back my own tears. "We have nowhere else to go." The three of us huddled together, refugees, perhaps orphans.

Three unhappy years passed. Aunt Katya was quite old and grew increasingly unwell. Her son and daughter-in-law seemed to resent our presence. I became very protective of Anna and Andrei, trying to ease Anna's occasional emotional outbursts and Andrei's anger at being so confined. One day Aunt Katya called me to her.

"Come here, Sonya, sit beside me," she motioned to a seat by her bed. She hadn't left her room for days on end. "I have been very unwell these last few months and the time has come for me to secure your future." I nodded, wondering what she could mean. We no longer spoke of waiting for Mama and Papa. "There is a Count here who has approached me for your hand in marriage, and I have agreed. He is very well positioned and is willing to take you on with no inheritance. He knows your situation. That is a big concession, Sonya; you must realize this. He is older but a very good match, considering everything. His wife died and left him only a daughter. His hope is to have a son from our line."

I was speechless. This was beyond my wildest imaginings. Marriage! I couldn't believe what I was hearing. Could she be serious? "It is the best I could do, Sonya. I hope you realize that."

"But I don't want to get married," I cried firmly, "at least not yet. I am still so young and want to study. Mama would never approve . . ."

"And pray tell me what the alternative is? You cannot wait forever for your parents. You must live your life, Sonya, and you must have financial security. That is what your parents would want for you. The Count has agreed that Anna can live with you until she is settled. And I have arranged for Andrei to go to school in Germany, an excellent school. I still have money left from what your parents sent that can cover this."

"But my education? I want to study. Papa would have wanted that for me." The tears flowed freely and I made no attempt to stop them.

"I must see to this marriage before I die, and I fear that I don't have much time left."

It was like a death sentence. My immediate thought was to take Anna and Andrei and run away. But where would we go? When I mentioned the terrible fate before us to Anna, she was even more determined.

"Let's go to Paris," she said. "Mama must have some relatives there." Mama was an only child and, after her parents died, she had not stayed in touch with any of her relatives, so we knew none of them. I remembered Mama's jewels that I had hidden in the closet, buried beneath a floorboard, as Mama had directed me to do. Certainly they must be of some value. But how would we sell them? We knew nothing about the world. The more I thought about it, the more I realized that I had no alternative.

Aunt Katya died, and I was married off to the Count. Andrei was sent to school in Germany, and our life in Russia drifted further and further away. I clung to the memories, refusing to admit that they were becoming mere embers of a flame whose time had passed.

* * *

I was sitting with Jay going over the company's finances. He had done a spreadsheet to show me how the new acquisition would affect the company's bottom line. It was a struggle for me to keep my mind on what he was saying. My strength was not in numbers, but rather ideas. I didn't like the kind of business the new company did and so was not eager to find value in this new merger.

"Are you following, Denashka?"

"Yes . . . no . . . I mean, well, not really."

He laughed fondly. We had liked each other from the start but the friendship had grown in recent weeks. Our conversations about the business were interwoven with many other matters, and I was intrigued by how much he knew about so many things. Despite the time we spent together, he was still very much of a mystery to me. Why would an African-American who grew up in Harlem be so drawn to Judaism? How was he so fluent in Russian? And why had he come into my life at this particular time? There was more to it than I could understand at that moment.

Whenever I was with him, I felt a friendship beyond what our relationship was at this time, beyond business, and yet we spoke little of our personal lives. It was very odd to feel so close and yet to know so little of each other. It was very comforting to hear him speak to me in Russian, which he often did, and to have him refer to me as "Denashka," but he didn't resemble any of the people that I remembered from my childhood in Russia. I couldn't help but wonder who he was to me.

"Your mind is far away, I can tell. What are you thinking?"

"I was thinking of Russia." I studied his face as I spoke these words, to see whether any memories lingered in him.

"Russia? Have you been there?" he asked.

I shook my head and asked, "What about you?"

"I've spent a lot of time there. I have had business deals . . . But let's get back to these spreadsheets." He gave me no clue, no hint of anything but the present moment.

"Why did you learn Russian?" Again I watched his expression carefully, searching for any clue to his past.

His face clouded. "I have had business there," he said. Jay had a way of letting you know when not to pursue a line of conversation. From the tone in his voice, I knew not to press him. We returned to the spreadsheets. "Do you see why this acquisition was necessary for the Washington office? It will help stabilize the office, and hopefully even make it profitable."

"That's not the only issue for me," I replied. "They defend and try to whitewash corporations that have an environmental problem. I would rather that they help corporations become environmentally responsible."

He smiled. "You are an idealist. One has to be practical and the most important thing for a company is to stem any losses."

"But should one compromise one's principles for that?"

"Sometimes compromise is necessary," he responded. I was quiet, not yet willing to concede. I listened as he went through the spreadsheets. When he was done, he said suddenly, "I've got to go away on business, so I won't be around for a few weeks. But we can pick up where we left off when I return."

I was sorry he was leaving. The office was much more attractive to me when he was around, but his coming and going was becoming routine. He would be present for a few weeks and then he was gone without saying why, except to say it was business. I was becoming more and more curious about Jay. I had ended a relationship a few months before I met him and couldn't help but wonder if there wasn't something more than just our business relationship. I greatly admired his intellect. He seemed to know something about everything, but I was also wary of his mysterious and aloof nature.

* * *

Months passed and I could remember no more than my marriage to the Count. Perhaps there was nothing more to remember. Perhaps I had spent my days unhappily married to that man, whose name I couldn't recall. But there was a pain that lingered in my heart, a pain that egged me on to try to remember more.

Then the floodgates opened.

Anna and I had been living with the Count for a number of years. I had had two miscarriages and the doctor said it was unlikely that I could bear children. Thankfully, the Count ignored me after that. I took refuge in reading and spent as much time in my studies in literature and philosophy as I could. My dream of dancing died along with my life in Russia. My ballet shoes were hidden away in my closet, along with the family jewels.

Anna had grown into a lovely young woman, but she was restless. She found relief in riding horses, but she was more daring than prudent. She had always had a rebellious streak and yearned for more stimulation that life in Bucharest could provide, so she decided to leave and go to Paris. When I asked how she would manage there, Anna replied, "I am sure we have relatives. I'll find them. I will die if I stay here any longer!"

"Don't be so melodramatic, Anna." How would I bear my life if she left me? But I couldn't expect her to sacrifice her life for me. She deserved more than to be stuck in the prison of the Count's house. At least I could escape into my books, but what did she have? I asked her, "But what will you do for money?"

She was silent. I had never told anyone, even her, about Mama's jewelry. Perhaps now was the time to share this with her. It had been many years with no word from our parents, but I still clung to the hope that they were alive and someday would miraculously appear. "I will get the money for you, Anna. Just give me some time."

"So you approve?"

"Anna, I can't imagine being here without you, but I also can't expect you to stay here forever. I know that. Go to Paris and start a life for yourself." My voice was trembling.

"Come with me, Sonya. I can't leave you here in this dark and gloomy place. Neither of us belongs here."

I shook my head. "I can't leave, not just yet. I know that when Mama and Papa come, they will look for us in Bucharest. If both of us leave, how will they find us?"

"We can leave word, an address," she said. I looked away. "You can't spend your life waiting for them, Sonya. Mama wouldn't want that. At some point we must accept the fact . . ." She couldn't finish the sentence. Regaining control, she said, "I will send for you as soon as I get settled. Then we will have an address to leave for them."

"That is a better plan." I feigned a smile. "But you must take one of the maids with you. You cannot travel alone. Mama would never have that." She nodded.

I planned to go that week to a jeweler in the city to see how much I could get for one of Mama's rings, but it was not to be. A few days later, Anna was out riding and hadn't returned when it was near dark. After sending the stable boy to look for her, I learned there had been an accident; she didn't survive.

My brother Andrei married a German woman and settled in Munich, where he worked in her father's bank. I had seen him only sporadically over the years, when he was on vacation from school, and he stayed with me for a few weeks after Anna died. But now years had passed and I had gotten used to my solitude.

My greatest fulfillment came through reading. I poured through the library seeking knowledge, and my reading eventually led me to Theosophy. This spiritual movement opened a door into the internal world, rich and exciting with unlimited potential for exploration. Over time, this inner world became more real to me than the outer one. To my surprise, one day I found that I was no longer holding onto the idea that my parents would rescue me. I also realized that my new interest in the occult was no accident. I remembered tagging along to the spiritualists Mama used to visit, and now I had come to the same place on my own. She would have understood and encouraged me; I began to carry on a one-way conversation with her so I could share my spiritual journey. After all, I couldn't speak with anyone else about these matters.

One day a letter came from Andrei, pleading with me to come visit. The Count assigned a companion, which I resisted but in the end had to accept. Olga was like my shadow, giving me barely enough room to breathe. On the long train ride to Munich, I was anxious. Letters between Andrei and me had been far and few between. I had only met his wife at their wedding. But as soon as I saw Andrei waiting for me at the station, all my concerns vanished. We embraced for a long time—the only family we had left.

I found that I liked Munich very much, and greatly enjoyed Andrei's circle of friends. To be among intellectual and creative people, with stimulating conversation, was a world away from my life in Bucharest. One of Andrei's friends in particular, an art professor from the university, introduced me to Art Nouveau, and also shared some of my spiritual interests. At Andrei's insistence, I extended my stay in Munich, first by weeks and then months. Finally I put Olga on a train back to Bucharest. I had little reason to return there, even though I knew I would have to do so eventually.

One day I went with Andrei to a salon with many people from the academic world. Although Andrei was in the world of finance, he had become friends with many intellectuals and artists. My life of solitude had left me very shy, so I withdrew to a quiet corner. My German wasn't very good, which made it even harder to interact with the others. I reached for a book and began flipping through the pages, more to look occupied than out of any real interest in the book.

Suddenly, a deep voice greeted me in Russian. I was startled. He immediately apologized. "I didn't mean to interrupt you."

"Not at all." I looked up at the broad bearded face that had greeted me. "How nice to hear Russian here." I began to introduce myself, "I am Sonya"

"I know who you are," he assured me. "You are Andrei's sister. I am Yuri Abramovich, a professor of physics at the University of Heidelberg. You are visiting, aren't you?"

I nodded. "This is my first time coming to such a gathering."

"I am also new to these salons, but I am visiting a professor here and so I tagged along with my friend."

We spent the evening chatting in Russian, speaking mostly of his life in Heidelberg. His description of the university made me eager to visit. I spoke little of my life in Bucharest; there was so little to share. I said nothing of my marriage. He had a wife and child in Russia, but he had left long ago and they were unable to join him. I thought of my parents, also stuck back in Russia.

My expression must have changed, because he quickly added, "I hope the mention of Russia does not disturb you."

"No, it's only that we were young when Andrei and I, and our sister Anna, were sent away. My parents never made it out." My voice trembled.

"I'm so sorry. I should not have mentioned the past."

"I don't know what happened to my parents. Some people say they may have been killed, but I don't believe it. I feel they are alive, somewhere."

"Let us not talk about Russia. Here we are now in Germany and we have met. It is unlikely that we would have met in Russia, Princess Sonya!" He gave a little laugh.

I smiled wryly. "I am hardly a princess now. That world is long gone." I liked him. He was not particularly attractive, but there was something very appealing about him. I think what drew me the most was his intellect. He didn't waste time on trivial matters. It was obvious he was a very serious man.

When Yuri rose to leave, he said, "Please do visit Heidelberg before you return to Bucharest. I so enjoyed our talk."

I couldn't get Yuri out of my mind. I felt so comfortable with him. My shyness evaporated in his company. I knew that I couldn't go back to Bucharest without visiting him first, so I mentioned it to my brother.

"You realize he is a Jew, don't you?" my brother asked.

"Andrei! What difference does that make? You sound like Papa!"

"I just want you to be aware. You know the situation here in Germany."

"Is it any different than it was in Russia? You know, Andrei, Mama had Jewish blood. Her grandmama was Jewish."

I saw the surprise on his face. "I don't believe it, Sonya. Papa never could have married her."

"It's true. Papa didn't know."

"She kept that from him? Well, you mustn't say anything about that here. You must be careful, Sonya, here in Germany. Go to Heidelberg if you like. The university is something to see, and I have friends you can stay with there. But don't get too friendly with that professor. It will cause you trouble."

I went to the visit the University, and Yuri was thrilled to see me. One evening I asked him about the situation for the Jews in Germany. "Until now, Germany has been a good place for the Jews," he said. "We have had more opportunity here than in Russia. There are many Jewish professors at the university, and some are from Russia. You can come to the physics department and meet the Jewish professors there," he laughed. "But there is reason to be concerned now. Things are changing here."

Yuri told me very little about his past, but I began to speak to him about my life in Russia. I told him stories about my mother and the secrets she would share with me. It was such a relief to be able to speak with someone about things that mattered to me. For the first time since leaving Russia I felt free to be myself. I thought the past was dead to me, but now I began to feel alive again. I told him about my aspiration to be a dancer.

"In Russia I was training to be a ballet dancer. My father was very opposed, but I kept training, even though I knew I could never dance on stage. I kept hoping one day he would change his mind. Then I was sent out of Russia when I was 14 years old. I haven't put on ballet shoes since then, and that was a long time ago."

"You are still young, Sonya. Put on your ballet shoes again."

I laughed. "I still have many pairs of toe shoes, wrapped away in my closet with a few other things I took from Russia. But I have other interests now."

"What are your interests?"

"Philosophy. There must be more to life than our brief material existence. Where do we come from? Where do we go when we die? I want to understand it all."

"I can tell you from the perspective of physics, but if you are looking for philosophy, I will take you to the university library. Everything is there."

Yuri was right. Many books in the library pointed me in the direction of the East. One day I was browsing and, as I reached to pull a book from a tightly packed shelf, a neighboring book fell to the floor at my feet. I reached down to grab it and place it back on the shelf when something made me pause. I approached the librarian and asked in my broken German if she could find a copy of this book in French. "The Bhagavad Gita," she said in German. "Let me look for you." A few minutes later she said, "I am sorry, we only have a German copy."

I don't know why, but I said I would take it. I could barely read German. That night I struggled to make sense of the book. Yuri asked if I wanted him to find a copy for me in a language I could read. I nodded gratefully.

"I must read this book," I said with conviction. "Please try to find it in French. I will come again to visit as soon as you find it." I was very serious.

"You will travel all the way from Bucharest for this book?" He was amazed. "Is that a promise?"

I blushed and looked away. "It is a promise."

Yuri smiled. "Then I will be sure to find it very quickly."

A few months after my return to Bucharest, I received a letter from Yuri informing me he had a French copy of the book. I made plans to travel again to Germany, with a quick stop in Munich to see my brother. When I arrived in Heidelberg, Yuri gave me the Bhagavad Gita in French. My heart leapt with joy. "Somehow I feel that the answers I seek are in here."

"You don't know how hard it was to find this," he said with a smile. "I had to practically bribe one of my colleagues in Paris to search the city for it."

It was on this visit that we became lovers. It happened very naturally one evening, when he bent over to kiss me and, without a second thought,

I responded. For me it was truly the first time. I had had sex for procreation with my husband, but there had been no pleasure in it. Quite the opposite: I had been repelled by his touch. Yuri awakened my sexual desire and gave me a deep sense of fulfillment and joy. This second visit to Heidelberg turned from a few days into a few weeks, and when I left I knew I would be back again soon.

On the next trip, I passed briefly through Munich on my way to Heidelberg. Yuri had left a key for me and I let myself into the flat. I knew he would still be at the university, so I started to tidy up. I had been shocked to discover that Yuri had no servants, nobody to cook or clean his flat. I didn't know much about cooking, but I could tidy things up. If Papa had seen me cleaning the flat of my Jewish lover, my god! What would he have said? I couldn't even imagine the scene. I sank into the couch in a fit of laughter.

"What's so funny?" I hadn't heard Yuri enter the flat. What could I say without hurting his feelings?

"I don't know what came over me," I said. "It was just . . . well, I am so happy to be here." That was enough.

My frequent visits to Germany were beginning to annoy the Count. He had no fondness for me, but he was annoyed at what people might say if I was not present at the functions he attended. As his health began to decline, he fussed every time I prepared to leave. "You are not to make so many visits to Germany. You are needed here," he pronounced one evening as I was preparing to depart.

"For what?" I asked him coldly.

"My health is not good."

"Olga is here to look after you." The companion he had sent to spy on me in Germany had moved in and become his personal caretaker. I didn't know or care what their relationship entailed.

"I don't want you leaving." His voice was brusque.

"Why must I stay? So you can torture me here? I don't have any life with you. In Munich, I have my brother and his wife. They also need me." My voice rose and I was surprised at the tone of my words.

"Then perhaps you should consider staying in Germany." His voice was like a thick sheet of ice. I shuddered as he left the room.

It was the first time I thought of leaving the Count. I didn't see myself living with Andrei, but perhaps with Yuri. We were friends and lovers, but could we be more to each other? On the train to Munich, I began to think seriously that perhaps I could have a life with Yuri. He didn't share my spiritual inclinations, but I loved his intellect and admired his knowledge.

I didn't mention the Count's displeasure with me during my short stay in Munich. I didn't want to worry Andrei, who still did not approve of my relationship with Yuri. Before leaving for Heidelberg, Anton, the art professor friend of Andrei's, stopped by for a visit. He had a special liking for me, but he was married and we never allowed our friendship to become anything more. He knew of my interest in spiritual matters and had come to tell me that a friend of his had told him about a certain *swami* from India who was passing through Germany on his way back East from America. Would I be interested in meeting him? I could barely contain my excitement. I had never expected to meet a real mystic, not just read about one, but actually to be in the presence of such a sage!

That evening we went to a private home to hear the swami speak. The room was crowded and we couldn't make our way up close, but it didn't matter. As soon as I caught sight of the swami, my body froze. I needed no more than a glimpse of him. There was something about the energy of the room, something I couldn't describe, explain, or even understand, but I felt something shift in my awareness when I entered his presence.

He was in the middle of giving a talk. He spoke in English with such a thick accent that I could hardly understand a word. Again, it didn't matter. What mattered was that after he finished speaking, there was a momentary opening in the crowd of people surrounding him and he turned his gaze on me. Our eyes met. It may only have been for a few seconds, but it seemed like a very long time. There was such familiarity in those eyes, as if he were a long lost love, as if he had come just for me, as if he had come to claim me. We didn't need to exchange a word. I had come for that glance from beyond, from the ancient past and distant future. What took place inside me was unlike anything I had ever experienced or imagined. I hadn't known there could be such a connection without exchanging a word.

"Do you want to speak with him?" whispered Anton. I didn't answer. I couldn't speak.

"Sonya, are you alright?" I nodded. "Do you want to approach him, or should we leave? There is a crowd of people around him and it may take some time to greet him."

"Let us stay a few minutes," I whispered, not wanting to move from the spot. I didn't need to speak with the swami; it would have broken the magic of the moment to utter even a word.

Anton finally pulled me away. Our ride back to Andrei's was in silence. When Anton said goodbye to me that night, I realized that I didn't even know the name of the holy man. "What is his name?" I asked. "The holy man."

"Swami Yogananda," replied Anton.

I repeated it with closed eyes. "Could you write it down for me so that I will not forget?" I took out a small piece of paper and watched as Anton wrote down the name.

"I think this is how it must be spelled. I don't really know. I heard some people call him Swamiji. I think that is like calling a monk 'brother.' That is how he is addressed."

Andrei and his wife were asleep when I entered the flat. I was glad not to be questioned. Once in my room I took off the locket Mama had given me on that last night in Russia. Without hesitation, I removed the picture of Mother Mary and put in its place the piece of paper with Swamiji's name on it. "You will be my protector now," I said, grasping the locket tightly against my chest.

Chapter 4

I said nothing to Yuri about my visit to the swami. The experience was too dear to me to share with anyone, even him. One night we had finished our evening meal and I was sitting on the sofa reading the Bhagavad Gita. He said, "You are really studying that book."

I looked up and saw him smiling at me. "What do you mean?"

"The look on your face is so intent. I have not seen you so engrossed in anything. I'm glad to see you are enjoying it."

"Every word of it rings true to me." He didn't say anything. We rarely discussed my interest in philosophy. Yuri was a physicist and had a different way of looking at the world. I put the book aside. I was to return soon to Bucharest and had been meaning to have a conversation with him. I had not forgotten the angry exchange with the Count before I left. I knew I would have to face him again soon.

"Yuri," I started slowly. "I am thinking of leaving the Count." I waited for him to respond, but he didn't. "What do you think?"

"Where would you go?" My heart trembled at his question. It was not exactly an invitation.

I gathered my courage and asked, "What about me coming here?" I had come to realize that Yuri had a secretive side. He kept many things to himself. Often it was difficult to know where he stood, and he didn't share his emotions easily.

"That's not practical, Sonya. You know that."

"Practical? Why does it need to be practical?" I couldn't hide my hurt.

"Our relationship means a lot to me." His voice was gentle. "I had hoped we could continue as we are."

"We can." I returned my gaze to the book, not wanting to let him see the tears welling up in my eyes. He sat beside me and tried to put his arm around me, but I pulled away. We had been seeing each other for several years, but now a wall had come between us. I could not deny the limitations of the relationship; after all, we were both married. Why did I push for more? I wasn't sure, except that my life with the Count was becoming more difficult.

"Sonya, I don't want you to be hurt. If you need to end this, we can. Both of our lives are complicated. We can't change our circumstances, but we can enjoy our time together, if you can manage that."

"I can manage it."

It was six months before I was able to return to Heidelberg. At home, I retreated more into my reading, with the Gita as my daily guide, my lifeline. When I arrived back in Germany, I was shocked by the change that had taken place. Signs saying "No Jews" were posted at various businesses and other locations. Officers were more visible on the streets, on the lookout for unwanted characters amid the heightened level of anxiety.

A worried and distracted Yuri greeted me. "Several Jewish professors have been let go from the university. I am trying to help them get out of the country and find positions elsewhere."

"But what about you?" I asked in alarm. "Will you have to leave?"

"I am all right at the moment. I am on good terms with the head of the physics department. But some of the others are very, very concerned."

"Yuri, let me help."

"What can you do?"

What could I do? Andrei and I were refugees ourselves and had little standing anywhere in Europe. We had not kept up with any of our relatives who had also fled Russia.

Yuri was often gone, presumably to meetings. There were visits from other professors and whispered conversations, which led me to believe the situation was graver than he admitted to me. I was at the library one evening when I suddenly heard Mama's voice, the first time since our separation that I actually heard her speaking to me. "The jewels," she said. "You still have the jewels. Use them to help the Jews, Sonya."

I rushed back to Yuri's flat. I asked, "Would it help if I could get you a good sum of money to enable the professors to leave the country?"

"Of course that would help, but where would you get the money, Sonya?" He knew my situation with the Count.

"Never mind that. I will bring money for their travel. Let me know how much you need." He calculated the amount needed to cover the travel of the professors who had been let go. I left the next day and went straight back to Bucharest. Alone in my closet, I ripped up the floorboards and took out all thirty pieces of jewelry that Mama had sewed into my dress. I had no idea of their value. A few weeks later I took a necklace and several rings and went to Germany. I told Andrei that I had a ring from Mama that I wanted to sell, and he put me in touch with a jeweler in Berlin. The pieces fetched more money than I had expected. Yuri was surprised when I showed up in Heidelberg with a large sum of money.

The situation deteriorated further for the Jews in Germany. The University of Heidelberg, which had been a refuge for so many Jewish intellectuals and Russian Jews, was not immune. One by one, Jewish professors were fired and forced to flee. Yuri's connections helped them get out of the country and settle elsewhere. Yuri himself seemed safe from the treacherous arms of the Nazi regime. I ferried back and forth between Bucharest and Berlin, carrying my mother's jewelry, the last remnants of my life in Russia.

One evening I arrived in Heidelberg with money for Yuri, only to find him more sullen and withdrawn than usual. Our relationship had changed since I said I wanted to leave the Count. He never asked where the money came from, and I never volunteered any information. He took it gratefully, but I felt he resented having to take money from me, so the distance between us had grown. And I resented that he didn't confide in me. He said very little about the plight of the Jewish professors, what was actually taking place, where they would go, or how they would escape. I knew none of the details.

"What is wrong?" I asked not long after I arrived. I had been away for several months. He didn't respond. In the following days I could see what had happened. He was no longer teaching at the university; he, too, had been let go. Yuri hardly spoke to me, and barely ever left the house. The window shades were kept drawn and he would peer out nervously once in a while. Finally I couldn't contain myself.

"Would you please tell me what is going on? I am on your side, Yuri. I am not the enemy."

"It is no longer safe for me to stay in Germany. But how can I leave the others here to fend for themselves?"

"Is it that bad now?"

He nodded. "One by one they are being arrested. The Jews are disappearing. We don't know where they are being taken."

"Then you must leave. You must! I am begging you, Yuri, to get away from here." Tears formed in my eyes. I felt helpless. "And I am coming with you," I said firmly. "I can't live in a place where there is so much hatred. We will go to America."

Suddenly it all seemed clear to me. The swami lived in America. Yuri and I would go there and find the swami. "Yuri, I have been selling my mother's jewelry, and I have only one piece left. It is my grandmama's precious ruby necklace, which has been in the family for generations."

"Selling jewelry?" he asked in surprise. "Is that how you have been getting the money?" He seemed relieved.

"I have been selling the jewelry that Mama sewed into my dress the night I left Russia. I have kept the pieces all these years waiting for her to come, so we could start a new life in Europe. But she and Papa . . . I know now they will never come. I have sold all the jewelry now but this one piece, and it will bring a lot of money, more than enough to get us to America.

"So the jewels from Tsarist Russia have helped the Jews escape. How ironic," he mused with a wry smile. "I was afraid you were taking money from the Count."

"No, I would never have asked him. The money comes from my dear Mama, who had Jewish blood. It is she who is to be thanked."

"I will have to work through my connections to see how we can get passage to America. I hesitate to leave now, but I think I have no choice. The authorities are watching my every move. It is too dangerous for me to stay. I know that."

"I will leave for Bucharest tomorrow. But Yuri, it may take me a bit of time to sell the necklace if I want a good price."

"Don't take too long, Sonya. Take any price you can get. We will make do with whatever money you have. Things are getting worse day by day . . ."

Yuri didn't take me to the train the next day as he usually did, so we said a hasty goodbye in the early morning hours, away from the many watchful eyes. I arrived home to find doctors by the Count's side. He had taken ill. I ran to my room and reached under the floorboards to get the last of Mama's jewelry. I would take none of my possessions with me. I had left a small suitcase at Yuri's, which would be enough. If I hurried, I could catch the evening train to Berlin.

Then I paused. I suddenly realized the step I was about to take. What would await me in America with Yuri? Was I being foolish to leave behind the security I had for the unknown? Doubts assailed me. What if things didn't work out with Yuri? Did he really love me? I sank onto a chair in confusion, unconsciously grasping the locket. "Mama," I whispered. "I need your guidance." Would Mama be disappointed in me having an affair with Yuri? Perhaps he would not make me happy after all. Perhaps I didn't really love him. I began to call to my mother in desperation, then my calls shifted to Swamiji. "Please give me a sign," I begged.

Through the veil of tears I saw the beloved form of my mother and heard her voice, as clearly as if she were standing before me. "Leave," she said firmly. "Leave this place, Sonya. You don't belong here."

That was all I needed. I started down the stairs, only to be called by my husband's voice. "Sonya, is that you? Are you leaving again?"

"Yes," I replied.

"You've just returned. Where are you going now?"

"Back to Germany."

"Back to your Jewish lover?" he asked sternly. I was shocked. How on earth did he know? Only Andrei and a few of his friends knew about Yuri, and Andrei did not interact with the Count. "You are surprised that I know, aren't you? I have friends in Germany in high places, and they know all about him and you. You are not to go back there, Sonya. My reputation is at stake."

I stood halfway down the stairs, too stunned to say anything. Then I raced down the rest of the steps. In the background I heard him shouting, "If you go back to him, don't think that you will be able to return here. You will be subjected to the same fate as he."

I ran as fast as I could, more frightened than I had ever been. I knew in every part of myself that America was calling me.

It took me longer in Berlin to sell the necklace than I had hoped. It finally fetched a good price, although not as much as it was worth. How odd. Mama had hoped her jewels would enable our family to begin a new life in Europe, but in fact they were enabling me to begin anew in America.

I arrived in Heidelberg with high hopes, but my dreams were soon dashed. Yuri's flat was boarded up, with the word "Jew" written across it. Nobody would give me any information. Neighbors just shook their heads and shrugged their shoulders when I knocked on their doors. First I thought that things had become too dangerous and he had fled. I remembered where he kept a spare key. I pulled the boards off his door and entered the flat. In the bedroom, I saw an open suitcase with some clothes. Why would he leave a half-packed suitcase? There was no note for me. I sat on his bed and cried. Where was I to go?

I remembered one old lady down the street who had liked him. Surely he must have said goodbye to her. As I was thinking this, there was a loud noise at the door. Suddenly SS officers surrounded me. "What is this meaning of this?" I asked in a trembling voice.

"You have broken into this flat," an officer replied. "You must come with us now." He took me roughly by the arm and led me away.

* * *

It was Monday, and an Executive Committee meeting had been scheduled for 9:30 a.m. I had a long commute and often didn't get into the office that early. Monday traffic was usually congested and I was especially delayed on this day. My mind was in turmoil and I was having trouble functioning. The memories of Nazi Germany had deeply disturbed me.

I arrived at the office after 10:30 a.m. and ran to see my father, but the meeting had already ended. "You're late," he said, with his usual affectionate smile. My father was very accommodating. He knew how difficult it was for me to manage the children and the commute, so he most often excused my tardiness. He said, "Jay will fill you in on what happened at the meeting."

"He's here today?" My father nodded. "Okay. I will find him."

I went to my office, closed the door, and meditated for a few minutes. I was hesitant to call Jay. My mind went back to Germany. I remembered being picked up by the Nazis, but couldn't recall anything else. Did I find

Yuri again? Was I sent to a camp? I had to know, but this was the way with these memories. They would come in spurts and then nothing more for weeks or months. I couldn't do anything to bring them on but wait, sitting with the emotions they awakened. It was exhausting, since it would be weeks before the emotions would subside. First it had been the loss of Mama that caused me so much distress, and now Yuri. I opened my eyes and went to Jay's office without calling. As usual, his door was shut. I knocked.

"Come in," said the deep voice. "Denashka, you missed the meeting. Sit down and I'll fill you in." I stood there dumbfounded. I had no doubt but that I had found Yuri. Now he was Jay, with no memory of that life. "Come in, Denashka, and close the door. You look as if you've seen a ghost." I sat across from him, struggling with my emotions. "I am sorry to say that very little was accomplished today. We started to go over the financials, but there was a disagreement between your sister and brother. Then your sister had to take a call and the meeting ended. Your father seemed frustrated." He paused.

"Can I ask you something?" He nodded. "It has nothing to do with the business, but about another matter. Is there a university in a place in Germany called Heidelberg?"

He laughed. "A very old and famous university. It is one of the great places of learning. Why do you ask?"

"I hadn't heard of it before. How strange. And in the 1930s, would there have been Jewish professors, Russian Jews, there?"

"Actually, it was a refuge for many Russian Jewish intellectuals. Until Hitler, they had many Jewish professors, some very prominent. But why do you ask?"

"And did they have a good physics department?"

"One of the best. Their physics department was renowned."

"What happened to the Jewish professors?"

"Why do you ask these questions, Denaskha? Many escaped when the Nazis came to power. Some went to England, others to America."

"Then the professors did escape the Nazis?" I was hoping for a clue to what had happened to us back then.

"Some did, and some didn't. They were picked up one by one," he said quietly, looking away. "But some left early, and there were people helping the Jews get out."

"How do you know all of this?" I asked.

He smiled. "Why do you want to know?"

I didn't know what to say. I had never heard of Heidelberg before these memories came to me. I knew nothing about the university of the Jewish intellectuals of that time. But I remembered it all now as the movie passed before my consciousness. *Oh, Yuri*, I thought, *if only you could tell me the end of the story. Did you escape or not? Did Yuri escape? Did we find each other again?*

He looked at me thoughtfully and said, "You always ask me about Russia. You know, there was a time when I was younger when I would only date ballet dancers; some of them were Russian. I never understood why it was that way." He grew quiet.

Oh, Yuri, I said to myself. *I know why. If only I could share it with you. If only you could remember.*

"Well, let's get back to company business," he said suddenly. "I will show you the P&Ls that were distributed at the Executive Committee meeting. I took a copy for you." He took out the sheets and started going through the details, while I pretended to pay attention. When he got a call, I slipped away, eager to be alone with my thoughts.

Weeks passed, and I still struggled with my emotions. Sometimes I was back in Russia with my mother, sometimes in Germany with the artists and intellectuals of that time. I was in and out of the present, living in two time periods at once. By now I recognized that the most important event of that birth was meeting my guru, however brief it was.

When I read *Autobiography of a Yogi*, Yogananda's book, as a 20-year-old, I yearned to meet him in person, but he had already left his body. The fact that I could not meet him was a sadness that stayed with me for many years. But gradually he became such an internal presence that it no longer mattered. It gave me great joy to know that I had met him in my previous birth. In fact, Yogananda returned to India only once after coming to America in 1921. He passed through Germany in 1935 on his overland trip back to India. Some say he had tried to meet Hitler, believing that a meeting with him could change the course of history, but it never took place. Thankfully, my meeting with Yogananda did, which is probably why my yearning was so intense in my early adulthood in this life. The memories were lodged in my subconscious, buried, waiting to be revived. When I began to put all of this together, I was flooded with gratitude and relief. Slowly I turned away from memories of my mother and Yuri to focus on those minutes in the presence of Yogananda.

Then more memories returned.

* * *

"I told you, he was my tutor. I met him at a soiree in Munich and he was teaching me German." I replied once again to their questions. My voice was weary and breaking. The SS officers had been questioning me for two days, wanting to know everything about my relationship with Yuri. They had taken my papers and tried in vain to reach my husband. I prayed that they wouldn't be able to contact him, as I knew he would take no responsibility for me. I had tried to call Andrei, but he was away in Prague, seeking a transfer there.

They didn't seem to care what I said. I knew they didn't believe me, but they dared not treat me too rudely because they knew of my husband. He was a friend to the Germans, a sympathizer. For the first time since I was a child, I began to pray. As a child, I had prayed to the Mother Mary, but now I prayed to Swamiji. I clung to the locket around my neck that held his name.

At the end of the second day, a senior officer entered the room. "Let her go," he said. "She doesn't know anything. But make sure she is on a train back to Bucharest. I am sending a telegraph to her husband. He will take care that she doesn't meddle any more."

They took me to the station and made sure I bought a ticket to Bucharest. SS officers were all over the train, watching my every move. But when the train stopped in Vienna, I managed to slip away. I knew I could not return to Bucharest.

Once in Vienna, I made my way to a hotel and collapsed in my room. I was in bed for days with a fever. I hardly noticed whether it was light or dark. I was in and out of sleep; sleep was my dearest friend since she took away my pain. One day I felt strong enough to sit in a chair and peer outside. For the first time I felt well enough to eat the soup the woman at the front desk had been bringing me. As I looked out the window, I saw officers patrolling the streets. Vienna was overrun with German officers and it was hardly any better than Germany. Where could I go? How would I find Yuri? How would I get to America to find Swamiji? I was in a desperate situation.

I fell into a trance, half asleep and half awake, my mind churning, trying to find a solution, when I suddenly saw Swamiji standing before me. He was looking at me with his beautiful eyes, just as he had that night I saw him in Germany. Such joy came over me. My heart lifted.

"I am coming to take you to America," he said, in a voice so sweet, so soft, so unlike any voice I had ever heard. His words chased away all my cares. I awoke with the realization that it was not I who was to find him, but rather he who would find me.

"I am going to America after all," I whispered. "He is coming to take me." I spent the next few days awaiting his arrival. Still feverish and weak, I could not leave my room.

A few days later there was a knock on my door and my heart leapt up. Was it Swamiji? I dragged myself to the door and opened it, and standing before me was not Swamiji, but Andrei, pale and drawn. "I have been searching all over for you," he said. "I didn't know where you had gone."

"How did you ever find me?" I asked in a daze. "What day is it?" My head was throbbing. I had no notion of time. I had no idea that weeks had passed since I left Germany. I realized I was sicker than I had thought.

"You are not well, Sonya. I am taking you back with me to Prague."

"But I am going to America," I said faintly.

"You cannot possibly go like this. Look at your eyes. You are not well." He helped me to a mirror; I was shocked at what I saw. My eyes were bloodshot, my face pale and thin. I looked terrible. I couldn't let Swamiji see me this way. "No arguing, you are coming home with me to Prague. Greta has found a place and the family has moved. First we must get you some food and get you ready." I had no strength to argue. I could barely eat the food he ordered for me. I knew I could not travel on my own, especially with all the checkpoints making travel even more difficult.

Before leaving, I left Andrei's address with the woman at the desk. "If a man in an orange robe from India comes looking for me," I said, "give him this address. He will understand." She nodded, but I could tell she thought I was not thinking clearly.

"Come, Sonya. We must rush," called Andrei.

"How did you find me?" I asked Andrei as we sat in the taxi on the way to the railway station.

"It was not easy to track you down," he said. "Some day I will tell you what I have been through."

I didn't need to know. All that mattered was that he had found me. I might have died in Vienna. I needed to get to his new home to rest and get well enough to go with Swamiji to America. The thought of meeting Swamiji again kept me going. Whenever I felt faint or depressed, he would come to mind, and I would remember that I was going to America with him. I had finally found a teacher who could give me the answers I was seeking. The fact that he had come to me in dream was a sure sign that he was that very teacher I had been looking for. I was so eager to see him again.

Andrei's flat was a lovely place on the main boulevard in Prague. Slowly I recovered some of my strength, but began to have pains in my lower abdomen and knew that something was not right. I didn't dare tell Andrei, who was hovering around, trying to tend to my every need.

A few months earlier, Andrei and Greta had had a little girl, their first child. When we had been on the train to Prague, Andrei told me all about her. They had named her Marie. "After Mama," I said. "How sweet. I will love this child." Andrei hardly remembered Mama or anything about Russia. I was his only link to the past and I knew that he had named her Marie for my sake. In those last years with Andrei, I treasured the little girl, treating her as if she were my own.

On days when I felt well enough, I would walk the streets of the old city, beautiful Prague, winding my way to the Jewish quarter, musing over the history but also waiting for Swamiji to arrive. I often sat alone by the river than ran through Prague. I was strangely attracted to this river and received much comfort sitting by her side, speaking to her as if she were an old friend. I poured my heart out to her. I couldn't speak out loud, lest someone hear me and think me deranged, but she was truly a living presence for me.

As the weeks and months passed, I still wasn't well, but I thought I'd be able to travel when Swamiji came. I had no more dreams of him and began to feel despondent. Perhaps he couldn't find me. I couldn't stay in Prague with Andrei much longer. Although I knew I was welcome, I didn't feel at home there and was eager to continue my spiritual journey.

"What do you think happened to Yuri?" I asked Andrei one day. "What has happened to all the Jews who have disappeared?" Every now and then, when I wasn't thinking of Swamiji, my heart would feel anxious about Yuri's whereabouts.

"I hope that Yuri made it to England or America, or perhaps France. I don't know where else he could have gone," Andrei replied somberly. "Things are very bad now in Germany. Greta has little news from her family. We almost don't want to know."

"Where will this all lead?" I muttered more to myself than to him.

"I dare not think, Sonya, but we lived through that terrible time in Russia, so we will make it through this as well. At least we are safe here in Prague."

All too soon those words proved untrue. Not long after this conversation, I watched out the window as the Nazis marched into Prague. My interest in life began to ebb. I was trapped in Nazi Europe. I yearned for Swamiji and tried to call to him in my heart, believing he would hear me. "I am here in Prague, waiting for you. Come get me." But he didn't come.

The pain in my abdomen grew more intense. I felt guilty that I had never told Andrei about the jewelry. One day I came to him with a bag of money. "This is from one of Mama's necklaces. She gave the necklace to me when we left Russia and I kept it all these years, waiting for her to come so she would have something. Then I sold it. Most of the money is still there. It is a large sum. Save it for little Marie so she will have something from Mama."

"Won't you need it? I don't want to take it if Mama gave it to you . . ."

"No, what need have I now?" He didn't ask anything else; there was no need to say more. What I had done with the rest of the jewelry was between Mama and me. I began to spend most of the days in bed. Andrei fetched a physician, but I hardly cared. What was there to live for?

"You will get better, "Andrei said one day, with tears in his eyes. "Please try, Sonya. You are the only family I have. I can't lose you. Please try to get well."

"I am trying, Andrei." I fell silent. It was difficult for me to speak. Suddenly the image of our Russian dacha came to mind and I asked him, "Do you remember our country house in Russia?"

"I don't remember Russia."

"You don't remember," I replied quietly. "I remember. How I loved that place! Our summers were the happiest times in my life." I began to describe the house to him, and how he and Anna used to play on the upper landing. "I loved the smell of the pine trees, the freedom we had.

There was so much about it that I loved."

"Get well, Sonya. Perhaps one day we will be able to go back."

I didn't get better. I felt life leaving me. Then one evening as I lay in bed, the pale light of dusk already fading, I saw him again. Swamiji, radiant in an orb of light, brighter than the sun. I didn't know if my eyes were open or closed, but it didn't matter. He was more real than anything I could see or touch. He stood there smiling, his face glowing. "I have come to take you to America." He had kept his promise.

I had waited so long for this moment. I had no thought of my bodily condition. I rose to meet him. My waiting had not been in vain. He stood there smiling, his hand outstretched. "Come," he said. "Come with me."

I felt joy again, light and free of pain, free of sorrow. Then the thought of Yuri came to me. *I must find Yuri first*, I thought, *before I go to America.* Swamiji stood patiently, as if he understood my hesitation. Then I saw him, my dear, dear Yuri, looking like a pale ghost, gaunt and sickly, with so many other people crowded like cattle in the dark and gloomy barracks. I shuddered and cried out to him, but he seemed not to hear me. As I looked more closely, I began to perceive lights that took the form of celestial beings that were trying to provide comfort. These beautiful beings emitted light of radiant colors, but the people seemed not to notice them. I heard a celestial song rising amidst the groans of people suffering from starvation or illness. It became clear that the celestial beings were helping them prepare to cross over, to die. Overcome by the sight, I looked away and saw Swamiji standing there, patiently, his hand extended out toward me. I glanced back at the darkness where Yuri was trapped. There could be no greater contrast between the two worlds I saw. I was paralyzed. My heart was breaking with pain; I could hardly bear the agony of what I witnessed. Then I heard a voice that said, "You can help from there as well."

Turning back one last time, I called out, "See the beings of light, Yuri. They have come to help." Then I turned to where Swamiji had been, but he was now gone. In the distance, very faintly, almost like a soft hum, I heard Andrei crying out my name. I was caught in multiple realities: Yuri, Andrei, and my desire to follow Swamiji. I paused for a moment, or a decade. I couldn't tell. Time was suspended. I was being pulled in so many directions until finally I just let go. The moans of the dying Jews became faint; Andrei's cries withdrew into the far, far distance. My only thought was of Swamiji. He had finally found me and I had to follow.

And so I died.

Swami Yogananda had come to take me, as he had promised, from the grip of a tormented Europe through death into rebirth in America.

* * *

"Why does he need to go?" I asked my father, trying to hide my feelings. This was the third time he told me that we could no longer afford to have Jay as a consultant. My brother was tasked with the assignment to cut costs, and Jay was one of those costs. After each conversation I had pleaded his case, saying how much value he was providing.

"We must cut costs," my father sighed. "Jay has been very helpful to you, I know, but we can manage perfectly well without him now. You and I are fond of him, but we can't let that influence our decision."

"Okay. You are right, Dad," I said, looking up into my father's caring eyes. He had put on his practical hat. I often wondered how my father could move so easily between the creative and practical sides of his nature, something that I struggled to achieve. My interest in Jay was purely selfish, and had nothing to do with the company. He had played a major role in reviving the memories of my past life saga. Now that I had recalled so many of the major events, he was being taken away and I had to accept that. Perhaps his role was done, both with the company and with me personally.

I stood before Jay's closed door, hesitating before knocking. I knew that this would be one of my last visits with him.

"Come in," he said in that typically deep voice. "Denashka, how good to see you. Have you spoken with your father?"

I nodded. "Yes, he told me. I am so sorry about this."

"No, no, the company has to cut costs. As an advisor to the Executive Committee, I totally agree with the decision."

"Can I continue to call on you?" I asked meekly, still somewhat intimidated by him. I didn't know whether it was his large presence, or his distant and mysterious air that kept me from feeling completely at ease with him.

"Of course. You and I will stay in touch." He smiled and I smiled back. It was becoming increasingly clear that there was nothing more for us to do together. There had been some unfinished business, perhaps my desire to see him again and know that he was okay, but that business was now done and it was time to move on.

I didn't see Jay much after that. On occasion he would stop by to visit my father. Every now and then, I would get a call from him, but our relationship seemed to fizzle out after he left the company, the timing of which coincided perfectly with the completion of my past life recall.

A short time after Jay left the company in the mid-1990s, a colleague and friend invited me to join her on a business trip to Vienna. "I have always wanted to see Prague," she said. "After my meeting in Vienna, we can spend a day or two in Prague."

I immediately agreed. I wanted to see if I could find the site that I remembered from my previous birth, where I watched the Nazi army march into Prague from the window of my brother's apartment. I remembered so many details of that scene. After my friend and I spent two days seeing the many tourist attractions, she left to go home and I was able to wander the city alone. I did find the boulevard that matched my memories, and although it had been many decades since the Nazi invasion, I was able to reconstruct the scene. This was one of the clearest confirmations I had that my memories were real.

The following year I took a trip to St. Petersburg with the same intention. Although I found streets that resembled the neighborhood of my childhood home, I couldn't find the exact location, as I had in Prague. These memories helped me neutralize two strong bits of unfinished karma—the desire to reconnect with my Russian mother and to find again my Jewish lover. Once the narrative completed itself, the pain of loss that had been submerged during much of this life vanished. I was released of those tailings from the past.

These experiences helped me to understand many things about myself, but they also raised a host of new questions. Why was I born in Russia into an aristocratic family? Where did my love for dance come from? My desire to know more, to understand the workings of karma, increased as I progressed on the spiritual path. I was spending much time in meditation working out some of the emotions that remained from my previous birth. I still felt the sting of leaving my mother standing at the train station in St. Petersburg. It took years for these feelings to dissipate, but as soon as they did, new memories began to stir.

PART II

EARLY 19ᵀᴴ CENTURY AMERICA

That which pervades the entire body,
know it to be indestructible.
No one can cause the destruction of the imperishable soul.
Only the material body is perishable;
the embodied soul within is
indestructible, immeasurable, and eternal.

—*Bhagavad Gita* 2.17-
18

The soul comes from without into the human body,
as into a temporary abode, and it goes out of it anew...
it passes into other habitations, for the soul is immortal.

—Journals of Ralph
Waldo Emerson

Chapter 5

N ot long after I had recalled the memories of my life in Russia, another vision came to me in the same manner as the first. I was roused in the pre-dawn hours, not asleep, not awake, not dreaming; my consciousness was somewhere in between, in a dimension not normally accessed by the conscious mind. The vision was like a still photo.

I was a young woman, very beautiful, dressed in a full-skirted flowing white gown, with bows and lace, and a wide satin sash tied around my tiny waist. My coal black hair was tied up in an elegant style, with bits of tight curls cascading down along the sides of my cheeks, framing my pale white face. My dress was a style from the early 19th century. I could tell I was in the American Deep South. I seemed to be around 18 or 19 years old, with a few other young people on some sort of outing in the country, a picnic. I stood a bit apart from the others in front of a large tree, where I saw an African boy hanging by the neck, limp, dead. Every cell in my body rose up in revolt. I screamed and screamed and couldn't stop screaming.

When I came back fully to the normal waking state, I was very shaken by what I had seen. Later, as my emotions calmed, I questioned the vision. I never would have guessed myself to be born in the American South. Growing up in New York in this life, I had almost an antipathy toward the South. I had childhood memories of the civil rights battles and, for most of my life, had great resistance to even visiting there. No, I couldn't possibly be that southern belle I had seen in the vision.

"I have a new project that will interest you." My father called me to his office. He alone among my family members understood that I wasn't exactly cut out for the business world, but that I had a strong creative side that could be very useful for the work the company did. He was always trying to find projects that would spark my interest and tap my talents. Most often these projects were in the area of the arts.

My father's passion for the arts was what first brought him to the business world. As a young man he studied painting and loved to paint, mostly nature scenes. This love never left him. After his marriage, when he needed to find a business that would support a growing family, he developed the concept of corporate support for the arts and founded a company called Art & Industry, which later grew into a large full-spectrum public relations company under a different name. Soon my father found himself deeply engaged in the museum world and, to this day, the company maintains a division devoted exclusively to the museum and cultural world. Later he found a way to merge his love for the arts and business even further: he became a photographer of sculpture and over time published more than 100 books on sculpture from different cultures and parts of the world. This satisfied his creative urge and still allowed him to be a very successful businessman. This was the model he wanted me to follow.

For several years my father had involved me in editing a sculpture magazine that had become a client of the company; I knew that he had orchestrated this project so that we could work together as well as to develop my writing skills. He took the photographs of the sculpture and I edited and in some cases wrote a number of the articles. It was a perfect collaboration, and I enjoyed working with him. I was content with this work. But now he was about to introduce me to something quite different, a project much more aligned with my character and interests.

He said, "We have started working for a new museum in Japan that was created by a spiritual organization. We are bringing journalists to the opening of the museum and inevitably they will ask about the organization's spiritual philosophy. None of us here knows how to explain it; none of us really understands their philosophy, but perhaps you will. This organization needs help articulating their spiritual message so that we can relay it to the art journalists. I think you can be very helpful. We can work together on this."

At the mention of spirituality, my ears perked up. By now I was used to the art projects, but I yearned for something more relevant to my spiritual life. "That sounds wonderful," I replied with visible enthusiasm.

"Read this background material." He handed me some brochures and booklets. Their museum is world class. They have hired us to help with the opening of the museum. This is a perfect project for you."

I had never been to Japan and didn't know much about the culture. In fact, I had done little travel. As a single mom I had not been able to leave my sons. But now my youngest had just gone off to college and I was eager to embark on something new. I began working with the group, helping to find the right language to express their spiritual philosophy to an international audience. They were headquartered outside of Kyoto, but their main U.S. branch was in Los Angeles and I was invited to meet with their leadership and members there. I was always glad for a trip to L.A. as Yogananda's headquarters were there. For many, many years I had been making retreats at Yogananda's seaside ashram just south of Los Angeles. I welcomed the opportunity to travel there to begin this new project, and to sneak in a visit to the ashram.

It was at one of my first meetings with the U.S. leadership of the Japanese organization that I met Clyde, an African-American lawyer who had left the practice of law to focus on his spiritual life. What was so unusual and special about him was that he was a member of both this Japanese organization and the organization founded by my guru, to which I also belonged. When I met Clyde, he had recently lost his wife, a white woman who had been an environmental lawyer and had similarly been involved with both the Japanese group and Yogananda's teachings.

Clyde spoke frequently and lovingly of his wife Dorothy, and I relished the stories of her. As he and I became friends, I became friends with her as well, that is, with her spirit. For a brief time after our meeting, there seemed the possibility of a romantic relationship with Clyde, but this thought did not last long because Dorothy was always with us, and I could no more betray her than I could a sister.

One day, after we had known each other for a few months, Clyde picked me up at the airport in L.A. and was taking me to the center of the Japanese organization for a meeting. Suddenly he started to laugh. I looked at him curiously and couldn't help but smile.

"What's so funny?"

"I just remembered an incident with Dorothy," he said, somewhat apologetically. "It took place here on this very road."

"Tell me," I urged. "I love to hear about her."

"She was passionate about anything that was alive, any little leaf. Once she was driving and spotted something in front of us, a branch with some leaves, I think it was, and she nearly drove off the road to avoid crushing it. She nearly killed us to avoid running over some foliage, but that was Dorothy."

I smiled and nodded my head as if to agree. Yes, that was Dorothy.

"She was passionate about whatever she set her mind to, such an independent spirit," he continued lovingly.

"I feel like I know her," I replied quietly. "When you and I are together, I feel her spirit very much alive. I think she is happy that we have met."

"You two would have gotten along very well," he said with a smile. Whenever Clyde spoke of Dorothy, there was never sadness in his voice, only love. Somehow I reminded him of her and our connection seemed to call her to us. This was comforting for us both. I understood well why he felt this way, but why did I? Why did I feel such a tender connection to a woman I had never met?

That night as I was sitting in my hotel room, meditating before bed, I felt myself being sucked back into the past, tumbling through the vortex of time. It was the same process and experience that I had had when the memories of my life in Russia began to bubble forth. It was happening again and I had no power to resist or control it. The present faded away and I began to see images of another time, and to hear conversations that had long ago ceased. And I saw her, my sister Dotty, living with me in the South back in the early decades of 19th century America.

* * *

I was born to French parents in the early 1800s on a plantation in Louisiana. My mother died when I was very young and I never knew her. My name was Elisabeth Bonnet and since childhood I called my elder sister Dotty. There were only the two of us, and we were very close, although she was quite a bit older. Our temperaments were very different. She was practical, almost manly in her approach to the world, strong-willed with an incisive mind. She expressed herself forcefully. Her speech could be cutting, but my father respected her and depended on her a great deal. In many respects, she took my mother's place in the family as my father's guiding hand.

I played a different role with my father. I think he saw in me much of my mother's artistic nature, with a strong aesthetic sense, more given to the world of imagination than practical affairs. I didn't always speak my mind and kept to myself a great deal. Dotty and I were so different from one another, but there was no shred of jealousy between us. Occasionally Dotty would get irritated with me for not paying attention to everyday matters. Her constant refrain was that my head was in the clouds, but actually she was quite content for it to stay there so she could manage my father's affairs. I was also quite happy with this arrangement as it gave me much freedom.

As a child, I found myself drawn to the subdued rhythms of the Africans who worked in my father's fields. I found their presence oddly soothing, and I sought refuge in their midst. Many days I spent watching their world from a distance, wishing in a way that I could be part of it. I never thought of the labor they endured, only their closeness to the earth, the earth that emanated such fragrance as they tilled the soil. Sometimes their quiet chanting would drift through the soft southern air at night and lull me to sleep. In dreams I would travel to unfamiliar places, to lush forests where birds of many colors sang. I loved the sultry summer nights with their thick moist heat, when open windows provided entry to their world.

What Dotty and I loved most about the plantation were the grandfather trees that lined the path to the house. As children we referred to them as our guardian angels. Their trunks were so thick that to encircle them would take several people. Dotty used to try to embrace them, getting some childhood friends and me to join hands in a ring around the tree. Then we would look up at the sunlight dancing through the full leafy branches and pretend that the sun was sending each of us a message. Even in its flickering appearance, the sun would be so bright that we would be forced to close our eyes and listen. What was the sun in its gleaming radiance telling us?

One day as we were playing this game, one of the children asked, "What is your message, Elisabeth?"

I replied without thinking, "The sun is telling me that I came from Africa, that Africa is my home." I was as surprised as the others to hear these words.

They all laughed. "How silly," he said. "Look at your skin, Elisabeth. It is as white as milk."

My eyes flew open. With great embarrassment, I blurted out, "I don't know why I said that."

"Because you have a strong imagination, "replied Dotty caringly, "and you can go to places where none of us can follow. For that you are fortunate, Elisabeth. Perhaps your soul did come from Africa."

There was a middle-aged African woman on the plantation known to have a way with medicinal plants. Bessie was always cooking up a brew and Papa would send for her whenever anyone got sick or hurt. Intrigued by her knowledge, I was always glad when she would come up to the house. A subtle scent of herbs accompanied her, bringing the dream memory of forests and broad leafy trees, surrounded by plants of all sizes and forms. Her medicines had a magical effect on people, who almost always recovered after being treated by her.

Sometimes Papa would go to her cabin to talk about a particular ailment. If I saw him heading in her direction, I would run to accompany him. She always had piles of fresh and dried herbs, and I could not keep myself from picking them up one by one to smell them and ask about the properties of each one. Papa would say, "Hush, let Bessie do her work," but she would smile at me and briefly explain what she was doing. I loved going to Bessie's cabin. The smells were mysteriously soothing. Even the smallness of the cabin had its appeal. There was barely anything in it—a small table with two chairs, and two small beds. Bessie had no husband; she had only Joseph, her son. Joseph was never around when we were there, always off doing some work, but I would never fail to ask after him.

I used to wonder as a child why we lived in two completely separate worlds: Dotty and I in one world, Joseph and the other African children in another. Why was there this impenetrable barrier between us, a barrier that could not even be discussed? I had learned early on it was not a matter for polite conversation. Once when I asked Papa why I could not play with Joseph, he told me that we had to accept this and not question it, so, on the surface, I did.

One day when Papa and I were collecting medicine from Bessie, I asked in the usual manner after Joseph. "He's working in the fields now," she replied with a touch of sadness.

"Oh," remarked Papa in surprise.

"Yes, Mr. Tallow says he's old enough, but it's hard work in the fields from dawn to dusk and Joseph, well, he's not really strong enough."

"How old is he now?" Papa asked.

"Just ten," replied Bessie looking down.

There was agitation in Papa's voice. "I will take care of it. We will bring him to the house. We are short-staffed and need more help there."

"I would be most grateful," she replied, raising her eyes. There was an awkward moment and a glace exchanged between Papa and Bessie, the acknowledgement of something I couldn't then understand.

Joseph was coming to the house to help in the kitchen, so I would be able to see him every day. There could be no better news than this. But although he was now physically present, we had no contact. Whenever he would enter a room where we were, he would respond to Papa with eyes toward the floor. The years passed and I kept my fondness for Joseph hidden in my heart, not sharing my feelings even with Dotty.

Then one day Papa announced that there had been a proposal of marriage for me from a man named Charles, the son of a wealthy plantation owner. I must have been around 18 or 19 years old. "It is a good match," Papa said. "One of the best families."

"But I don't love him," I replied angrily. "And besides, I don't want to get married, at least not now."

"Love is something that grows. It doesn't happen all of the sudden," Papa responded with a faint smile. "You will learn to love him. He is a handsome boy. At least give it serious thought before deciding. It would not look right for us to reject this family."

Papa had just about given up on Dotty getting married. She had refused every prospect and made it clear she had no interest. I knew I was Papa's last hope for a son-in-law and heirs. I ran from the room and up the stairs, struggling with my emotions. Just then I passed Joseph coming down the stairs. I paused and looked at him; he paused as well. I could feel my face flush. "Joseph," I whispered in a rough voice. "Why do you never look at me?" He didn't answer. "There is nobody here," I said. "You can look at me." His eyes were downcast. "Please, Joseph, look at me." He turned his eyes to me—they were rich and deep and beautiful. What was it in them that touched me: a certain pride perhaps, a strength and a manliness? Then I heard Papa's voice and hurried to my room.

It was not long after that Joseph ran away. I was glad for him. He deserved better. Papa agreed not to go after him. "But he will be caught," said Papa. "And it will not be good for him. There is nothing I can do. He should not have run away."

The weeks went by and no word of Joseph. "Perhaps he has found his freedom," Dotty said to me one day.

"Let us hope so," I replied.

I still had not given my response to Charles. Papa had told Charles's father that I was still young and needed more time to think it over. I knew the day was approaching when I had to either accept or refuse his proposal. In order to help me make my decision, Charles invited Dotty and me on a picnic. I reluctantly agreed.

We went to a lovely spot by the river. Tall trees lined the riverbank, stretching their lanky, moss-draped branches over the fast running water. There were several of us on the outing. Dotty began to set out the blanket and lunch. I wandered off among the trees, glad for a few moments to myself. I sought out one of the tallest trees and stood under it. I dared not press myself against the trunk as I did in my younger days for fear I would stain my beautiful white dress. It was a new dress of the latest fashion, with satin bows and a wide satin sash. Dotty had laughed at me for wearing it to a picnic, but I could not resist. It was my nature to love to dress in beautiful clothes even if I had no place to go. I looked up through the branches toward the sun, as I had when I was a child. It was bright today. I closed my eyes.

"What message do you have for me, oh sun?" I whispered. "Do I honor the wishes of Papa, or do I follow my own heart?" I tried to still myself so I could hear the response emerging from up above or deep inside. In such moments it seems the external and internal worlds merge and they are one. What was spoken from outside only reflected thoughts emerging from deep within. But this day, the silence did not speak to me. I received no answer to my invocations. The sun was mute. I opened my eyes and looked up into the brightness. "I have my whole life ahead of me," I thought, as if speaking to the sun. "I cannot marry him now." Yes, that was the answer the sun was trying to convey. I would have to tell Papa as soon as we returned. Now that I had my answer, I should get back to the others, I thought.

As I turned to go, I felt dizzy from the glare of the sun. Staring into that brilliant, flaming eye even for those few seconds caused me to lose my step and stumble. I gained my footing and found myself but a few yards from the body of a boy hanging from the branch of a neighboring tree, limp, a rope around his neck. It was Joseph. I knew at once that he was dead. I screamed and the others came running. I could not stop myself from screaming. And long after my voice fell silent, the screams kept racing through my body.

After that incident, I did not leave my room for days. I was in a state of shock and could not pull myself out of my numb condition. It was only Dotty's words that brought me back to life about a week after the incident. "Look at me, Elisabeth," she said in a calm but forceful voice as she cradled my face in her hands. "I promise you, on my life I promise you that I will avenge Joseph's death. I will not let them get away with this. No matter how long it takes, I will avenge his death." Her eyes and voice were firm.

"That won't bring him back," I said through my tears.

"But I will make sure he did not die for naught. It may take some time, but I will make sure. Do you understand me?" Her voice was firm. Nobody had a stronger will than Dotty and I knew she meant what she said. I nodded. "Papa is distraught as well. He blames himself, although there was nothing he could have done. We are all victims." Then she added, "I have been to see Bessie."

"He is all she had," I murmured.

"She expected it after he ran away, but I told her the same thing that I am telling you. I will not let his death be in vain. I promise you that." I looked at Dotty. A distant and steely look had crept over her eyes. She was gazing off into the distance, no longer gazing at me.

"What will you do, Dotty? What can we do?"

"I don't know," she said. "It will take time for me to figure this out. But I take a solemn vow that, before I die, I will make sure that because of his death, others will be free."

I refused the proposal from Charles. Papa was disappointed, but accepted my decision. The months passed and I couldn't shake off the shadow cast by Joseph's murder. The image of him hanging from the tree refused to leave my mind. It haunted me night and day. I would see him in dreams with the rope around his neck, and I would scream out. Nothing could ease the pain I experienced from what I had seen. And then came the guilt. Perhaps it was the incident on the stairway that caused him to flee.

My spirit had lost something precious and I didn't know how to recover it. A year or two passed. Proposals came and were rejected. Papa didn't know what to do with me. Finally he appealed to a woman relative living nearby to accompany Dotty and me to Paris, where we would stay with my mother's aunt. It was my first trip away from home.

Chapter 6

D otty found little of interest in Paris, but I marveled at the life there. It renewed my spirit. I found the people so much more cultured than those in our society at home. Everyone seemed to have a passion, a creative endeavor—painting, music, literature. It was a world I easily slid into, hardly noticing my sister's boredom. And the styles! I had never seen such creative and magnificent outfits.

We had been there only a few months when my aunt announced that she was taking us to Vienna to attend a Grand Ball. As was to be expected, Dotty resisted, but when I refused to go without her she agreed to join us. She saw how Paris had brought the glow back into my life and she was truly pleased. Papa's scheme had worked. But she cautioned, "Don't get carried away, Elisabeth. This is not our world. Eventually we will have to go back home."

If Paris was the center of creative life, Vienna was the epitome of extravagance. The palace where the ball was held was beyond anything I could have imagined. Everywhere I looked there were gilded adornments of the most lavish nature.

"Try not to stare," whispered Dotty. "You are giving us away."

It was both comical and entrancing. As I cast my eyes around the ballroom, my glance fell on a woman standing near us who was wearing the most extraordinary jewelry, and I drew closer to get a better look. I couldn't help but stare at the large glittering necklace adorning her neck. I was so absorbed in the scene that I didn't notice one of her companions approaching until he stood before me, held out his hand, and asked for a dance.

Embarrassed to be caught off guard, my first impulse was to decline, but then I thought otherwise and took his hand.

"What is your name?" he asked as we began the formal steps of the dance.

"Elisabeth," I murmured shyly.

He waited. "Just Elisabeth?" he asked.

I nodded, not wanting to give away too much information about myself.

"Okay, just Elisabeth," he smiled, "I am just Pavel from St. Petersburg. May I ask where you are from?"

"Paris," I mumbled, hoping that my French was good enough to hide any hints of an American accent.

"I could not help but notice you from across the room," he said in a genteel tone. "You are by far the most beautiful woman at this ball." I blushed at his words. He continued, "The woman you were admiring is my sister."

I felt my checks grow redder and I looked away, not knowing what to say. Had I been so obvious? He saw my embarrassment and tried to make me feel at ease. He was much older than I and not particularly handsome, but there was something very attractive about him, perhaps his cultured and elegant manner. He talked on and on about all sorts of things, and the more he spoke, the more he sounded in many ways like my sister Dotty. He made fun of the extravagance of Vienna life and the frivolity of the people, saying that all this show had nothing to do with true culture. He preferred the country to city life and went on to extol the virtues of living a quiet life in a natural setting. I was listening attentively, nodding occasionally in agreement, intrigued by the conversation, and slowly I began to feel at ease with him. One dance passed, and then another and another, until the evening faded into late night. I hardly noticed the time fleeing. I didn't feel weary at all. I could have kept dancing had not my aunt finally intervened, saying it was time for us to leave.

"I should apologize for having taken up your whole evening, leaving no opportunity for the other gentlemen," he said as he let go of my hand and bowed.

I thanked him profusely and told him that I had never enjoyed myself so much. In fact, I had never danced with such joy and delight. Until that evening I did not realize how much I loved to be swept across the dance floor as if nobody but the two of us existed.

"I am in Vienna for the week. May I invite you ladies to the ballet tomorrow night," he addressed my aunt, but his eyes continue to rest on me. "My sister will join us," he said.

I glanced at my aunt with pleading eyes, hoping that she would agree. Dancing with Pavel had given me a sense of freedom that I had never experienced before. "We would be honored," she replied, giving him our address.

"Then it is set. I will pick you up tomorrow night."

Once in the carriage, I allowed myself to express my joy. I had never been to the ballet and was so excited to be invited. "Do you know whom you were dancing with?" asked Dotty in amazement.

I nodded. "His name is Pavel and he is from St. Petersburg, Russia, I suppose. I know that he is much older than me . . ." I stopped fearing Dotty was about to scold me for spending the evening with an older man. "But, Dotty, he is so cultured and so intelligent . . ."

"You suppose! Elisabeth, you are probably the only one at the ball who doesn't know who that man is."

"I know only what I told you," I replied, annoyed at her tone. "He is a very nice man, and very cultured as well. I hope he is not married, for the attention he paid me . . . well, it would be inappropriate if he were a married man." I was pleased by his apparent interest in me and felt an attraction as well.

"Elisabeth, he is a Russian prince!"

"Dotty, no. You are mistaken. It couldn't be true. He is a most humble man." I smiled that she would mistake Pavel for a prince.

"There is no doubt about it."

"Say you are kidding." Dotty loved to tease me and sometimes it was hard to tell when she was serious and when she was jesting, often to provoke me.

She shook her head. "It is for real. He is a prince, Elisabeth, and you are probably the only one there who didn't realize it."

My eyes flew open as wide as they could, and a shocked look crossed my face. "And I spoke to him as if he were just another gentleman, like anybody else. Oh, Dotty, I am so ashamed."

"That is probably why he didn't let you go all evening. Every woman there was eyeing him, and they were probably all wondering who the noble lady was dancing the night away with him. But don't worry. He is a bachelor I am told."

"We must cancel tomorrow night," I murmured. "I can't go. I can't face him and his sister."

"You must go. You have made a commitment. He is like any other man. Don't let what I have told you change anything."

Dotty decided not to join us the next evening. Aunt Margaret and I went to the ballet that night, and the next and the next. Of all my experiences in Europe, it was the ballet that left the deepest impression. I had never seen any art form so graceful, so magical, and so ethereal. The dancers were more like spirits than people. I could have kept going every night to the ballet. Pavel seemed to enjoy my enthusiasm, and the more I marveled at the dancing, the more pleased he was.

"Come with me to St. Petersburg, and I will take you to as much ballet as you desire," he said in a serious tone. I didn't respond. Dotty was right to caution me. I was growing very fond of the prince and the world he was showing me. The plantation was becoming more and more remote. There was a part of me that could have followed Pavel to Russia without a backward glance. But it was not to be.

The next morning my aunt received a telegraph and we had to return to Paris right away. She dashed off a note to Pavel to say that we could not join him that evening, as we had to leave for Paris. I settled back into Paris life with dreams of Vienna still in my mind.

It wasn't long before Dotty came into the sitting room one day to announce: "There is someone to see you, Elisabeth." I looked at her quizzically. I didn't know anyone in Paris aside from my aunt's acquaintances. Who would come to visit me? "I've shown him into the parlor," she said.

"Him?" I asked meekly.

She nodded.

I couldn't imagine who it might be, but my heart leapt as I saw him from the doorway. Pavel had followed me to Paris. For the next few weeks he took me somewhere grand every night, to opera, ballet, theater, dinner. My head was truly spinning. Louisiana became like a forgotten dream, and everything faded away but the magical world in which I was now living.

One day Dotty cautioned me again, this time in a more serious tone. "Be careful, Elisabeth. Don't let your heart get carried away."

"I know," I replied solemnly. "I know we must return home."

"In two weeks time," she said. "Aunt Margaret has purchased the tickets for our travel home. You must tell him." I nodded, not sure of how I would broach the subject. "It is only fair that you tell him now."

"I don't want the world he is showing me to end," I replied in a quiet voice. There was much sadness at the thought of returning to America.

"You and Pavel live in two different worlds," she said, "and they can't be bridged. Bring yourself slowly down from the clouds." After a moment of silence, she added with great regret, "Sometimes I chide myself for allowing you to get so carried away by him. You know he can't be serious, and you are too fine a woman, Elisabeth, to be toyed with."

Her words jolted me. It was like the sudden appearance of storm clouds on a calm day. Until that moment, I had not thought of the future, not his and not mine. I was too busy enjoying myself in the present.

The next evening on the way home from the opera, as the carriage stopped in front of my aunt's house and Pavel was about to step out to open the carriage door for me, I rested my hand on his arm and stopped him, saying, "Pavel, the time is approaching when I will have to return to America." He seemed startled. He had found out soon after his arrival in Paris that I lived on a plantation in Louisiana, not in Paris.

"Must you go so soon?" he asked.

I smiled. "I have been gone a long time, many months. America is my home, and my father is waiting for us."

"How soon?"

"Two weeks."

"I wish we had more time, Elisabeth." An awkward silence followed and then he broke it by saying, "Then I will have to say to you now what is in my heart." We were both quiet. "Elisabeth, these have been the happiest weeks of my life."

I nodded and smiled. "I also have enjoyed this time immensely. You have opened a new world to me, and it will be difficult to return to the world I knew."

"Then why return?" he asked in a serious tone. "Come with me to Russia." I must have looked startled because he hurried to add in a low tone, "Elisabeth, I want to marry you."

My mouth dropped open. This was the last thing I had expected, especially after Dotty's words. Perhaps I had been naïve not to consider that all of his attention to me indicated some sincere intention. But truly the thought of marriage had never entered my mind.

He saw my shock. "I know there are many differences between us, but they are of no importance to me. I am twice your age but I have never felt a distance due to that." I still couldn't utter a word. I didn't know what to say. "I hope your silence does not mean rejection, Elisabeth. Please do consider seriously my proposal."

"No, no rejection," I finally uttered. "I am just so surprised. Do give me time, a few days to consider all of this. There is so much to think about."

"I will call for you in three days and, hopefully, you will have a positive answer for me by then," he smiled.

I must have looked dreadful when I entered the home of my aunt. As soon as Dotty saw me, she dropped what she was doing and ran to take me in her arms. "You have told him, and that is the end of it," she exclaimed. 'Was he angry?"

"No, nothing like that."

"Then why do you look like you are in shock?"

"Dotty," I cracked a half smile. "I don't know whether to be happy or sad. He has asked me to marry him and go with him to Russia."

"Marry? Are you serious? Is he serious?"

I nodded. "It is the last thing I expected."

"What did you tell him?"

"Dotty, I didn't know what to do. I asked him to give me a few days."

"Are you in love with him?"

"I don't know. I don't know what it is to be in love."

"You have enjoyed his company and the world he has shown you, but that is not necessarily love, Elisabeth." She led me to the sofa and sat me down.

"How do I know if I am in love with him?"

She thought for a moment. "Does your heart beat fast at the sight of him?"

I shook my head. "But the very thought of him makes me smile. He is so kind and considerate."

"Do you think of him every moment when you are not with him?'

Again I shook my head. "But Dotty, I am happy when we are together.

I take great comfort in his presence."

"I can't help you, Elisabeth," she said briskly. "I don't know what it means to be in love either."

"If I do decide to go to Russia, would you come with me?" I asked meekly.

"And leave Papa all alone? Beside, you know how I feel about the cold weather."

I was quiet. "I don't think I could bear for us to be parted, Dotty."

She turned her eyes away. "You mustn't think of me. This could be your chance for happiness." She was quiet and then added, "But do think of Papa. He is very attached to you, Elisabeth, more so than to me. You are his heart and I don't know if he would survive losing you."

For the next few days my mind went back and forth, considering both options: leaving behind all that was familiar and following Pavel into an unknown world, or saying goodbye to him and the world he had shown me. In the end perhaps I didn't have the courage to leave what was familiar, or perhaps deep inside I knew that something else awaited me in the new world.

It was a sad and confusing parting with Pavel. He said that perhaps I was too young and needed more time to consider his proposal, but I knew in my heart that once I returned to America it would be difficult to leave. It was now or never, and I chose to return to the world I knew.

It was on the boat back to America that I found my love for Pavel.

"I do love him," I cried, burying my head on Dotty's shoulder. "I do love him. He is in my mind always. What am I to do, Dotty?"

There was not much she could say. We were well on our way home to America.

* * *

I was to see Clyde again before leaving for the airport to return to New York. I had spent the whole night reliving my early years in the South. Clyde was a spiritual friend and would surely understand the recollection of past life memories, but I wasn't sure whether or not to confide in him. I had not told many friends about my memories of Russia, because it was difficult to speak of the experience, but I thought perhaps

Clyde would understand. I had a desire to share these experiences, but I also instinctively felt to keep them private, as the teaching was really a personal one, providing great insight into my current life.

When Clyde came to pick me up at the hotel, I suddenly asked him out of the blue, "Where were you born?" He had an accent but I couldn't place it.

"Alabama," he replied.

"So you are a southern man!" I exclaimed.

"Well, yes, but I have been away for a long time."

I was quiet for a while and then said slowly, "I have come to feel that Dorothy and I were sisters, perhaps in the south, sometime in the last century." He didn't respond. "What I remember most about her was her strong will, and independence. She was fiercely independent, wasn't she?"

"The most independent woman I have ever met," he confirmed. "She was an ardent feminist. That was one of the qualities I loved about her," he said quietly. Then he added, "The three of us clearly have a connection. When I am with you, I feel close to Dorothy and feel her presence. But I don't know any more than that. Only you can say what your relationship with her in the past has been."

I needed time to process what I had experienced the night before in meditation. On the flight home, I tried to piece together what I had seen. Perhaps my love for ballet originated from my time in Vienna and perhaps I did follow Pavel to Russia by being born there after my life in America. But I had to understand more. Was there a deeper reason for my return to the South and what course did my life take after my return? So many questions arose, but one thing I had learned was that the answers came in their own time, and I could not press for more information than was given.

My work with the Japanese organization continued and I began to delve into their spiritual philosophy. It was very fulfilling and I was very aware that this was a rare work opportunity, one that would enable me to use my communications skills to bring spiritual principles to a wider audience. My father was very pleased that I had found something that I could fully embrace, yet also paid the bills. The organization was a paying client, and yet for me, my work with them was part of the unfolding of my spiritual journey.

As had been my experience with the recollection of my life in Russia, I had to wait for the memories to return. For many months I remembered no further than the boat ride back to America. But eventually, during an evening meditation, I found myself sucked back into the 19th century and I was again living the life of Elisabeth.

Chapter 7

T he time in Europe changed me. I did not come back to Louisiana the
same girl who had left. Papa expected me to return home ready to
marry, but my meeting with Pavel made it impossible to settle for any of
the gentlemen at home. Dotty told Papa of my time with Pavel, but he did
not take seriously my brief flirtation with royal life. The more he made
light of it, the more solemn and determined I became that I would not
marry a man I did not love. I could see his despair. One of his daughters
had to marry. Who would look after the plantation when he was gone?
He knew that his elder daughter had no intention of marrying. Without
my compliance, there would be no man to assist him, no heirs.

"Papa, you know that I am as smart and capable as any man," Dotty
proclaimed one evening when the subject of my marriage came up. "I am
going to run the plantation with you." Her voice was firm.

"And you, Elisabeth?" asked Papa beseechingly. "Don't you have a
desire for a husband and children? The most eligible men in this town are
after you. Won't you give any of them a chance?"

"I don't want to be treated like a flower," I replied firmly. "Pavel gave
me a taste of something deeper. If I find a man here who will love me for
what is inside, not outside, then perhaps at some point I will consider it."

"I had hoped the trip to Paris would knock some sense into your
head," he said shaking his head. "You don't know how difficult life will be
for the two of you when I am not around."

"We will manage just fine," replied Dotty with an assured smile. "But
we have you with us now and it makes no sense to worry about the future."

I had an idea of my own. I had seen how the women of Europe were
so much better educated, and I thought to bring something of that to the
young girls at home. I would start a school.

Papa gave in to the desires of his two daughters. Dotty began to assume more responsibility for running the plantation. She took it up with enthusiasm and before long was insisting to Papa that we needed to be progressive and reform the way things had been done. Increasingly, she and Papa began to argue about how to manage our affairs. She insisted on letting go the manager of the plantation as she said he was a hard taskmaster. Papa demurred, claiming the man had been with the family a long time and was to be trusted, but Dotty was unmoved. He had to go. This was the first of the many changes she was to make, changes for the better. I retreated more and more into my own world, busying myself with setting up a school for the daughters of other plantation owners, but on occasion I had to intervene on Dotty's behalf.

One day, Papa heard that Dotty had been working in the fields, alongside the Africans. He was shocked and upbraided her for the scandal this would cause, but Dotty didn't care. She claimed she could not give others work that she herself would not do. I admired her for the way she was able to stand up to Papa, and I saw the way she was quietly making life better for the Africans who worked the plantation. Papa seemed not to notice this, but I realized what she was doing and praised her often in Papa's presence, hoping to awaken in him the same respect for her that I had. He never came around to recognizing her gifts, and I know that was a source of sorrow for her.

Many months after returning from Europe, Dotty handed me an envelope. "It is from him," she said. I grabbed the letter and hungrily drank in every word. Pavel's letter was filled with anecdotes about his life in St. Petersburg. It was intelligent, amusing, and brought back such fond memories of our time together. I wrote him of my dream to start a school for girls, and so began a correspondence that was to last until his death.

My life now was devoted to the organization of the school. It was an enormous undertaking, far more than I had realized, but Dotty gave me much assistance and soon I found others to help. I had managed to collect the funds to purchase land and a building and hire staff, but soon the expenses of the school ate up everything I had collected. We had no money to open the school. I became desperate. Would all my efforts come to naught? I had exhausted all my options and had nowhere to turn, when out of the blue a very official looking gentleman arrived at our door one day with a package from Russia. Pavel had sent a large sum of money for the school. My eyes filled with tears as I realized what he had done for me. On two more occasions when the school was desperately in need of funds, Pavel somehow knew intuitively to send me money, and this allowed the school not only to keep open its doors, but also to grow and flourish.

The years passed. I had other proposals of marriage, but Papa no longer was surprised when I refused. One winter Papa took ill and died. Dotty had already taken over running the plantation, so there was no disruption in our lives. My girl's school was thriving and gaining a reputation in many parts of Louisiana and beyond; we could not accommodate all the applications from families wanting to send their daughters to the school. One day I was surprised to receive an invitation to visit a girl's school in Boston. I eagerly accepted this first trip to the north.

As I was leaving, Dotty handed me a package. "You would do me a great favor if you could deliver this to Mr. Jeremiah Brown. Here is a letter to accompany the package and this is the address in Boston."

"Who is he?" I asked, taking the package.

"A very special man," she replied quietly. "I have not met him but know a lot about his work and have great admiration for him. We have been corresponding for a while now."

"So there is a man who has finally caught your interest," I exclaimed with amusement. She shot me a chiding glance and I pried no further.

It was a long journey to Boston, with numerous coaches and trains. Finally I arrived and was surprised to find the atmosphere as stimulating as Europe had been for me so many years earlier, but in a much different way. It was not the beauty, artistry, or wealth that struck me, the formality or history. It was the intellectual activity, the new thinking, the breaking of traditions. For the first time I encountered Africans who were free men, and women who spoke their minds publicly and led independent lives. Education was of a wholly different order. Girls were being taught to think for themselves, not to be mere showpieces for their husbands.

After I had finished my business, I remembered the package Dotty had entrusted to me and set out to find Mr. Brown. A tall, elegant looking African man opened the door.

"I am looking for Mr. Jeremiah Brown," I said hesitantly.

"Yes, I am Mr. Brown." He must have sensed my surprise, because an awkward moment ensued. Dotty had not mentioned that he was an

African.

"I have a package from my sister," I said somewhat meekly, after introducing myself. I handed him Dotty's letter and he broke into a warm smile. He graciously invited me to come into the house.

"Your sister and I have been corresponding for a few years now. She informed me that you would be coming." He took the package and opened the letter. I watched his face carefully for any clue of the nature of their correspondence, but there was no expression on his face. He nodded, put the letter and package aside, and invited me to stay for tea. A middle-aged African woman came to serve us. "This is my wife, Cornelia," he said. She held out her hand and I took it, glad to be able to meet this African couple on an equal footing.

"Your sister is an admirable woman. Please express to her our deep gratitude," said his wife. I nodded. I made some casual conversation with her, but my eyes kept turning to her husband.

Mr. Brown had the demeanor and look of a fine gentleman. Once I got over my initial surprise, I found myself to be quite comfortable with him. His straight hair was parted on one side and brushed back. His face was long, framed by sideburns that almost reached his chin. His skin was an autumn brown color, lighter than many Africans. His eyes were gentle and wise. When he addressed me he looked me straight in the eye with a calm and steady gaze. There was such grace about him. I had never met an African who spoke with the confidence of an equal. I wondered about his history, how he attained such a position in society, but it was to take me many visits to uncover his story—a story of courage, determination, and accomplishment.

As I sat sipping the tea his wife had served me, now and then casting my gaze around the room and noticing the care with which everything had been organized, with books neatly arranged in various corners, I turned my eyes to find him gazing at me thoughtfully. He had taken off his glasses and I could see an almost tender look in his eye.

"Is it possible, Miss Bonnet, that we have met before?" he asked quietly "There is something about you that is so familiar."

I smiled. "I don't see how that is possible. This is my first trip to the North." Suddenly I shivered involuntarily and tears flooded my eyes. I couldn't explain the tears. It was something about his look. For the first time I saw pain etched in his face, a pain different from mine. His was a deeper suffering, far deeper than I could imagine, and yet there was a grace with which he wore his pain. In that moment, his pain became my pain and I felt it in the core of my being. I knew that we were somehow connected, although it made no sense to my logical mind. It took me quite a few minutes to regain my composure.

"Please excuse me," I said wiping my eyes. "For some reason our meeting has evoked something from the past, something very painful." Perhaps it was Joseph, I thought, the memory of him, of what Joseph could have been, but no, it was something different, beyond what my mind could comprehend.

"I am sorry," he said, replacing his spectacles. "I didn't mean to upset you."

My tears were gone and I felt a quiet joy being in his presence. "Our society has brought pain to all of us. None of us are spared the grief of our present situation. If only people could realize that we are all victims. I am most pleased to meet you, Mr. Brown, and your gracious wife, most pleased. I will convey your greetings and good wishes to my sister." I got up to leave.

"Yes, please do," he said holding out his hand. "I do hope that we meet again."

I lingered for a moment, gazing at him curiously. "Yes, perhaps we have met, somewhere, at some time. That may well be," I murmured.

The visit with Mr. Brown had been both comforting and disturbing. Unable to understand my emotions, I brushed them aside and brought my attention back to the task at hand. I had only a few days left before I was scheduled to depart for home. My visit to the girls' schools in the area had been inspiring and filled me with many ideas to implement back home. I had been greatly impressed by the caliber of the students and depth of the studies.

Just before I was to leave Boston, my host invited me to attend a talk with her. "Mr. Emerson is giving a talk tonight. Before you leave you should hear him lecture." I was glad to go along. I didn't know anything about the speaker, but my host's praise was enough to make me curious.

The talk was being given in Cambridge, outside of Boston. We went together in a coach. I didn't know what to expect and I thought not much of it, until I saw the tall scholarly man enter the room. A calming air accompanied him, the chatter ceased, and a hush fell over the room. I sat up straight, my attention fully focused on the lecturer. I observed his physical appearance, but that wasn't what struck me about him. He would have been around my age or a bit older. He had a thoughtful visage and the demeanor of a pastor. I had no interest in religion, having been brought up by a father who had little use for the Catholic church of his tradition, but I could feel that Mr. Emerson had an almost religious air about him.

"Is he a preacher?" I inquired of my host.

"He is and he isn't," she responded quietly. I looked baffled. "I mean he was, but he has gone far beyond that now." I didn't understand what she meant.

As he began to speak, I listened with great attention, but then, slowly, his words trailed off. They became a background hum, a vibration with no discernable meaning. I was feeling very quiet and peaceful and so closed my eyes; my attention turned inward, drawn deeper and deeper as if pulled inside. It felt like I was falling into a great abyss, but it was a very pleasant feeling. I allowed myself to drift, no longer aware of my body, but very aware of myself. I couldn't tell where my point of being was. My body no longer seemed to contain me. I felt myself everywhere and nowhere at the same time. I was conscious, very conscious, but not of my outer surroundings, of another world inside, an internal reality that was vibrant and beautiful.

I was aware of a mellow light, unlike sunlight. I rested in this light for I do not know how long, and then gradually the outer sounds returned and I could distinguish words being spoken. I opened my eyes and there was Mr. Emerson expounding something with great enthusiasm. Perhaps another thirty minutes passed, but I was still embedded in the inner world and could not return to the lecture. I could not bring myself fully back until he brought his talk to a close. There was warm applause.

My host got up to leave, but I was unable to move, still basking in the experience. I did not want to speak or interact. "You are very quiet, Elisabeth. Did you enjoy the lecture?" I could only nod. I had to speak with the lecturer! I had to find out what he had done to me, but there was a crowd around him, so I followed my host from the hall.

I decided to postpone my journey home for a few days to hear Mr. Emerson lecture again. We went a few nights later, but I could not recapture the experience. I heard his words and they were inspiring, but when I closed my eyes and tried to relive what had happened to me there was nothing sucking me inside, no light, no hum, only the darkness of closed eyes. At the end of the lecture I again thought to approach him, but once more there were many waiting to speak with him. However, I could not leave the north without some exchange of words between us, so I extended my journey home for another week. After the third lecture I decided to wait as long as it took to speak with him. Finally the group around him dispersed. He was alone, gathering his papers, as I fostered my courage and approached.

"Mr. Emerson, may I speak with you?" I asked hesitantly. He paused and looked up at me. His eyes were penetrating. "I've come to hear three of your lectures, and I find them very inspiring." He nodded. "The first night that I came, it was last week, I had a very strange experience. I was carried by your words into another world, far different from the world we know. Perhaps you can help me to understand it?" I paused.

"Yes, go on," he said.

"I don't quite know how to explain my experience. It was unlike anything I had experienced before." I fell silent, unable to find the words to go on.

"Most likely we will need more time than a brief conversation will allow. You may visit me tomorrow at my home in Concord, and we can discuss it," he said, writing his address on a piece of paper. "Come at 2 p.m. What is your name?"

"Elisabeth. Elisabeth Bonnet."

"Miss Bonnet, I will see you tomorrow." He smiled and with a nod of his head walked out.

I was left staring at the piece of paper, wondering what I would say to him. A wave of regret came over me. Perhaps I would make a fool of myself. Perhaps I had imagined the whole experience. He might think nothing of it, that it was some silly imaginings, but it was too late now. I had to go.

I awoke the next morning even more sorry that I had bothered to approach him, but at the appointed hour I knocked at his door. A woman received me, and with a warm smile invited me in. "Miss Bonnet?" she asked. I nodded. "Mr. Emerson is expecting you. I will show you to his study."

He was absorbed in writing when I entered and she motioned me to sit in a chair beside his desk. I waited for him to turn his attention to me.

After some time passed, he looked up and noticed my presence. "Ah, Miss Bonnet. I am so glad you have come. You wanted to discuss something with me, an experience you had during my lecture. Before you begin, please tell me a little about yourself. Where are you from?"

"A small town in Louisiana," I replied. "My family has a plantation that my sister now manages. I run a girls school there. I came to Boston to learn about the education of girls in the North and quite by accident was taken to your talk last week by my host."

"I see," he said. "Go on now about your experience."

The words froze in my throat. I didn't know how to begin, so sure was I that he would dismiss what I had to tell him. "Mr. Emerson, I'm . . . I'm so sorry to trouble you."

"It's no trouble at all, Miss Bonnet. I like to know how my lectures affect people. You know, I am the subject of much criticism these days, and I enjoy meeting those who think well of my words." He smiled.

"How shall I begin," I said nervously. "Mr. Emerson, I am not a religious person, not at all. I was brought up without any faith really . . ."

"Perhaps you are fortunate in that."

"But I had an experience the first night I came to hear you that I can only call a religious experience. You see, as soon as you began speaking, your words became a background hum and I lost consciousness of the outer world. It was as if my body had dissolved, as if someone had cut me free. I was conscious of existing everywhere. I was far more than only this body. It was as if I existed nowhere and everywhere at the same time. It was as if the whole universe was contained in me, or rather as if I was contained in an ever-expanding space. I don't have words for it really, but it was a very joyful experience, and I wonder if that was the soul I was experiencing, the soul that religion speaks of . . ." I paused. "I hope you don't think me fanciful . . ."

His attention was fully focused on me. "Not at all, Miss Bonnet, please continue."

"I don't know how long I stayed in that condition, but when I came back to the outer world, you were finishing your talk. I am sorry to say I didn't hear any of it. I came back again for your next lecture in the hopes that I would have the experience again, but I didn't. I heard everything you said then, and again last night," I smiled. "I am glad about that. I was inspired by your words, but I am most eager for this experience again." I looked at him inquiringly.

"Miss Bonnet, you are very fortunate indeed. I cannot explain your experience, nor can I take any credit for it. These experiences come upon us mortals every now and then to show us there is something more than our bodily existence, but they are very difficult to retain or duplicate. We are not the givers, only the receivers of such states. All I can do for you is to offer some reading materials in the hope they can provide some clarity. I have come upon some books from the Orient that may interest you. I can lend them to you as they may be difficult to find."

"I would be most grateful. I will be back up north in a few months and can return them at that time." The words tumbled out of my mouth. Until that moment I had no thought of returning to Boston.

"Take your time," he said. "If I am traveling, you can leave the books at my home. You have the address. Or better yet, come when I am in town so we can discuss them." He was thoughtful for a few minutes and then went over to his bookshelf. "Take this, the Bhagavad Gita, and here are a few others on oriental thought. These books have had a great impact on me," he said quietly, "and perhaps they can guide you."

"The Bhagavad Gita." I repeated the title. "Who is the author?" I asked. I had done much reading, mostly novels, and had never come across this book.

"It is one of the sacred texts of the Hindus. It is a conversation between God, in the form of the Hindu prophet Krishna, and man, in the form of the warrior Arjuna. I myself have been reading the Vedas, the oldest of their holy books, but the Vedas are quite complex and difficult to access. Better you begin with this."

"The prophet Krishna," I repeated softly. "Who is he?" At the sound of the name, a subtle and involuntarily tremor moved through my body.

"Krishna was one of the ancient Hindu prophets. There is much about his life that is similar to the life of Jesus, and he is revered in the East just as we revere Christ. Their civilization is a very, very old one. We would do well to study it. Have you heard of the book?"

"No." My mind was in something of a daze. "I have studied many subjects, but I know nothing of India or oriental philosophy. But there is something familiar in the sound of that prophet's name."

"Perhaps you will discover why," he smiled again.

"I cannot thank you enough," I said, taking two other books from him.

"I am so enormously grateful for the introduction to these books. I will bring them back soon, I promise."

"Yes, do come visit again." He rose from his chair and extended his hand. "My wife will show you out. Miss Bonnet, I suggest that you record your experience. It may be useful to write it down; it may help you recapture something of it when you feel the need."

"I will try to do that. Yes, thank you."

"Miss Bonnet, few of us are so fortunate as to have such an experience even once in a lifetime. Do not trouble yourself if it does not return. Having experienced a state beyond the body, even once, you will not forget it. You will see that your perspective on life and death will change."

I left the house feeling that I had received more than expected. It didn't matter that Mr. Emerson could not shed light on my experience. That no longer troubled me. I now realized that I had not really come for any explanation; I only needed to be pointed in a direction, and that he had done. The rest I would do on my own.

When I arrived back at the plantation, I did not share my experience with Dotty, afraid perhaps that she would mock me. I began to spend more and more time alone. In the evenings after dinner, I would go to my room and copy a page from the Bhagavad Gita, knowing that I would soon have to return it. I wrote the lines out and then read them over a few times, closing my eyes to focus on their meaning.

At night I would fall asleep with the book in my hand. Dotty found me thus a few times, and asked, "I found you grasping to your chest that book you brought back from the North. What is it?"

"Just a book on oriental philosophy," I replied, brushing it off.

"So, the North has turned you into a philosopher," she said half mockingly. I didn't respond and she changed the subject. There was less conversation between us these days. Dotty was also more withdrawn. I had little interest in the running of the plantation and so asked few questions. The weeks and months went by with only superficial interaction between us.

One day over dinner Dotty asked if I would be returning to Boston.

"Why do you ask?"

"No reason in particular," she replied. "But if you do go, I have another package for you to deliver to Mr. Brown."

"Perhaps it is time for me to plan another trip. I do want to develop further my relationship with one of the schools, and I have to return some books I borrowed."

A few weeks later I was again on the coach heading north. I delivered Dotty's package and was glad for an opportunity to spend some time with Mr. Brown and his wife. He received me warmly and was gracious as before, profusely thanking Dotty and me for our kindness and generosity. It didn't occur to me, I don't know why, to inquire into the nature of the package. My mind was on other things. I had checked to make sure Mr. Emerson would be in town and had made an appointment to see him.

"Well, Miss Bonnet, please sit down," Mr. Emerson greeted me as his wife showed me into his study. "How did you like the reading material I gave you?"

I took the books out and laid them on his desk. "I cannot thank you enough. These books have meant a great deal to me, especially this one," I said pointing to the Bhagavad Gita. "I copied the entire book, page by page, and read a few lines every night."

"Yes, it is one of the world's great texts. What in particular moved you?"

"I cannot even say. It touched a deep part of me, but I wanted to ask you . . ."

"Yes?"

"Mr. Emerson, you are a man of faith. I cannot say that I was, but after reading this book, my life has changed. I want to know the truth—about life, death, why we are born on this Earth. I never thought that man could truly understand these matters, and so never took an interest in religion, but this book seems to point a way, a way to knowledge. It explains much, but . . ." I paused.

"But what?" he inquired, eyeing me curiously. Perhaps he was surprised by the intensity of my interest.

"There are things in the book that seem contrary to our Christian teaching."

"Perhaps, but perhaps not. It depends on how one interprets our Christian teaching."

"This idea of the soul being reborn again and again, do you believe that?"

"I am yet a student of the Orient. I cannot say I have any first-hand knowledge, but I would say the same of our Christian teaching. One only truly knows what one has experienced. Experience must be our teacher. Have you had further thoughts on the revelation you had when you were here last?"

"I would hardly call it a revelation," I laughed.

"Indeed it was. You experienced yourself apart from your body. And if the soul can be and know itself apart from the body, can it not then take on a new body after the old one dies? I do not doubt the possibility of this."

"I do find that to be very logical," I replied. "I am inclined to believe it. In fact, everything I read in that book makes perfect sense to me. Most Christians would consider it heresy, but it is as if I am not hearing this for the first time, as if I knew it all before. I don't know how to explain my feelings," I said blushing.

"We must approach this as a science, not a matter of belief. We are all explorers, trying to make sense of this journey of life. What I do know is that a number of people have had experiences very similar to yours. They felt themselves expanding into an awareness far beyond the normal waking mind. They felt as if the whole universe existed within them, a kind of cosmic consciousness, and like you, they say it was a very joyous sensation. Perhaps that is the union with God that the Hindu prophet refers to." He was quiet for a few minutes and then continued. "Is the God of the Bhagavad Gita really any different from the God of Jesus Christ? I think not. There is much to learn from these books of the Orient. We find how much we have in common."

"I fully agree," I replied. "And yet, I dare not speak a word of this to any of my acquaintances, even to my own sister, at least not yet."

"That is wise," he cautioned, "or you will open yourself to much criticism, as I have experienced of late. Let me recommend a few other books. These you can easily acquire. You must continue your study of the Orient, Miss Bonnet, and of our own Transcendentalists. Our own philosophers have much to say about these matters as well."

"Transcendentalists. I have heard of them but don't know much about their philosophy."

"I will recommend some books that have just come out, and a new magazine as well. I do believe you will find them enlightening. And there is a woman you must try to meet when you are in this area, Margaret Fuller. I think you will like her very much. You may use my name as an introduction. She will introduce you to a society of well-educated ladies, with strong and independent minds."

Chapter 8

M y trips to the North became somewhat regular. On each trip, Dotty
sent a neatly wrapped package to our friend Mr. Brown. Initially I
would visit Mr. Emerson every time I came, but then his lectures began
to take him around the country and I began to seek out others in the
transcendentalist movement. I combined my interest in education with
my interest in the transcendentalists and other emerging writers who
were incorporating ideas from the Orient. I met Margaret Fuller, as he
suggested, and her group of women opened a new world to me, a world
of women thinkers far ahead of their time. They talked about full equality
and their ideas had a tremendous effect on me.

As I began to bring my new educational ideas from the North to the
South, adding a class in philosophy at my school, I noticed a drop in
enrollment, but I refused to compromise my ideals of education. I
dedicated myself to educating the girls whose families allowed them to
attend.

The years passed and, in the course of time, I began to notice changes
in our Louisiana household. Most of the Africans were now gone from the
house, with only one manservant and two women house servants left.
One night during dinner, the manservant Simon entered the room a bit
disturbed. "Miss Dotty, Mr. Jenkins and four other men are on the porch,
asking to see you."

She looked up. "What about? Tell them we are in the middle of
dinner."

"I told them, but they are insisting to see you."

I could tell by the look on Dotty's face that something was wrong. Her
jaw was set, her eyes held a steely expression. I knew that look. It was
one of unbreakable determination. "Simon, get me Papa's rifle."

"Dotty, what is this about?" I asked nervously.

"You wait here, Elisabeth. I will sort this out."

"I am going with you." I rose from the table and hurried behind her as she took the rifle from Simon and walked toward the porch.

"Good evening, Mr. Jenkins, is there something I can do for you?"

"Good evening, Miss Bonnet. We're sorry to have to disturb you."

"Well, what is so urgent that you fellas must interrupt our dinner?" she asked in an annoyed tone.

"There's been talk, Miss Bonnet, disturbing talk."

"Talk never seemed to bother the folks round here before," she replied wryly.

"We heard that some of your slaves have escaped, and we're here to help y'all capture them."

"People round here have nothing better to do than to make up stories. Nobody has escaped. I don't need your help, gentlemen." She spoke firmly, but then in a softer southern style added, "but I thank y'all for offering."

"Miss Bonnet," chimed in one of the other men. "Everyone knows your slave count is down. Everybody round here is talking."

"Let them talk," she replied in a curt tone. Then she added, "Without Papa, we've had to reduce our work here, and I've had to sell some slaves, but what concern is that of yours?"

"If you don't mind, Miss Bonnet, we'd like to see proof of sale."

Dotty's voice was firm. Her anger was palpable and I saw her grip the rifle. "I said it's no concern of yours. I won't stand here to be insulted." Then she added with greater control, "but I thank you for inquiring. If the need should arise, I will not hesitate to call on you gentlemen. Now if you will excuse me, my sister and I are in the middle of our supper."

"Miss Bonnet, if you women need help with the plantation, you know I have offered to buy it from you."

"My sister and I are perfectly capable of managing our affairs, but we thank you for offering," Her voice was steady and firm. "As I said, we are in the middle of supper, so I thank you gentlemen to please be on your way."

I stood beside her speechless, looking from Dotty to the men, most of whom I had known all my life. My heart was racing. I couldn't quite fathom what was going on, but I knew that something was amiss. We had never been overly friendly with the owners of the neighboring plantations, even when Papa was alive. He never quite viewed himself as an American and had kept his distance from the others. They resented this, we knew. We had heard Papa criticized for his "arrogant French ways," for thinking he was a cut above the others. After Papa's death, we had isolated ourselves even more from the others. My mind was racing. I knew I had to intervene and lessen the tension.

"Mr. Jenkins, why don't you and the others join us for coffee in the drawing room. We are almost finished our meal," I said, invitingly. Dotty and I shared a dislike for the other plantation owners, but I was better at hiding my distaste.

Dotty shot me a quizzical glance but I ignored her and encouraged them to enter. Instead of accepting my invitation, it seemed only to make him angrier.

"And you," he said bitterly, turning his eyes on me. "You stay away from our women. Polluting their minds with your Yankee ideas, that's what y'all are doing. We don't want any part of it. Stay away from them."

His tone was threatening. Dotty moved closer to me and in a raised voice came to my defense. "How dare you speak to my sister in that tone, when she has sacrificed so much to educate the girls here. Civility is gone from the south. Now get from here. Get off our porch." She clutched the gun and made a motion toward the men.

"I am warning you both," Mr. Jenkins called out as the men turned to leave. "You are no longer wanted here. You don't belong in decent society."

As soon as they were gone, Dotty exploded. She was furious, but I was shaken. I had never been spoken to in such an insulting tone, and it frightened me. Dotty saw my fear and this helped to calm her down.

"Don't worry, Elisabeth. They can't do anything to hurt us," said, putting her arms around my shoulders.

"They can. They were threatening us. We are two women here alone, Dotty, and I'm frightened. We don't belong here. I hate it here. I feel it every time I return."

She was quiet for a few minutes and then said. "Do you want to leave then?" I nodded. "Then go," she said in a cold voice. "You are free to leave any time. I don't want to hold you to a place you hate."

She withdrew her arm from my shoulder, but I took it and held it tight. "I wouldn't leave without you, Dotty. You know that." Then to ease the tension, I said, "Let's walk in the night air as we used to." I took her by the arm and led her down the path lined with the grandfather trees, thinking the soothing warmth of the summer night would help chase away the tension that had suddenly arisen between us. I knew something was wrong and I needed to find out what.

"Dear Dotty," I started. "I have left you all alone to manage this plantation, never thinking what a burden it must be for you." She didn't respond and so I continued. "And I . . . I have been lost in another world, letting my mind wander in the clouds as I always have." I glanced at her sideways to see if she would find this amusing. A slight smile crept over her lips. A distance had grown between us and I could feel it now keenly. We came to one of the old grandfather trees and I put my arms around it as we used to do, leaning my head against its aged bark. She also put her arms around the tree and through the moist night air I could see the tension easing from her face. These trees had long been our protectors, our guardians. "What has happened to us, Dotty? And what has happened to the plantation? Why did those men come here tonight?"

"Those men resent independent women. They can't bear that we can manage the plantation without them," she replied bitterly.

"Why did you say you sold some slaves? They are right, aren't they, that many of the Africans are gone from here?"

She cut me off. "I didn't sell anybody," she said angrily. "You know that I wouldn't. How can you think that? All those men want is to buy the plantation cheap from us, but I won't let them. I won't let them take advantage of us just because we're women."

"If you didn't sell the Africans, then what happened to them?" We both withdrew our arms from the tree's embrace. I stood looking at her through the pale moonlight, which was bright enough for me to discern her facial expressions. She seemed pained, and I put my hand on her arm. She looked away without answering me. Suddenly it dawned on me that her packages to Mr. Brown were connected to what was happening on the plantation.

"Dotty, tell me, who is Mr. Brown, and what is in those packages you have been sending him? I don't know why I never thought to ask, and I don't know why I never asked you what is happening here to the Africans." I didn't wait for her to answer. "I suppose that I can't blame you for not confiding in me. It was I who turned a blind eye and was so engaged in my own world that I didn't see what was happening right in front of me. You have freed the Africans, haven't you, Dotty? And you have been sending Mr. Brown money to help with this. Now I see it. I don't know how I could have been so unaware." It all became clear to me and filled me with admiration for my sister. She didn't have to respond, because I saw by the expression on her face that I was right. "Why didn't you tell me?" I asked pleadingly. "Didn't you trust me? Did you think I wouldn't agree?"

"Elisabeth, it is better that you don't know too much. There is danger."

"Danger! You and I are in this together. I would have given up my school and everything to help you with this."

"Would you have, Elisabeth? Would you really have come down from the clouds?" Then she added. "I have had to bear all the responsibility here, worrying about the money, having to make decisions. You wanted no part in that." Her tone softened. "I didn't mind. I took it on myself and did it gladly. Only don't accuse me now."

"I am not accusing you, Dotty. I just want to know the truth so that I can help."

"You have helped, Elisabeth, more than you know. The money from the school has helped a great deal, and as much money as I could save from the crops has gone toward helping the Africans escape North. And the rest I sent to Mr. Brown so that others can escape. He has a network and helps freed slaves get settled when they make their way to the North. He is part of the Underground Railroad that we have been hearing about, and he is the most courageous man, Elisabeth, a man of true character. All we have done is to provide the money; he has done the rest. About half of the Africans on this plantation are free now, just think of that Elisabeth. They have the freedom Joseph died for."

"Joseph, poor Joseph," I murmured. The image of him hanging limp from the tree came back to me. "You did this for Joseph," I whispered. Now it all made sense.

She looked straight at me and said in a slow, firm voice, "I told you when he was lynched that I would avenge his death. And I have. It is because of him that so many Africans of this house are now free. He didn't die in vain. I know that means something to you."

"It means a great deal," I said quietly. "I just wish you had told me so that you would not have had to bear this alone."

"Elisabeth, we are in this together. I have done my part and you have done yours. We have different strengths. I have always admired your courage and independence. Without you, how would I ever have gotten money to the North?" Her voice was filled with tenderness. "You know I never have been a good traveler. I have counted on you for that."

"Me, courageous? It is you, Dotty, who has had the courage to do what you did, alone, and to stand against these men. No, it is I who have always admired you. You are the most noble, the most dedicated woman I know, and I can't imagine what I would have done without you all of these years.

She laughed. "Then we are admirers of each other." I hugged her. It seemed as if she wanted to say something more but she refrained.

"What is it?" I asked.

"Nothing."

"I don't feel it's safe for us to stay here," I said. "Perhaps we should sell the plantation and move to the North. You will like it there, Dotty. The women are strong and independent. They are more like you. I can get a job in a school, I am sure of it now. I have many contacts. There is nothing left here for us."

"Except the rest of the Africans. We cannot leave them. If we sell this place they will never be free. When all the Africans are free, Elisabeth, we will move up North, I promise you that."

"When will that be?"

"Not long. If we have a few more good years, if the crops are good . . ."

"Then as long as we are here, we must try to live in peace and open up the minds of our neighbors."

"That will never happen," she replied. "Look how their girls have been dropping out of your school as soon as you introduce new ideas. No, Elisabeth, it will take a long time for change to come. The men here will hang on for as long as they can."

I knew her words to be true. We began to walk back to the house when she suddenly stopped and asked me.

"Do you regret not having married Pavel?"

"Why do you ask me that now?" Pavel had died many years earlier and since then his name had not come up.

"Things would have been much easier for you."

I shook my head. "I think I would have been happy with Pavel. He introduced me to a world of beauty, and I remember with great fondness the wonderful time we spent together, the friendship we had, but as magical as that world was, I wouldn't exchange for anything the wisdom I have now found through my reading." I began to get excited. "Dotty, I wish you could meet Mr. Emerson. He has shown me a world far greater . . ." A look of disinterest came over her face. "Anyway, it doesn't matter. Perhaps you will meet him when we move north."

Three years passed. I tried to engage with the wives of the plantation owners, keeping them busy while Dotty helped the Africans find their freedom, one by one, but my efforts were of little use. They continued to withdraw their daughters from the school until I had to close it. That was a sad day for me. Change would have to come slowly to the South. I was impatient and wanted to be part of the new thinking that was taking over the North. Dotty wasn't sure where she stood. Despite her resentment of many of the values of our society, the impingement on the freedom of so many, Africans and women alike, there was something that she loved about the South. I began to worry whether she would adapt to a different life and find the society of the North as enticing as I did.

After a few good harvests, it seemed that finally we would be able to move north. Dotty was not as excited as I hoped she would be. She loved the land above all else, the giant willow trees, the flower gardens that she so lovingly tended—this was home to her. She acquiesced for me, but I know her heart was not in the move. All we needed now was a teaching position for me.

One day I received a letter offering me the position of principal at a prestigious girls' school in New York. I was beside myself with joy. I let out such a scream when I read the letter that Dotty came rushing down the stairs.

I took her hands and started dancing across the room.

"This is our chance," I cried. "It has happened."

"What are you talking about? What is wrong with you?" she inquired with a frown.

"A job offer," I laughed, handing her the letter. "More than I could have expected, and at one of the most prestigious schools. Dotty, do you realize what this will mean for us? Now we can really leave this place."

I saw at once that she didn't share my joy. "I am happy for you," she said simply, handing me back the letter. "Nobody deserves it more than you, Elisabeth."

"You are coming . . ."

She feigned a smile. "We can no longer stay here, I know that, but I don't know what I will do up North."

"Listen to me, Dotty. The abolitionist movement is gaining force in the North. You can be part of that. You can work for the same cause there as you have here, perhaps you can even do more."

She didn't seem convinced, but I could see that she was doing her best not to shatter my joy.

The letter requested that I meet with the trustees of the school as soon as possible, and so I made plans to leave immediately for New York. Dotty once again gave me a large sum of money for our friend Mr. Brown.

"This is what is left from the sale of the school building," she said. "We have enough without this to manage the move. I think we will sell everything in the house," she added with a sigh. "We will take nothing from here, only memories."

I nodded. "We are starting life anew, Dotty. We don't need anything from here."

"Starting life anew at our age," she sighed again. "We are no longer young, Elisabeth. People don't start over at our age." She seemed tired and for the first time I noticed that age had caught up with her.

I left soon after, and on the journey I had a dream in which I stood before a man dressed in an orange robe. I couldn't make out the details of his face, as I was focused on his feet. As I knelt before him, I was overwhelmed by a wave of love. I bowed down, touching my forehead to his feet, and as I did so I seemed to dissolve. My body dropped away and I was everywhere and nowhere at the same time, a vast body of space, encompassing all. I awoke enveloped in a wave of love, but something new had entered my heart—a deep and powerful longing—but I couldn't tell the object. I could only identify it as a longing to preserve that tremendous feeling of love.

The dream was very similar to the experience I had when I first went to the lecture of Mr. Emerson. So many years later and the experience had returned. As I came more fully to the waking state, I wondered about the man in orange robes who awakened such love in me that I would touch his feet. Who was this man and where did he come from?

I was eager to discuss the dream with Mr. Emerson, but fate would not have it. Soon after I arrived in New York, I received a telegraph that Dotty had taken ill. I turned right around and headed home. By the time I arrived, she was very weak. She had contracted smallpox. I cared for her day and night, praying that she would survive. Oddly, I found my appeals directed to the orange-robed figure that had entered my dream. I could feel his presence, and he gently whispered into my inner ear that it was time for her to go, but still I clung to her.

"You mustn't leave me, Dotty," I pleaded one night as I applied cool towels to her feverish face.

She peered at me through her swollen eyes. "Little sister," she whispered. "You have been so dear to me. Don't cry. I don't mind dying." She was half delirious. "But there is something I have wanted to tell you for a long time."

I looked at her with sorrowful eyes. I would not let her die.

"Joseph . . ."

"What about Joseph?"

"He was . . . he was our half-brother."

I was stunned. "What are you saying? You are with fever, Dotty, and don't know what you are saying. You must rest and then we will speak."

"It's true. Papa told me right before he died. He never forgave himself for Joseph's death."

"You mean . . . Papa and Bessie?" She nodded.

I thought for sure she was imagining this in her delirium, but that night as I sat by my bedroom window, I closed my eyes and tried to discern what the truth might be and I received a quiet affirmation. I went back into Dotty's room and sat by her bed. I must have sat there all night, perhaps I slept or perhaps I let my mind wander back through the years. Dotty and I had struggled, it was true, but we had also given each other great strength. I liked to think that in some way my mental expeditions to the East had provided her with some silent support, some strength, some blessing for her work. I felt enormous gratitude that she was able to accomplish what I could not. I had ferried money back and forth, but she had made all the arrangements for the Africans to gain their freedom. She was a great soul, a woman of such courage and determination, and in her last hours I let my heart feel how much I admired and loved her.

I saw her breathing become less frequent and shallower. I knew that she was leaving me. My hand clung to hers. I wanted so to keep her with me but I dare not hold her back; she was heading to a place I longed to be. "Go, Dotty," I whispered. "Go into that great beyond. Let your body go and become one with the universe."

After Dotty died, I came down with the illness. Dreams of moving North faded away. All that remained for me was the memory of the one in my dream, the one for whom I had felt such love, who like a magnet was pulling me toward him. What was this love that so captured me, so personal and intimate and yet of such a lofty nature? I did not remember feeling this way toward any man, not even Pavel. No, not even Pavel. This was a love of a totally different order, and yet it was only a dream.

Did such a love exist? If I could imagine it, then surely it must exist, I reasoned. Perhaps one day I would find it. Perhaps I would find that man in my dream, clothed in an orange robe, whose face I could not see. Perhaps in the other world, the world I was moving toward, perhaps there I would find him. That was something to wait for, to hope for, even to yearn for.

One evening as I was lying with fever, my handwritten Bhagavad Gita gripped to my chest, I found myself back in Vienna. Pavel extended a hand to me. I took it shyly and the music began. My feet lifted and he swept me away. We danced and danced until the steps of the waltz suddenly turned into ballet, and I was dancing as I had never danced in life. What a feeling of freedom! I was twirling in the air, as light as a bird, drifting beyond earth, beyond the planets, beyond the stars. The music carried my body through the spheres and filled me with such joy. This was music of a different order and my feet knew naturally how to respond.

With this music pulsating through my soul, I let go of my clinging to life.

* * *

The memories of my life in the South returned to me over a period of many months, and the remembrance explained many things about my current life. As a child, I didn't like my given name. I didn't have a middle name, so my father told me I could choose one. I picked Elisabeth. As a young girl I wanted to be a teacher, and at the age of only nine or ten I set up a school for the neighborhood children in my family's basement where I tutored them, or so I pretended. When I became a teenager, I was very drawn to the Civil Rights movement, and later in college developed a love for the Transcendentalists. One of my earliest introductions to the East was during my college years when I came upon Emerson's poem "Brahma." I hadn't found my guru yet, but this poem awakened my interest and I began to search further.

Later in my 20s, my love for the Bhagavad Gita came forward; it has been my holy text ever since. During those early years, like Elisabeth, I kept it with me all the time, reading and rereading it until I knew many of the *slokas*, or stanzas, by heart. It was as if I repeated in my early years of this life many of the themes of my last two lives, like a fast re-run.

These memories helped me understand why I was subsequently born in Russia, and my love for dance. I began to put the two lives together and to see a natural sequence, a subtle pattern linking one life to the next. It was like putting together a vast puzzle. As each piece fit into place, the picture gained greater clarity, but there were still so many missing pieces. I was only beginning to understand the patterns. As more information filtered through, more questions arose: Was it my guru who had appeared in that dream, helping me once again make the transition through death? I didn't know. Why was I born in the South and what was my relationship to the Africans? Why had I felt such an affinity with Bessie, Joseph, and later Mr. Brown? And the meditative experiences, where did they come from? And when would I find my life in India?

Clyde and I became closer after my memories of Dorothy returned, but it also became clear to me that we could never have a romantic relationship. He would always be like a brother. I continued my work with the Japanese organization. My children were on their own, and I took many trips to Japan. I began to feel a strong affinity with the culture, but I didn't know why. On my first trip to Japan, I was traveling with a colleague and my father. We had been invited to a symposium at the Museum that had been founded by the spiritual organization for whom we were working. They took us to the old Sanjusangen-do Temple, famous for its thousand statues of Buddhist deities, many who came from Hindu cosmology. The atmosphere in the Temple was so elevating that I found myself drifting into another world and being sucked inward.

By now I was familiar with this process and knew that visions from the past were calling me. I withdrew to a corner and went into meditation. I saw myself fleeing from flames into the forest with my children. It was a chaotic scene. I saw a betrayal and flight from the beautiful burning villa. Fear overcame me and I abruptly pulled myself back to the present. My eyes flew open, my heart pounding. I didn't want to go there. I didn't want to peer any longer into the past. With great effort I pulled myself back to the present. At that moment, I said to myself, "I can't go back. I can't do this anymore. It takes too much out of me." And so that door closed. It was to be many, many years before it opened again, and I was to relive the scenes from that life in Japan, but I save that story for a later chapter.

One day I received a call that Clyde had had a heart attack. For the first years after our meeting, I had been seeing him quite regularly, but as time passed the visits had been less frequent and I hadn't seen him in over a year. I called him to say I would make plans to come visit.

"How soon can you come?" he asked.

"A few weeks," I replied.

"Come soon," he said in a foreboding tone. "As soon as you can."

I understood his meaning, but didn't realize the urgency. He was still young and I couldn't believe he would die. I was in the process of making travel arrangements when I got word that he had left his body. With his death a chapter closed and my memories of the American south began to recede.

My life was soon to be radically altered as older memories were calling to be awakened.

PART III

EARLY 18ᵀᴴ CENTURY AFRICA

As a person sheds worn-out garments and wears new ones,
likewise, at the time of death, the soul casts off its worn-out
body and enters a new one.

—Bhagavad Gita 2:22

I could well imagine that
I might have lived in former centuries
and there encountered questions
I was not yet able to answer;
that I had to be born again because
I had not fulfilled the task
that was given to me.

—Carl Jung

Chapter 9

A much welcome but unexpected opportunity arose that was to alter the course of my life significantly. My father came to see me in my office one day, with an excited look on his face. A few years earlier a dear friend of his had become Secretary General of the United Nations, and my father had been advising him on a pro bono basis. He loved the work with the U.N. and wanted to get me involved. The perfect opportunity presented itself in 1998. He told me, "The Secretary General has agreed to hold a meeting of religious leaders at the United Nations for the millennium year. Ted Turner's foundation will provide some of the funding. I want you to help organize this."

I had turned away from institutional religion long ago and considered myself to be somewhat of a hidden yogi, doing my meditation practice while supporting my children through my work. When I didn't respond, he exclaimed, "This is perfect for you. You'll be working with the Interfaith Center of New York." Another friend of his, Dean James Morton, an Episcopal minister, had recently founded the Center. Interfaith work had not yet become mainstream, and Dean Morton was one of the pioneers of the movement. It wasn't until post-9/11 that a tremendous acceleration of interfaith activity took place.

A central principle of my guru's teachings was the unity of all religions—one truth, one divine reality expressed through many streams, many narratives—and so the project did strike a chord. My father offered my services for this project at no cost, and for the next year and half I traveled the world with my colleague from the Interfaith Center, meeting with religious leaders, encouraging them to come to the U.N. for this historic event: The Millennium World Peace Summit of Religious and Spiritual Leaders. The Interfaith Center had assigned one of its staff, a man from India, to the project; he became the Chair of the Summit and I the Vice Chair. He was the outer face, the speaker and dealmaker, and I the behind-the-scenes organizer, the writer and content provider.

A number of incidents shaped my thinking at this time. My colleague and I had been invited to a conference in Oxford, England, organized by Dadi Janki, a great woman spiritual teacher from India. At my first meeting with her, I was very moved by her presence and spiritual power. Then, at a dinner with the other participants, I sat next to a Muslim leader from the Middle East. I tried to make conversation by mentioning the Summit we were organizing at the United Nations and the trouble we were having finding women religious leaders. One of the women from the Secretary General's office, who was working with us on the project, kept pressing us to make sure we had women at the summit. He responded by asking me coolly, "Why do you need women leaders? This is a religious summit."

I was taken aback and replied, "Well, we are half the world's population."

"If I were you, young lady, I would stay away from the subject, or you may find that nobody will attend your Summit."

I was shocked by his response and mentioned it to my colleague. He was sympathetic with me but was struggling with a number of political issues, like the fact that we couldn't invite one of the most respected and beloved religious leaders, the Dalai Lama, to the U.N. because it would create a huge protest from China. The U.N. had made it clear to us from the start that we could not invite him, but some religious leaders were very unhappy about this and said they would not come to the Summit if the Dalai Lama were not invited. This became a major challenge and the women's issue got sidelined.

After much effort and many challenges, the Summit took place in New York in late August 2000. Over 1500 religious leaders from all around the world participated. A few days before it was to open, my father came to see me and said, "You are going to open the Summit and give the welcome." I shook my head vigorously. He knew my shyness. How could he ask this of me? To speak at the General Assembly Hall? Impossible!

He insisted. I wrote and rewrote the one-page statement of welcome that I was to make, and with great difficulty forced myself to the stage. It was a tremendous achievement for me. I had always been too shy to speak out, even at a meeting of a few people, but since that day I have never felt any concern about public speaking before a large audience. I also rarely have to prepare talks in advance. I learned in the General Assembly Hall that day that if you open yourself to the inspiration and guidance of the divine presence, which is always there waiting to be tapped, you need not expend mental energy on preparation. The only preparation is attuning to the higher will. I have enormous gratitude to my father for having the insight to help me overcome a serious shortcoming.

Another incident on the opening day of the Summit shaped the future course of my work. A very senior religious leader was to be one of the first to enter in the religious procession, but there was a problem: he came from a very strict Hindu monastic order and could not look at women. The delegation from Thailand, ten monks and one nun, were sitting near the aisle, and as it happened, the nun was sitting at the end of the row near where this orthodox religious leader was to enter the General Assembly Hall. Everyone on my team tried in vain to get her to move, but she didn't understand English and resisted, indicating she needed to stay with her delegation. Finally my colleague approached me and in an agitated voice asked me to move her. I asked why.

"Because she is a woman, and the religious leader heading the procession is not permitted to look at women," came the desperate response. The clock was ticking and we were already past the hour when we were to begin.

I felt terrible. This incident cast a cloud over the grand opening for me. I went to her and sweetly asked her to come with me. She smiled and followed me to another seat. Later when the Thai delegation came to offer gifts to my colleague and me, I apologized profusely. She brushed it away with a smile. She became a dear friend and joined me in my later work.

The opening procession was full of pomp and ceremony. Religious leaders of the highest order, dressed in colorful ceremonial outfits and all sorts of head gear, led the way to the stage of the General Assembly Hall to begin the prayers and chanting. It was the first time religious leaders had gathered in the General Assembly Hall of the United Nations. It was a beautiful affair, but for me it was darkened by the lack of women's voices and the undercurrents of repression and religious competition that I perceived. If more women had been present, I thought to myself, some of the religious tensions could have been appeased. I chided myself for not being more determined to seek out women, but this aggressive approach was not in my nature, and I was still new to the inter-religious world.

Needless to say the women themselves were unhappy that they had so little role at the Summit and pressed me for a follow-up summit of women religious and spiritual leaders. I told my father, who approached the Secretary General, who thought it a good idea. He encouraged us to hold the Summit at the Palais des Nations, the United Nations headquarters in Geneva, Switzerland. So we began organizing another grand event.

The women's summit encountered much resistance. For reasons I couldn't then or even now understand, the idea of women religious leaders threatened many religious organizations. In 2001, when my colleague from the Interfaith Center and I began preparing the women's summit, we traveled to Geneva to meet with the religious communities there. They were far from welcoming.

"We don't want your American feminism here," one of the religious leaders told me bluntly. I was shocked. I hardly thought of this peace summit as a feminist initiative. I had never regarded myself as a feminist. Nor was I not a feminist. I had always resisted the effort of many leaders in the feminist movement to masculinize themselves; rather than seeking to change the prevailing paradigm, they sought to model it. I fully embraced and tried to exemplify the ideals of the Divine Feminine, which I felt were sorely needed in the world. We needed women to manifest these principles, not to suppress them and try to be like men. Of course, much has changed since then, but I remember when I first began working, I had been told to cut my long hair and exchange my flowing skirts for suits.

I did neither.

We couldn't get the funding for the women's summit that we had secured for the first Summit, but we found many businesswomen who gave small amounts to support the travel of women leaders. To our great satisfaction, many male religious leaders supported the summit and participated, so it ended up being not only for the women leaders. It was of great significance that quite a few men were eager to participate even though they would have only a supporting role. They were able to experience what women often feel at such events: that they are observers rather than shapers.

We called the gathering The Global Peace Initiative of Women

Religious and Spiritual Leaders. Over 750 delegates participated from more than 45 countries. Many of the most prominent women religious leaders from many traditions were present. While the first summit had been very political, there were no politics this time. It was a joyful and productive event. I made a promise to the women at the first Summit in New York and I had kept that promise: I gave the women religious leaders a platform at the United Nations, which is what they had requested of me. I had no thought to continue beyond that one event.

At the end of the Summit, a group of women from Israel and Palestine asked if we would come to their region and help them join together in dialogue. The second intifada was raging, and tensions were high. We agreed, and before I knew it I had committed to organizing a follow-up meeting.

Out of this initial Summit in Geneva we birthed The Global Peace Initiative of Women Religious and Spiritual Leaders, a nonprofit organization whose vision and leadership was held by a group of women spiritual leaders, but which was by no means restricted to women. We soon began to see our role as evoking the Divine Feminine energy and creating greater balance in the interfaith movement, bringing in gender balance as well as balance between West and East. We later shortened the name to the Global Peace Initiative of Women, known as GPIW.

One of my father's friends was the Under-Secretary General at the United Nations. His wife had a sister, who became my assistant. Marianne, a longtime Tibetan Buddhist practitioner, worked with me to organize the meeting in Geneva. Our energies were completely synergistic—a partnership that enabled us to do the work that lay ahead.

A few months after the Geneva Summit, in spring 2003, we brought about 50 women leaders from Israel and Palestine to the Nobel Peace Academy in Oslo for what was supposed to be a peace dialogue. We also brought a group of women spiritual leaders from different traditions—Christian, Jewish, Hindu, Buddhist, and Muslim—to facilitate the dialogue. Just before the event was to take place, there was a suicide bombing in Tel Aviv and the borders were closed. The Palestinians could not get out. We were frantic. We called one of the Israeli delegates, a Labor Party member of the Knesset (the Israeli Parliament), and she worked around the clock to make sure the Palestinians could get to Oslo. Security was tight and they had long delays. The Palestinians were angry and tired when they arrived. The Israelis were angry and upset over the deaths from the bus bombing. It was a difficult beginning and the first few days were full of accusations and yelling. It was a competition: whose suffering was greater?

I felt helpless, wondering what to do, thinking perhaps I had made a mistake in trying to engage in peace work. It was far too complicated. Then, on the last day of the dialogue, one of the Palestinian women stood up and began speaking. She was visually impaired and had suffered many ordeals in her life, but through these struggles she had developed tremendous courage, stamina, and wisdom. As she spoke, she broke into tears. While trying to regain her composure, she began singing "We Shall Overcome." One by one all the women stood up and joined the singing, Palestinian and Israeli alike. The whole energy of the room shifted, and the dialogue became a true peace conversation after that, each side sympathizing with the narrative of the other. That night the Palestinians and Israelis danced together, although we respectfully assured them that we would not spread photos of them embracing!

Along with two of GPIW's co-chairs—Rev. Dr. Joan Brown Campbell and Sister Joan Chittister, I spent the next two years shuttling back and forth between Israel and Palestine, bringing together in dialogue first women, then women and men. The irony of this work did not escape me. Some 70 years earlier I had been able to provide the means for Jewish professors to escape from Nazi Germany. Were any of these Israelis their descendants? Was I completing some karma that had been initiated with the selling of my family jewels? It gave me a deep satisfaction to be able to create a space for compassion and understanding to emerge in a region of the world where I had a karmic link.

I began to understand a little about how individual karma works, as I could see the continuation of themes from one life to the next, but what about mass karma? The Israeli-Palestinian conflict seemed an intractable outcome of World War II. Something that had been initiated during that time was unfinished. How could that karma be neutralized so that the cycle of suffering could end? I struggled with this question. In the years that followed, many other groups began to organize dialogues and other joint projects between the Israelis and Palestinians, and I felt there was nothing more we could do. We did not know how to untie the karmic knots that were stagnating the energy there. Perhaps it was just a matter of time, a healing task for the next generation.

I was coming to realize how complex collective karma is. I saw that among individuals in both Israel and Palestine, there were real shifts in consciousness. The narratives that were holding the conflict in place were losing their energy and reality for a growing number of people. However, the political structures were not responding to these changes; the collective that was changing was not yet large enough to affect a shift in the greater mindset. The karma would play itself out in time. It had to.

The war in Iraq was raging, so we turned our attention there. Partnering with the United States Institute of Peace, we brought to Dharamsala, India, a group of young Iraqis, women and men, who were working in some capacity to build dialogue in Iraq. We chose India because it is close to Iraq, a neutral country, and easy to get visas for the Iraqis. We chose Dharamsala because of its beauty and location in the Himalayas and the presence of the refugee Tibetan community. Little did we know that at the very time we were to gather, the Tibetans would rise up against increased restrictions imposed on Tibet by the Chinese in preparation for the 2008 Olympics taking place in China that year.

We arrived with the Iraqis to find thousands of Tibetan monks on the street in a silent candlelight vigil. The Iraqis had never heard of Tibet and knew nothing of their struggle with China, but their nonviolent methods of protest became a major theme of the meeting. At the beginning of the dialogue the Iraqis were deeply divided, Shia versus Sunni. Once again I struggled to understand the workings of collective karma. The Shia had been repressed under Saddam Hussein, so was it not natural that the reverse would now come into play? How long would this reversal need to go on?

After meeting with the Tibetan leaders, the Iraqis realized they had more in common with each other than differences. The Tibetans were a bridge for the building of unity, and the Iraqis went home with Free Tibet t-shirts. Witnessing the Tibetan monks in silent candlelight vigil affected them more than any words could have. I realized that the best we could do was to open people in conflict regions to the struggles of other people. This helped them to grow beyond their own situation and to realize they are part of a greater global struggle. The microcosm is merely reflecting what is taking place at the macro level. Each individual part, each conflict, reflects a greater movement of which we are all part. I was coming to understand interdependence in a much deeper way.

As was the case with the Israeli-Palestinian dialogues, I came to understand that our work was really about awakening consciousness.

We could do little to alter the political or economic causes of war, but we could awaken people to the reality of interdependence, and help others realize that we all suffer together. Together we can rid ourselves of this suffering by freeing ourselves from anger and animosity. We can take responsibility for our own negative emotions, which play a role in perpetrating conflict. The greater the number of people who take responsibility, the more we will be able to drain the negative energy and lessen the potential for conflict.

The work of GPIW grew and grew. As new conflicts arose, we organized dialogues in many places of conflict—Sudan, Lebanon and Syria, Afghanistan, Cambodia, and on and on. We traveled incessantly. As we became known in U.N. circles, we were invited by the United Nations Development Program (UNDP) to organize a series of summits with young leaders working in their communities to advance the United Nation's Millennium Development Goals. The first meeting was to take place with young leaders throughout Africa. The local UNDP offices were to choose the delegates from each country, and we were to bring the spiritual leaders to the gathering in Senegal. I was excited. This was to be my first experience in Sub-Sahara Africa and I didn't know what to expect.

As soon I landed in Africa, I loved the smell of the earth, the breezes, the vegetation. Africa had a distinctive feel unlike any place I had ever been, yet I felt very much at home.

The meeting of young African leaders was a huge success. We sat for days listening to the young people speak with such vision and enthusiasm for the future. Most of the world sees Africa through the prism of disease, poverty, and war, but they saw their Africa as a place of great opportunity and possibility. The world was theirs to shape, and I was deeply impressed by their intellectual and creative abilities. One young woman in particular struck me. Barbara was the 22-year-old daughter of a member of Zambia's Parliament and she had recently lost her mother in a car accident. Her mother had started a farming cooperative for women, and the women at the meeting were entreating Barbara to continue her mother's work. We were moved by her commitment and passion.

The spiritual leaders were seeking to bring a spiritual lens to the process of development, speaking of spiritual values as a foundation for a country's progress. That was our contribution, since our work was not in the area of development per se. One of the spiritual leaders was from the Japanese group that had started the museum for which my family's company worked. They also had extensive experience in natural farming, a version of chemical-free farming that did not apply any additives to the soil. They saw farming as a spiritual practice and knew that pure, chemical-free soil, pure water, and the right spiritual perspective were the keys to healthy food and a healthy environment. They were also impressed with Barbara's vision and leadership abilities, and in the years to follow were to provide much support for the women's natural farming project, which grew to over 5,000 women farmers. Barbara was to make many trips to Japan to bring back the spiritual philosophy of farming to Africa. I was coming to see that our work at GPIW was to facilitate such connections. We were conveners, setting the stage for a global spiritual network to emerge. The U.N. was pleased, and the African summit turned out to be the first of a number of such gatherings that we organized with the U.N.

After the gathering in Senegal, there was to be a day trip to the island off Senegal, which had served as the holding area for Africans before they were put on slave ships heading to the New World. Everyone went but me. For some reason, I couldn't bring myself to go to that place. The very thought filled me with great anxiety, feelings that I didn't understand but that prodded me to search inside.

After returning home and the memories came alive, I understood.

Chapter 10

I first saw her when I was but a child, no more than eight years old. My mother had given birth to my brother and was bleeding profusely. The woman attending her sent me to gather wood for the fire so she could boil medicinal plants to stop the bleeding. I went to the edge of the jungle, very close to our village. My father had warned me many times not to enter the jungle, but I was allowed to stay near the edges and collect fallen branches. I saw her peering out at me from the jungle. I was startled at first because she didn't look like an ordinary person and I worried that she might be a spirit. The elder women of the village used to frighten us with stories of spirits that dwelt in the jungle—their way of making sure we would not venture into dangerous territory.

She beckoned to me and, as I cautiously drew closer, I could see that she looked like an old woman, with a bent-over frame and long knotted grey hair that fell in strands to her waist. Wide black eyes dominated her thin and deeply-lined face, which held vibrant eyes, almost childlike in their liveliness. I felt pulled to her and began to enter the thicket of trees, but stopped, remembering my father's repeated warnings.

"No need to fear me, child," she said in a gentle voice, emerging from the trees. "I have only come to give these to you for your mother." She handed me some plants. "Boil them and feed the broth to your mother. It will stop her bleeding." I took the plants and ran back to our hut with my bundle of wood, stopping only once to glance behind at the strange woman who stood staring out at me from the edge of the jungle. It didn't occur to me until later to wonder how she knew about my mother's condition.

The woman attending my mother resisted, but when her recipe did not stop my mother's bleeding, she boiled the plants I had given her and fed my mother the broth. For two days my mother drank the medicine and her bleeding eased. When my mother regained her health, she asked me where I had gotten the plants. I told her someone had given them to me, but I didn't tell her about the woman in the jungle. She didn't press me and the incident was forgotten.

I didn't see her again for several years, although I looked for her every time I went to the jungle's edge to gather wood. When I was about 12 or 13, my younger sister became very ill, her face was swollen and her body burned with fever. After many attempts the village healer said she had tried everything and could do nothing more for her. Without telling anyone, I went in search of the woman of the forest. This time I entered the jungle. I didn't know her name, so I called out "Didi," which meant grandmother in our language. It was what I called her from then on.

"Didi," I called again and again. "You helped my mother once. Please help my sister now." My voice cracked as I called out, remembering the fear and pain on my mother's face. I didn't dare think of what might happen to my sister without Didi's help. There was no response. Perhaps she had been passing by that one time I met her. Or perhaps she had died. I sat down among the trees wondering what to do. I knew nothing about plants, and yet I felt as if my young sister's life was in my hands and I had to help her. Suddenly I heard a rustle in the thick brush. I swung around in fear, thinking it could be a lion, but there she stood.

"I have brought some plants for your sister," she said. "Take them and do as before, only make sure you boil the plants for a long time so the broth contains their essence. Do not let anyone else do it. I will work through your hands. Now go quickly because there is not much time."

I took the plants from her outstretched hand, but couldn't bring myself to leave.

"Go," she said, brushing her hand as if to shoo me away.

"Didi, I will go but then I will come back. I must see you again."

She nodded. "When your sister is well, come back and I will be waiting inside the forest. Now go to her quickly before she leaves this world."

I did as she commanded, insisting to my mother that I boil the herbs and feed my sister the broth. My mother stood by in despair as my sister's body burned and she slipped in and out of consciousness. As I prepared the plants, I kept the image of Didi in my mind. She said she would work through my hands. I didn't know what she meant, but somehow I knew to keep my mind fixed on her. Several days passed and I kept preparing the herbs for my sister to drink, pouring little drops into her mouth. My anxious mother kept asking me questions: "Where did you get these medicinal plants? How do you know they will work? How do you know the right amount?" I didn't know any of the answers, so I kept quiet, hoping that Didi was working through me.

My sister recovered. When she was able to stand up on her own, I went back to the jungle, penetrating the densely wooded area more than I was permitted to do. Didi was waiting for me. She greeted me with a nod, saying simply, "Your sister is well now."

"Yes." I was quiet for a few minutes and then said with much enthusiasm, "Twice I have witnessed your healing powers. I want to learn from you."

She laughed a loud hearty laugh, then suddenly grew quiet. "What do you want to learn?" she asked, eying me quizzically.

"To heal people."

"There are those in your village who can teach you."

"Not like you," I replied with conviction.

"Why do you want to heal people?"

"To help them, of course."

"To unlock the secrets of the Spirit takes much convincing. I cannot teach you," she said, walking away.

I did not expect to be refused. I stood there not quite knowing what to do.

She turned briefly. "Go back to the village. There are others there who can teach you." She slipped back into the dense forest, leaving me feeling rejected and forlorn.

I had a stubborn streak and was determined more than ever to unlock the secret of the plants, so I began visiting the woman in our village who was known as a healer. She taught me to distinguish one plant from another and the qualities of each. This one was soothing to the stomach, that one was cooling to the system and brought fevers down, and so I learned the basic elements of working with the plants. Sometimes the concoctions helped and sometimes they didn't. Often we would find ourselves helpless in the face of an illness or a wound, and my mind would always turn to Didi. After several years I began to realize that Didi had a deeper knowledge. Her healing powers came not from the plants themselves, but from a different source; I had to find out what that source was. So I regularly went back to the spot where she had last met me. I went again and again and again, but she was never there.

I was a young woman of about 16 when I saw her next. I was sitting by the edge of the jungle feeling particularly forlorn when I heard her voice. There she was, standing by the edge of the forest as she had been many years earlier. Although I had changed a great deal in the intervening years, she looked as she had when I first met her.

"Didi!" I cried, with a broad smile on my face.

"So you have not forgotten me after all these years," she laughed as I ran to greet her. I was overjoyed to hear her crackling voice. "I like your determination. Come tomorrow and we will see what you can do, but you must come deeper into the jungle. Follow this path and you will find me." With those words she slipped away among the trees. I tried to follow but minutes later I could no longer discern her figure. It was as if she had evaporated.

I could hardly wait for the next day to arrive. Although I had not been more than a few minutes in her presence in total, I trusted her implicitly ... or so I thought.

The next day I made my way to the edge of the jungle. Remembering my father's many warnings, I paused before entering, then advanced slowly and cautiously. I had gone a few hundred steps into the forest, a spot still considered safe from the wildlife, when I saw the narrow path that she had indicated and followed it. After some time I began to feel uneasy. I had never ventured this far. I knew there were dangers, but there was a clearing ahead and she must be there. Perhaps that was where she lived.

Indeed, I saw her when I arrived at the spot, but between us rested three lionesses. My body froze. The lions had not seen me and I could still creep back out of the jungle, but I saw her beckoning me, her eyes watching me steadily. In that moment I had to decide to go to her or not. If I turned back, I knew that would be the end of it. If I proceeded, I had to trust that she would protect me from the lions. Was she capable of doing that? I recalled her healing both my mother and my sister; surely she would not let me die. Still I hesitated. Then my body began to move forward slowly, almost against my will. There was nothing I could do to stop it. I dared not look at the lions, so I kept my eyes firmly fixed on her.

Her eyes were on me as well.

As I approached and stood about midway there, I saw her place her hand on one of the lioness's heads, and she began to pet her, speaking softly in a calm voice. I drew closer and was not far from the lions when I felt a magnetic power emanating from Didi's eyes, protecting me like a large sheath of light encasing my body. Certain of her protection, I gained confidence and walked with steadier steps, passing the lions as if I were invisible. Up until this point, they seemed not to notice me or to mind my presence, but as I drew close, one of the lionesses lifted her head and let out a ferocious sound. My whole body shook and I froze again, too frightened to proceed or turn back.

My eyes were fixed on Didi. Her gaze was calling me forward. If I am to die, I thought, I would die by her side. She took a few steps toward me, reached out her hand and drew me to her. We walked past where the lions rested to a small rock and she sat me down. I could not release my gaze from her as my body was still in shock over what I had just done.

"Didi, the lions!" I gasped, afraid to turn around least I see their ferocious gaze fixed on me.

"What lions, child?" she asked in her sing-song voice, her eyes full of laughter.

I swung around to find the lions gone and in their place sat three large boulders. My heart was racing, as much from confusion as fear. I turned my gaze from the stones to Didi and back to the stones again. "There were lions there," I murmured faintly. "I didn't imagine them. I saw them and heard them."

Didi smiled. "Our mind sees many things, which are not as they appear to be. You did see lions, but they have served their purpose and are now gone. You are brave indeed to have come this far." She took hold of my hands and sat me down beside her. My body was still shaking. I didn't understand her words. If the lions had been there, then how did they disappear? Was she playing magic tricks on me?

Didi smiled. "You have great faith, Thema, so I will teach you," she said with a beaming face. I could not answer, caught as I was in confusion. Seeing my distress she began to rub my hands and arms. The shaking eased and a great peace came over me. I followed her as she got up and walked further down the narrow path. She sat me down on a fallen tree in another small clearing. Having stepped out beyond the umbrella of trees, I could feel the hot sun peering down, and I put my hand above my eyes to shade them from the glare. Perhaps it was the heat, I thought, that caused me to see things that weren't there, or did she have magical powers? My gaze must have given away the questions that assailed me.

She laughed and then said in a more serious tone. "What is it you want to know, child? Why have you come to me?"

I ventured in a hesitating voice, "Was that magic, Didi?"

"What is not magic?" she replied. "The whole world is a magic show, one vast magic show created by our Mother."

"But Didi, where did the lions go and how did you do that?'

An enigmatic smile crossed her face, but she kept silent.

Feeling more at ease, I changed the subject. "How did you know about my mother's condition when you first met me, and then my sister's? How did you know these things?"

"I know many things, child, as you will discover."

"Why haven't I seen you in all these years, Didi? I come quite often to gather wood, but you have not been here."

"Do you think I sit here waiting for you?" she replied in an almost chiding voice. "I have other things to do, my child."

"But then why now, Didi. Why?"

She shook her head. "So many questions." I looked at her, expecting an answer. Finally she replied, "It is I who should be questioning you. What is it you want from me, child? I am here because you have called me. It is your desire that has brought me here. I am only responding to what is in your heart." I wanted her to tell me something about herself, but was too shy to ask. "You can call me Didi. I have many names, but that one will do."

"Didi, I have learned many things about the medicinal plants, but . . ."

Her laughter interrupted me. "You have not even begun your training," she replied. "You must forget all that you have learned."

"Why must I put aside what I have learned?" I protested

"You still don't understand, child. It is not the plants that heal; it is the mind of the one who allows the Mother to work through her. The plants are but a vehicle. You can heal with any piece of grass, or stick of wood. It makes no difference."

I looked away, baffled by her words. I didn't want to contradict her lest she disappear again, but I had seen the power of the medicinal plants. "Didi, it was you who healed my mother and sister with the plants."

"Was is it the plants that did the healing, or were they only an instrument?" I was now totally confused. "I am not belittling the power of the medicines," she explained more gently. "I am trying to teach you a greater secret. Keep all your knowledge if you will, but learn to use the power that is behind the plants, that gives them their life energy. Do you understand me, child? If one of the women in your village had given your sister the same medicine I gave you, it would not have saved her life. It was your sister's time to die, and only an intervention saved her."

"Intervention?" My confusion grew deeper.

She nodded and said in a matter-of-fact voice, "I had to speak with the Great Mother Spirit and seek an extension of her life. That is not an easy task." A look of great wonder and admiration came over her face when she spoke of the Great Mother, a look that I could not fathom. I gazed at Didi in amazement. If what she was telling me were true, then she had a power that surpassed anything I had ever seen. She was not merely a woman of the healing medicines, but something else; I couldn't quite understand what that might be.

"We will begin your training," she said amused. "And we can begin with the plants, if that is what you wish."

Without comprehending the implications of my words, I replied quietly, "No, Didi. I want to learn from you the greater secrets, not the healing properties of the plants. You are right, there are others who can teach that. I know that you have a greater knowledge."

She looked at me intently. "You will not be able to share with anyone the things that I will show you." I nodded. "And it will do you no good to talk to others in the village about me. Do you understand? There may be times that you feel confused and afraid, but you will have to confront your fear. Only you can chase away your doubts."

"I am not afraid," I replied firmly, thinking that there was nothing that could surpass walking past three lionesses!

"You possess a faith and determination of which you are not yet aware. I can teach you how to uncover these qualities, but you must be patient. It takes years to unfold one's abilities. In time you will learn to see beyond what the mind says is real, to see the Spirit nature behind the physical form—the Spirit that can transform one object into another.

I looked down as she spoke these words, trying to take in her meaning. Two birds flew down beside us and I watched as they hopped about on the forest floor. Suddenly my eyes caught sight of something else. A large and deadly looking snake was slithering toward us, its hood raised as if ready to attack.

Suddenly I jumped up from the rock on which we had been sitting and pointed to the snake a few feet away. I began to back away. A wave of fear rushed over me, and I could not even let out a cry. I had a particular fear of snakes as a deadly one had crept into our village a few years earlier and bit my brother. The poison rushing through his system had nearly drained his body of life, but the herbs had healed him.

"What is all this fuss?" she asked, shaking her head. "You must learn to be calm in the face of danger."

I continued to back away as the snake approached Didi from behind.

"Watch out, Didi!" I finally found my voice again.

"Watch out for what?" She innocently inquired.

"The snake!"

"What snake?" she asked looking around.

I turned to face her. "There." When my eyes turned to where the snake had been, it was gone. "It must have slithered away," I said. I looked around, fearing that it was still lurking somewhere in the vicinity. She smiled. "Didi, I saw it. I really did," I stammered. "It was right behind you and it looked like it was about to attack."

"Did you not just tell me you are not afraid? Where did your faith go, child, the faith that I spoke about." She gazed at me intently.

My heart was racing. Only minutes before I stood before the lionesses and now a deadly snake. First they were there, and then they were gone. What kind of magic was this? Whatever games she was playing with me, I didn't find them amusing at all.

"Child," she chided, "how am I to teach you if you are so afraid of our sister creatures? When it is your time to die, you will die. If it is not your time to die, no lion or snake can harm you. You must trust in the Mother's protection. They are her children as we are."

I looked at Didi in confusion. Was she what some in our village would call a witch? The very thought sent shivers up my spine.

"The mind creates its own reality," she replied casually. 'You must learn to distinguish and see beyond appearances. Don't be fooled, my child, by what appears to be. You think you saw lions and now a snake, but were they really there?"

"I saw them. It could not have been my imagination. I am sure they were there, but where did they go? What kind of magic, Didi . . . ?" My voice had become faint. Fear had entered me again. This time it was not fear of lions and snakes, but of her.

"It is for you to decide what is real, child."

I was quiet. Perhaps Didi was a spirit and not a real person after all. The animals had seemed real enough, but perhaps she had cast a spell. I began to shift nervously from one foot to another. I was overcome by the thought that she had magical powers of which I needed to be wary.

"That is enough for one day," she said quite suddenly. "Come, I will see you to the edge of the forest."

My heart sank when she spoke those words. I was torn between fear and the desire to learn from her. I had failed whatever test she had given me, but despite the questions racing through my mind, I was deeply attracted to her, to her knowledge, to everything about her.

"When will I see you again?" I asked in a hesitant voice when we had reached the place of parting.

"You must resolve your doubts before I see you next. As long as you question me, I can be of no use to you," she replied, then hurried down the path that we had left behind.

I stood at the forest's edge for a long time staring at the trail she left. Who was this woman who drew me to her like a magnet and yet also awakened fear? Who was this woman who could create animals out of thin air and then make them evaporate? Who was this Mother Spirit of whom she spoke? I had come to the forest to find answers, but left with far more questions and uncertainties.

I stayed away from the forest for the next few months, struggling with my feelings, quite dispirited by the thought that I had let Didi down. I reviewed the incident again and again, sometimes believing that Didi had played a magic trick on me, but more often feeling that she was testing my courage and trust in her. The latter was to win out, and soon I was back gathering wood and calling for her every chance I could.

My relationship with Didi had gotten off to a difficult start, but I was determined not to let it end there. When she didn't appear after many visits to the forest, I began to long for her, a feeling that I couldn't explain or understand. When I went to gather wood and she wasn't there, my heart sank. Emptiness set in. I had to see her again.

Chapter 11

T he next time I saw Didi was about a year after the incident with the lions. I had begun to believe that I would never see her again. Then one day when I was collecting wood by the edge of the forest, I heard her call. She stood a few feet away in the jungle. My heart leapt at the sound of her voice. I jumped up, letting the branches I had collected fall from my hands, and rushed to her full of enthusiasm.

"Didi," I cried. "I am so happy to see you again."

She smiled. "And I am happy that you have called for me."

An awkward moment followed. I wondered whether I should say anything about our last meeting, but instead I said, "You have been away a long time."

"I have not been away," she replied mysteriously. "It is you who have been away. I have been here waiting for you."

"But, Didi, I have come often to the forest looking for you . . ."

"Your eyes could not see me, is that it?"

Confusion once again set in. When she saw this, she laughed. Suddenly I felt quite forlorn. I could not understand her, but I loved her and wanted to be in her presence as much as I could. I didn't want to say anything that might keep her away. "I have missed you a great deal," I replied with some sadness.

"Yes, child, that is why I am here." Her voice was gentle and loving. She took my hand and we walked in silence into the forest. When we stopped she sat me down and asked, "What is it you are seeking, Thema?"

"Seeking? I don't know." Until that moment I had not thought that I was seeking anything.

"The last time I saw you, you had fear of me. That fear is now overshadowed by your love. It is natural, Thema, to fear what you don't know. You should not be embarrassed or ashamed about that. Never think that I would judge you. Nothing that you can do or say will make me think less of you. I have waited silently among these trees, because your love had to emerge and chase away your fears. I am not in the habit of playing with the forces of nature, but on occasion, the great Mother Spirit allows it, when there is a purpose." Her eyes were twinkling. "The things that you saw here in the forest with me can be done, but such things are not due to any magic spells. They are simply the power of the Mother at work. You may doubt me, Thema, but never doubt her. Out of her mind came the lions, the snakes, and all that you saw. Her mind can make them change shape, make them appear or disappear. We are all creations of her vast being."

I didn't know how to respond. I knew nothing of the great Mother of whom she spoke.

"You needn't understand all I am telling you, but one day you will."

"You asked me what I am seeking," I replied slowly. "I don't know. All I know is that I need to see you. You fill an emptiness that I feel inside. When I don't see you, I miss you terribly, Didi."

"My child, you came for love, not knowledge, but in the end they are the same. You will learn everything you need to know through love. It is this love that has drawn you to me. Many people want magical powers and I was testing to see if that was what you seek, but it is not. You are seeking love and only the Great Mother can give you that. Only she can satisfy your heart's desire. I am but her messenger, the one who can bring you to her."

She was right. It was love that truly drew me to Didi, not her powers or magical abilities, not her healing, not any of the extraordinary things she could do. It was simply out of love that I had come. My feelings for Didi made no sense to me. We had only met a few times and our conversations had been brief, but she held a special place in my heart. I thought of her as my dearest friend. I felt that she knew me inside out and was aware of my thoughts and feelings before I even spoke them.

"When you speak of the great Mother, I don't understand." Then I added with something of a chuckle, "and I don't understand why I miss you so much when I don't see you."

"Am I not lovable?" she asked in a teasing tone. I gazed at her and smiled. "It is not this old woman who you love, child. It is the One you see in me, the One who sent me to you."

"Who is that? Who is the Great Mother of whom you speak?" I asked, once again baffled by her words.

"You will find out in good time. You will discover everything you need to know through love. Nothing else is required, only love."

I didn't quite know what to expect. I had imagined that my last experience with Didi would be repeated, but there were no lions, no snakes, nothing to fear that day or in any of our subsequent meetings.

I went to the forest regularly after that. Sometimes Didi would be there but often she would not. I never knew when I would meet her. Inevitably she would appear when I had a great need to see her, when my heart would be aching to be in her company and hear her laughter. When we did meet, she stayed for only an hour or so and her words were always enigmatic, without much explanation, leaving me to wonder about the deeper meaning. I understood much later that she was seeking to develop in me faculties beyond the thinking mind, the "spirit sense" as she called it. "It is through the spirit sense that you can know all things," she once told me. "But it is not easy to develop this."

I knew that my trips to the forest were not for what she could teach me but out of pure love for her. She had become an indispensable part of my life. She knew this and on occasion would respond with tenderness, but at other times she would be as remote and distant as the stars. I would feel as if she was pushing me away, but when I would be back in the village reflecting on this, I realized it was not a lack of love that made her seem inaccessible. It was something else, something that I couldn't understand. Didi remained an enigma.

Soon, time came for my marriage. I stood before Didi one day and told her of the arrangements that were being made. She nodded, already knowing the course of things to come. I sought her advice.

"It is determined already," she said. "If you do not marry, you will have no standing in the village. Your family will shun you. You will have no place to go.

"I could come live with you," I said.

She laughed her deep and hearty laugh. "You are young still. You have duties to fulfill. Your place is not with me."

"Didi, you have never told me about your past. Did you ever marry?"

Didi never spoke about her life. When I would ask any personal question, she would change the subject, carefully avoiding any clue to her past. I yearned to know something of her history. She didn't answer my query but instead said, "The man you are to marry is the son of a fine warrior. He will also become a good warrior. He is very good looking, and of fine character too. Yes, marry him."

I looked at her in amazement. How did she know he was handsome? "Have you seen him?" I asked with surprise.

"Do you think I see only what is among these trees?" she asked equally surprised.

I had not told anybody in the village about Didi, not even my sister, who was the closest person to me. There was fear of such women. They were regarded as having only half a mind, inhabited by dark spirits, and I remembered Didi's warning early on in our relationship when she told me to speak of her to no one. On one occasion I had thought to bring my sister to meet Didi, but as soon as that thought entered my mind, I heard Didi's voice telling me no, my sister would be afraid.

Since my encounter with Didi and the lions, she took a softer approach to me, trying to teach me through subtle messages. I was far from the perfect student and often could not grasp what she was telling me, but it didn't matter, I was happy just to be with her. The whole world was alive to her and she was in constant communion with the life forms around us, but what I loved most was not when she spoke of the animal or plant life but when she spoke of the Great Mother, the Mother of us all. Gradually, over time, this Mother became a presence to me as well, and I began to feel, if not fully understand, a little bit of who Didi was.

"We are one family," she used to say. "One family emerging from one Mother, the Great Mother Spirit. Humans have separated themselves and created a world for themselves apart from all the rest. But this is not the way it truly is. We are part of one great expansive body, each part working in harmony with the rest, just as our human body functions. Suppose the heart were to go live alone and separate itself from the rest of the body. The whole system would die. Could our legs or arms live apart from the whole? How crazy to think so," she would say with a shake of her head.

The day before my marriage ceremony, I went to the forest to find Didi. I so wished she could be there for the ceremony, but I knew this was impossible. She was waiting for me. "I'll be there with you," she said. "You may not see me, but I will be watching you."

My husband was indeed a beautiful man, tall and sleek with a strong chest and arms. His facial features were very fine. His dark skin was silken, so smooth to the touch. His hair was cropped very short, as was mine. I also was tall and sleek, and from what the village people said, we made a handsome couple.

I was happy with him and in the early days of my marriage I didn't visit the forest much. I had made the mistake of telling my husband about Didi, but he dismissed the very notion of a woman living in the jungle. I should have known better, but in my effort to fully join myself to him, I felt I should confide all my deepest secrets.

"No such woman exists," he insisted. "These are stories people like to tell to scare the children and keep them out of the jungle. Don't pay any mind to those tales. If you think you saw someone, it was your imagination. Nobody could survive in there, certainly not a frail old woman. And you should not be going to the jungle alone. You cannot protect yourself."

"But I have spoken with her many times. I know Didi to be real."

He laughed. "It's your imagination, my Thema. Don't give it any thought." And so for a while I stayed away.

It was during my first pregnancy that I was overcome with a longing to see her and wandered into the jungle silently calling her. I found her seated on a large boulder as if she had been waiting for me, a lioness lying peacefully beside her. Remembering my first experience with her lions, I assumed it to be one of her creations and so paid it no mind. I was not afraid. Didi smiled at my calm demeanor. As I sat beside her, she motioned to the lion to leave, and off it went. I watched as it marched off down the wooded trail.

"So it was real!" I exclaimed.

"Do you think I go around creating lions?" she protested with a sparkle in her eye.

"Didi! Will you never stop teasing me?" I was so glad to see her. In the back of my mind I had thought that perhaps she would chide me for being away so long, but scolding was not part of her nature.

She put her hand to my stomach and said very sweetly, "Your son will be coming soon."

"A son?" I asked, pleased at this news.

She nodded. "The birth will be long and difficult, but I will be with you so have no fear."

I sat beside her. It seemed as if no time had passed since our last meeting, and we picked up right where we left off last time. Ours was a continuing conversation with no interruption despite the long intervals between meetings.

I was feeling quite relaxed this day and so thought to inquire once more into her past. Every time I had done so previously, she had evaded my questions, but today might be different. "Didi you have never told me about yourself, your village, your past. Where do you come from?"

She pointed her walking stick up to the sky and said, "From the stars, like you."

"Be serious, Didi."

"What makes you think I am not serious?"

"But where is your village?"

"I have no village."

"Surely you have a family, a husband once?"

She laughed. "What makes you think so?"

"But where do you live now? Not in this jungle."

"I live everywhere and nowhere, my child. Why all these questions? What is it you really want to know?" She stared at me intensely.

I realized she would yield no information. I dared not speak out loud the thought that had recently entered my mind. Sometimes I wonder if you are real Didi, or just a figment of my imagination, as my husband claims. She responded to my thought with feigned indignation.

"What a question to ask someone! Am I real? Feel my body. It is flesh and blood like yours, my child." She took my hand and ran it over her arms.

I looked at her apologetically, embarrassed that she had read my thought.

"I am as real as you, Thema, and as unreal. Look at me, child, I can disappear into the sun beams." Suddenly the air was filled with a heavy mist and I could not discern her figure. I heard her voice but couldn't see her. "And I can emerge from those very beams of light." The mist lifted and again I saw her seated beside me. "Does that make me unreal? You can do the same if you attend to what I have tried to teach you. There is nothing magical about it."

I was speechless. My husband's dismissal of Didi had left an imprint on my mind, more than I had realized. I was embarrassed now that I had allowed his way of thinking to affect me.

"Don't let doubts set in, Thema. It is you who have called me, and I am here in response to your call. I have told you not to speak of me to anyone. Your husband is a good man but he does not have the love that you have. I only make myself known to those who are my own. You have a yearning in your heart. That is why I have come. It is the Great Mother you yearn for, not an old jungle woman, and the Great Mother knows the yearning deep inside of you."

I was at a loss for words. It was true there was a yearning in me for something that I didn't understand. But the Great Mother Spirit, She would know of me and of this yearning? I was an insignificant young village woman amidst Her vast creation. How was it possible that She would respond to me? That was too much to comprehend.

Didi smiled. "She sees into the heart of all her children," she said, and added, "There are mysteries to be uncovered and in time you will uncover them, my child. But the time is not now. You must go home and give birth. Take these plants and do as I have directed in the past. It will ease your pain." She got up and with a parting glance took off deeper into the jungle.

My labor was very intense. It went on for several days and I was so exhausted I thought I would die giving birth. But Didi's words rang in my ears. I did as she had told me, drinking the broth throughout the labor, and in the midst of the worst of it, I felt her presence beside me. Finally my son was born. He kept me very busy for the first few months and I was unable to get to the forest. I wanted very much to present him to Didi.

Finally, one warm bright day I took him to the forest. I didn't know if Didi would be there, but usually when I had a strong need to see her she would show up. I entered the forest light-footed, feeling very happy to be bringing my son to her. I wandered in deeper but she was nowhere in sight. I called and called. Suddenly I heard the roar of a lion not far off. Despite all she had taught me, I could not face the lion without her nearby to protect me. I had not mastered that ability! There was a rustle in the bushes nearby and I swung around to find not Didi but several men from our village.

"What are you doing here in the jungle?" One of them asked in a stern reprimanding voice.

"I am here to meet . . . What are you doing?" I responded.

"One of the goats in the village was eaten last night. We are out to find the lioness. They are encroaching now. You should not be here, especially with the child. We will see you to the jungle's edge."

I had no choice but to leave. Word got back to my husband that I had wandered into the jungle and he kept a watchful eye on me after that.

"Are you still chasing that imaginary old woman? For once and for all, put her out of your mind," he chided me in a harsh voice. "What will the people of the village think? They respect us. Do you want us to lose our standing?" His scolding was the beginning of the erection of a wall between us, a barrier that made me feel alone and dejected, as if I had no voice, no say in my own affairs.

I did not see Didi until some years after my second son was born. After the birth, I was busier than ever. That child was a special one to me. There was something about him that made me cling to him, something precious, almost vulnerable. I took great pleasure in watching him grow from infancy to boyhood. And so the months passed into years and I busied myself with the children. There were times when I was overwhelmed by all the family work and I felt Didi slipping away from me. I had not a minute to myself. Then one day, when my sister had come to watch the children, I slipped away and went alone to the jungle's edge and sat down forlorn. I was overwhelmed by emotions that I couldn't understand. I loved my husband and my children, but I had begun to feel a sense of futility inside. I longed for even a glimpse of Didi. My time with her had been the happiest in my life. It was only then that I felt a sense of freedom, of possibility, of being valued. With Didi I was more than just a wife, a mother, a village woman. There was something about her smile, her laugh, which brought such joy no matter what we were discussing. She made me feel connected to the vast universe beyond our small world.

I had not seen her in a number of years and I longed to hear her voice, her laughter, which seemed to shake the whole of the forest, to smell the flowered fragrance that her body shed. I could not imagine going on much longer without a visit from her. Suddenly I heard her voice booming inside of me.

"Come in two days' time. Your family will be away and you can spend the night." I jumped up in joy and ran back to the village. When I arrived my husband was making preparations for travel. We had been invited to a festival in a nearby village and it would mean two days travel. I expressed fatigue and asked to stay behind. It was to be my first separation from the children, and I hesitated.

"Are you sure you want to stay behind?" my husband asked.

My second son clung to me, insisting that he would not leave without me. I vacillated but then remembered Didi's words to me. Gently and somewhat sadly unwrapping my son's arms from around my neck, I pushed him in the direction of his father. "It is better that you all go. I need some time to rest." And so off they went, my husband and the two children, with many members of the extended family.

The next day I made my way deep into the jungle, looking for Didi, calling her name. When I couldn't find her, I thought that perhaps I had imagined hearing her voice inside of me. In fact, I had not seen her that day. I had only heard her voice and it had come from within. Perhaps it was my desire that made me think I heard her. My mind was full of doubt. I walked and walked. Didi was nowhere in sight. I was deep in the jungle now but I felt no fear. I was desperate to find her.

Then her playfulness began. I heard her laugh behind me, but when I turned to look, nobody was there. Then I heard her laugh a ways off in front of me. I rushed ahead and again nobody was in sight. After this continued for some time, I called out, "Didi, please, show yourself."

There was no answer, only silence. Her laughter stopped.

"I miss you, Didi, please." The tears started to flow. Never had I felt so much love and yearning. Suddenly my voice became almost stern. "I must see you today," I called loudly. "I must!"

"That is the determination I was waiting for," came her melodious voice. I saw her bent body standing beside a tree.

It was like the sun breaking through the clouds. I smiled and my tears turned to laughter. So happy was I to see her. For the first time in the many years that I had known her, she allowed me to embrace her.

"I saw that sadness has entered your heart and so I came," she said. "Why are you not happy, child?" I had no answer. I didn't know why I had this empty feeling inside. "You feel overwhelmed by family life?"

I nodded. She was expressing what I dared not admit to myself.

"And your husband does not understand you. I see. Thema, this is the way of family life. You must accept it and not expect more from your husband than he can give. I have told you he is a good man even though he is limited in understanding. That is not his fault. In time he too will grow. You must find happiness within yourself. No one can give it to you."

Only then did I realize how much I longed for freedom, time alone to look up into the night sky and ponder the mysteries held there. I yearned to be more than a mother, the wife of a village warrior. The tears began to form in my eyes.

"Sometimes I miss you so much, Didi, that I can hardly stand it," I blurted out.

"I know the yearning in your heart," she replied. "It is not a yearning for me," she said, "but for the great Mother."

"But it is through you that I know of her," I murmured. "Without you . . ."

"That yearning is a great gift, Thema. Don't wish it away. In that pain there is a sweetness that brings you ever closer to the goal."

"If only I had more time with you, more freedom," I complained, drying my tears.

"It is not possible now, Thema," she said gently, shaking her head. "You have family duties. Just remember that no matter what you are doing, the mind can always be free. Nobody can control your mind, child, nobody. You can be roaming the jungle with me while you are busy caring for your children." She was quiet for a few minutes. A strange look came over her eyes as she glanced off into the distance.

"I don't want to spoil our time together by complaining," I said. "I am grateful that you have come, so grateful, Didi, so grateful." I looked at her lovingly and all my disappointments faded away.

Her attention returned to me. "You must be ever joyful, Thema," she said taking my hands in hers. "It is not your husband or children who will give you joy. It is life itself. Life was born out of the inexpressible joy of the Great Mother. That joy is embedded in every part of creation. It is yours if you will but take it." She let go of my hands, rose from the rock on which she was seated and began to walk quickly deeper into the jungle. I hurried to keep up with her.

"Where are we going?" I asked. Despite her aged and bent body she sped like a lioness herself, and I had to walk quickly to keep pace.

"I am taking you on a journey, a journey that will put an end to your sadness."

I had never been so far into the jungle but I had no trepidation. I felt free and happy to be with her. After a few hours of walking, mostly in silence, we came out of the forest to a beautiful meadow by a rushing river, surrounded by gentle hills. The area was filled with fragrant flowers and many small animals. I had no idea where we were and I didn't care to ask.

"It is beautiful, almost magical," I exclaimed, taking in the scene. I didn't know such a beautiful place existed within a day's walk from my village.

She nodded. "We can rest here. I will prepare some food." There seemed to be the remnants of an abode of sorts because Didi was able to find the needed items to make a fire and fill a pot with food. There seemed to be, in fact, an abundance of food.

"Is this your home?" I asked as I watched her work.

She smiled. "Still that same question. I have told you that I have no home, or rather, the whole universe is my home. How could I call only one place my home?"

I should have known that I would get no more than a typical Didi response.

She prepared a delicious meal. "I didn't know that you could cook, Didi?"

"Have I never made a meal for you before?" I thought back to all the times we were together. I shook my head.

"My, my," she said. "I am a very good cook. We can do anything we put our mind to. I have taught you that."

I nodded. "But you made all of this out of nothing.

"Why does that surprise you? Haven't we all come out of nothing? Out of what ingredients did the Great Mother make us? Out of her dream, Thelma. I have taught you that."

Every conversation now always came back to the same topic, the Great Mother Spirit. Increasingly Didi spoke to me of her. She wanted me to understand something, but I had not yet grasped what she was trying to teach me.

"Didi, where are you when you are not with me?" I asked.

"Many places," she replied, poking the embers of the fire.

"So you don't live in our forest, do you?" She shook her head. "Do you come only to meet me?"

"Questions, questions, so many questions. Why not ask me something important?"

I lay my head down on some nesting grass and looked above me. The sun grew dimmer as it inched its way toward the horizon. A beautiful pinkish red light beamed across the sky, but that too was fading fast.

"It is so beautiful here," I mused. "And I am so happy. I could stay here forever with you."

"My child. I have many things to do. I cannot rest in one place for too long."

"Tell me something about your life, Didi, anything at all."

"The universe is more beautiful than you can imagine, Thema. This world, with all its beauty, is but a pale reflection of what lies beyond."

"What does lie beyond, Didi? Have you ever seen that world?"

She didn't respond. I looked at her and saw that her eyes were closed. She was still as a rock. She did this sometimes, slipping away from the outer world. I knew to keep quiet at those times. Usually I felt a bit restless and was eager for her return. This time, I didn't mind. I had the whole night ahead of me. There was no rushing back, no one to check on me, to question and confine me. For this one night, I was free.

One by one the stars began to make their presence known. The stars were like jewels strewn across the sky, the Great Mother's necklace, I thought. I smiled to myself. Now I was beginning to think like Didi. I saw her eyes slowly open. A small smile broke across her face as she looked at me. I was filled with excitement. "Tell me about the beginning, Didi. Where did we come from?"

After some time she said, "That is a very big question, Thema."

"I want to know."

"What is it you really want to know, my child? The beginning of what? Your tribe, where your people came from?"

"No, not that. The beginning of it all."

"You mean creation." I nodded. "Well, that is a longer story, but I will begin." And so she started her tale of how at one time, very, very long ago, there was only the Great Mother Spirit absorbed in Her own Being. But there came a time when the love flowing from this Mother became so abundant that it began to express itself, bursting out of her and giving birth to many different forms. "That was the beginning of creation," Didi said. "We were born out of Her love."

She began to describe all that was created and, as she spoke, her voice faded into the distance and my eyes got heavier and heavier. I felt great peace and happiness lying there under the stars at Didi's feet, listening to her melodious voice. Before I knew it, she was standing erect and tall before me. Her form had expanded and transformed into a very tall and beautiful young woman, with glowing black skin and shining hair that fell in waves almost to her knees. Her eyes shone like diamonds, both soft and fierce. Her walking stick had turned into a spear. She took my hand and we moved through the heavens, passing world upon world until we entered a place full of light, a beautiful world, beyond any earthly description. The thought came to me, "This is where the Gods live." She led me through beautiful vistas of multi-colored lights with many heavenly beings, passing trees of many colors and translucent waterfalls. I felt such joy, such joy on seeing this beauty beyond description.

"This is where I live, child. Now you know. This is where you come from and to where you will return. Only joy lives here. Only joy." I heard those words echo from everywhere.

The sun was pouring over me when I awoke the next morning. Didi brought me a hot drink. She was back to her normal self, a bent over woman with knotted gray hair. I looked at her in disbelief. Had I dreamed the whole experience?

"Didi . . ." I began.

"Did you have a good sleep, child?" There was laughter in her eyes.

"I had a dream last night."

"We all have dreams," she said quietly as she offered me food.

"But this was no ordinary dream. I saw you as the Goddess and you took me . . ."

She smiled, "And I see you as the Goddess, my Thema. Where is the Goddess not? She is everywhere, in all of us."

"But was it real or was it only a dream?"

"What shall I do with you, with all your questions and doubts? Have I not told you many times? It was as real as anything is real, and as unreal."

She saw the puzzled look on my face. I turned to gaze out at the distant landscape. In this meadow I could see far across the seas of grass and flowers. After so many years she was as much of an enigma as ever.

Then she addressed me in a more serious tone. "Why do you think a dream is not real? All of what you experience will pass away when you die, Thema, and your life will seem to you then as only a dream. Am I sitting here with you now? Do we exist? At some point our meeting will become a dream to you, one you may not even remember. But nonetheless it has a reality that will never die. The fact that you and I are here together will always be, because what comes into being can never die, only transform. Our meeting exists outside of time, which continually flows like a river, ever changing, but there are those things that exist beyond time. One day you will know this."

Her words created a shift in my understanding and I began to grasp what she was saying. She looked at me lovingly and said, "You must decide what is real. Only you can remove your doubts."

I knew that what I had experienced that evening was no ordinary dream, and I knew I would never forget what she had shown me. In my heart I recognized that she was far more than I could ever grasp. She was not the old jungle woman she appeared to be. But who was she? I didn't know. My family life seemed far away now. At that moment the only thing that was real to me was Didi, and nothing seemed more real than what I had seen during the night.

Real or not, the dream filled me with an inexpressible joy that was to last a long time. We walked back in silence through the jungle. It had taken us hours on our journey the previous day, but today the journey back seemed half the time. When we arrived at the jungle's edge, she said to me. "I will not see you for a while, but keep this joy with you, Thema. Keep the memory of the Great Mother in your heart. She is the only One who is real. The rest of us are but her dreams. Remember that, and remember her." I didn't want to leave and stood frozen in the spot at the forest's edge.

"Didi, I don't want to go back. I beg you to let me stay with you," I pleaded.

She smiled. "How would your husband and children feel if you were to disappear into the jungle, never to be heard from again?"

"Then I will come again soon."

"I will not be here," she shook her head. "I will be busy elsewhere. Before I meet you next, you will have two pregnancies that will end before their terms, and then a daughter will be born. Come see me after that."

"How long will that be, Didi? I can't wait that long."

"I have taken you on a great journey and shown you many things. Do not forget my words or what I have shown you."

"But Didi . . ."

"Learn to see me between the beams of sunlight, child, and in the grasses that blow in the wind. I am all around you. I never lose sight of you, so you need never lose sight of me." With those words she turned and walked away.

As soon as my family returned, the busyness of daily life also returned, and I had hardly any time to let my mind travel to other worlds. Sometimes when the children were asleep, I would sit outside our hut and look into the night sky, wondering if Didi was traveling somewhere among the stars. I would close my eyes and try to recapture the image of her that I saw in the dream. I wanted to remember that form of hers, standing tall with spear in hand. She was so beautiful, so powerful, so strong, and as fierce as any warrior I had known. I would never have believed such strength could exist in a woman's form. But then again, little did I know of the Great Mother Spirit before meeting Didi.

I was pregnant again but, remembering Didi's words, I did not have much hope that the baby would survive. I lost the child somewhere in the middle of the pregnancy. I was soon with child again, and again lost the child. My husband was in despair. Our sons were growing older and he wanted more children to fill out the flock. I feared he might think of taking a second wife, but then I conceived again.

"This time the child will live," I told him confidently.

"You must take care not to exert yourself," he said. And so he pampered me throughout the pregnancy. A beautiful girl was born, as Didi had predicted. I remembered her words to bring the child to her.

Chapter 12

A shift was in the air in our region. Aside for minor skirmishes, there had been relative peace among the tribes for some time. We had been hearing about raids in faraway villages, and the capture of young men and woman, but now those raids were coming closer, and some of the villages were cooperating with the foreign forces behind the raids. Some people said evil spirits were coming in the form of white men with powerful weapons, but we never saw them. The elders of our village did many ceremonies to keep the evil spirits away but, despite our efforts, the sense of insecurity grew stronger. The alliance we had among the tribes threatened to shatter. There was talk among the village elders that it was time to call a meeting for the wider region and find out who was betraying the trust among us.

I could sense that our peace was being threatened, although nobody would speak openly about it. The warriors were visibly guarding the village at night. The elders were meeting more frequently after we all retired and the village settled down from the day's activity. I asked my husband why there was such concern among the elders, but he brushed it away. I knew that he didn't want me worried, especially since I had just given birth. Months passed and the situation did not improve. It was difficult for me to get away because every path to and from the village was under careful guard. I remembered Didi's words and knew that I had to go to her. One evening I sat outside, looking up into the vast sky. The memory of that night I had spent with Didi under the stars came back to me. Then I heard her voice inside, "Come tomorrow," she said. "The path will be open."

I watched throughout the day for an easing of the guard in the village. Around noon, I could see the elders gathering. I told my husband I was going to fetch something from my sister. He nodded and I left with my infant daughter tied to my chest.

Didi was waiting for me just outside the forest. As soon as I saw her,

I knew something was amiss. There was a distant look in her eyes, and she didn't greet me with the same loving smile. Her body was there but her mind seemed elsewhere. She took the child into her arms and passed her hand over her head, then her heart, then down her body to her feet. "She will be protected," Didi said. "I will look after this one."

We didn't walk into the forest, but sat by the edge of the trees where long ago I used to come gather wood. I knew that I didn't have much time, so I began to tell Didi about the tension in the village. "My husband won't tell me much, but I fear there will be a break in the alliance and that will be bad. Then each village will be on its own." Didi listened quietly, nodding as if she knew it all. "There are outside forces coming who are turning one tribe against another. These forces are very strong. They have weapons we don't have. I fear things will take a turn for the worse. Didi?"

She was silent for a while and then said, "I can't interfere with the will of man. Fate must take its course. Whatever must happen, Thema, accept it and don't fear. But what will take place here will need a long time to undo, a very long time. How foolish is man." Then after a few minutes, she said, "I will teach you something now. I will show you how to enter another's dreams. It will be useful for you to know this. You must concentrate." I closed my eyes and tried to focus my thoughts, but my mind was restless.

"No, not like that, not with force, but with a letting go. Let everything else drift out of your mind and align your mind with that of the person with whom you seek to communicate. It is as if you become one with that person and enter his body and mind. Think with complete focus what it is you need to communicate and repeat it over and over. That person may receive it in a dream, or as a thought. It works in different ways. The success will depend on your concentration and their receptivity. It will take time but you have the skills. You have many abilities, Thema, of which you are not yet aware, but they will be useful in the future. What I have shown you is also for your future, not only for this moment."

All of this time Didi was holding the baby. Now she handed her back to me.

"Thema, when the tribal chiefs meet, ask your husband to bring you along. He will resist but, if you can find a way to convince him, I will assist you. Try any means you can to go along with him, you and the children. There is the possibility of re-building trust among the tribes and this can help guard against the impending threat." She was silent for a few minutes and then calmly said with great firmness, "Do not remain in the village. Do whatever it takes to go along with your husband."

"He would never allow a woman to go," I replied shaking my head. "He is adamant about this. So often he has resisted any counsel from me."

She sighed. "If only the men would realize the great power of women—that we bring benefit to them, not a challenge to their authority—so much suffering could be avoided." Then she added with a crack in her voice, "This time may be different. Do what you can. It is not safe for you and the children to remain there." At this sign of emotion, something I had never felt in her before, she turned her eyes away and gazed into the distance. When she turned her eyes back to me, I thought I saw something I had never seen before, the faintest flicker of sadness, like a shadow creeping across the sun of her face. As long as I had known Didi, I had never seen her when she was not bubbling over with joy. Her face, her eyes, her whole body seemed to exude joy, but not today. I was struck by this change and it brought fear into my heart.

"There are things, Thema, that I cannot change as much as I would like to. Even I have to accept some things as they are."

Her words sent a shiver through my body. It was almost as if she was saying goodbye. "You are not going to die, Didi, are you? I asked in consternation.

"How could that which was not born ever die? No, child, I am not going to die."

"You are not leaving me?"

"I will never leave you."

"Then why is it that I feel something ominous, some impending sorrow entering my heart?"

She didn't answer. She got up and began walking toward the edge of the jungle. I followed in silence. My stomach was in a knot.

"Go child," she said simply.

"I cannot, Didi. I cannot. I cannot leave you."

"Go," she repeated again, more firmly.

I burst into tears. Why did I feel that I would not see her again? "Will I see you again?" I tried to control my tears. She looked at me long without answering. "Didi, I love you. I cannot bear to lose you."

"You will never lose me."

"Then I will see you again."

"Yes, I will come to you." Her voice was barely audible.

There was something so unnerving about this parting, so much left unsaid. I walked into the fields beyond the forest, but fear gripped me and I turned to run back.

Standing at the edge of the forest was not the familiar form of Didi but the Great Mother I had seen in dream, her long black hair flowing smoothly like streams of dark water. Her form had doubled in size and in her hand was the same spear I had seen in my dream. Even from the distance I could see the light flash from her eyes, sending currents of love to me. I had hardly taken in the sight when she disappeared and was gone from view. Once again I saw the familiar form of Didi. I stood frozen in my place, but Didi lifted her hand in blessing and motioned me to continue on.

"Goodbye, Didi," I whispered. "I love you more than I can ever say."

My husband was making preparations to leave the next day for the meeting of the regional council. He was taking the best of our warriors in case violence broke out. I pleaded with him to take me along, but he insisted the council meeting would be no place for a woman. He said harsh words could be spoken. He would take only our eldest son, who was soon coming of age, to be counted among the men.

"But perhaps I can be helpful," I said meekly.

He smiled. "I know, Thema, you are always eager to help, but you must keep your place among the women here, looking after the children."

That night as I was preparing for sleep, I felt dark clouds enveloping me. They came closer and closer until they were hovering over me. I felt a strange pressure around my neck, a pressure that I couldn't free myself from, as if I was being strangled. I struggled to catch my breath. I knew I wouldn't be able to sleep and so spent the evening hours pacing the room, calling silently to Didi for help. My husband saw my anxiety and coaxed me to bed.

"Let me hold you," he said. "Nothing can harm you when you are in my arms." I was restless with frightening dreams. I saw ships coming and cried out. I woke up sobbing. My husband was alarmed but took me again into his arms. I clung to him throughout night.

In the morning, he and two dozen of our strongest warriors prepared for the journey. "I will only be gone four days." He unwrapped my clinging arms. "I can't image it will take longer to sort this out. The village will be guarded, but promise me you will not leave the village." I nodded. "No walks to the forest, no venturing out."

"I promise," I said. I walked him and my eldest son to the edge of the village and watched with heavy heart as they and the others walked off into the distance. I didn't know what danger lurked, but in my mind I thought the dark clouds were a foreshadowing of what might happen to them. What if hostilities broke out, betrayals were revealed, and tempers flared? What would happen to my son should violence break out? He was not prepared and would be vulnerable.

A hush came over the village. Life seemed to stop. I went about my duties, caring for the children. My sister came to stay in our hut as an undercurrent of anxiety also gripped her. The first day passed uneventfully, as did the second and third. We had no word from the men and I was beginning to feel more at ease. I went to sleep that night thinking they would return the following day, the fourth day. But I couldn't sleep. Finally in the early pre-dawn hours I got up and made a fire. I put a pot over the flames to heat some water and watched as the water came to a boil.

I was about to remove the vessel when I heard footsteps running and a bloodcurdling scream. I froze. Before I could think what to do, an arm had grabbed me by the waist. Without realizing what I was doing I swung around, pot in hand, and threw the hot water at the man behind me. He screamed a curse at me. The man was from a different tribe, one I didn't recognize. Three other men ran into the hut. By now my sister and the children were awake and huddled in the corner. All four men attacked me, throwing me to the floor. Out of the corner of my eye I saw my sister run out with the children. I kicked and struggled to get free but I was no match for them. One man held open my legs while another ripped open my clothing and forced himself into my body. As the second man did the same, I bit his cheek with all my might, clamping down until his blood spilled onto my face. He grabbed a knife that had fallen to the floor and dug it into my neck. I felt the life leaving me and I lost consciousness.

When I came to, all was quiet. I saw my body lying there on the floor in a pool of blood. I stared at my body, wondering what to do, how to revive it, and soon came to realize that I was separated from the body that was lying there lifeless. Was I dead or alive? I didn't know. Nobody was there in the hut. I was alone. I walked out into the village, but saw only a few small crying children and some elderly people lying in the dirt, either dead or hurt. I wandered in a daze, trying to piece together what had happened. It had all taken place so quickly. I went from hut to hut trying to understand. I was confused and dazed and didn't know what to do.

I had to find my sister and children. Perhaps they were safe. I remembered seeing them escape. My feet took me automatically to the forest. I found Didi there with my daughter in her arms.

"Didi, what happened?" I cried.

"There was a raid on the village last night," she said quietly.

"Am I dead?"

"Yes, my child."

"My son, where is my son?"

"Your sister came with the children. She hid the baby behind the trees there, and then they ran. I will look after your daughter, Thema, until her father returns. I will see her safely back to him."

"But my son . . ."

"They caught him, Thema, and took him away. Your sister also. There was nothing I could do."

"I must find him."

"Yes, go to him."

"But how, Didi, how?" My heart was breaking at the thought that he, my very dearest child, was captured somewhere."

"Enter his dreams as I have taught you and you will find him. Go now, quickly."

"But why, Didi? Why did this happen?"

She shook her head sadly. "Who can understand the ways of man? I could not change your fate. It was death or captivity. You chose death. You must travel now to another land . . . your journey will continue."

"But, Didi . . ." I began to protest, but she disappeared and I was left alone.

I didn't go anywhere. I didn't know where to go. The world around me grew dim and I didn't know where I was anymore. I was no longer in the village or the forest. I was in some dark place, wandering in the mist, wandering, wandering, looking for him, my beloved son. Wherever I looked, there was only darkness around me, but I had no fear. My only thought was of him. I had to find my dear son. Slowly Didi's words came back to me, every word that she had spoken about entering a person's dreams.

"Concentrate, not with force but with a letting go." It was as if I heard her say, "See your son before you. See him clearly there, his face, his hair, his chest and arms, his legs. He is lying there in front of you."

Time seemed not to exist. Everything was clouded in a dark haze. It could have been days or weeks, but at a certain moment the haze cleared and I saw my son standing before me. He had a smile on his face; he was so happy to see me. I smiled back. He called out to me. I bent down and took his head between my hands. I looked into his beautiful brown eyes and said in a calm and steady voice, "You must be brave now, my son, strong and brave like your father. You must be a man now so that your father will be proud of you."

"I will be brave," he said.

"Do you promise me?" I asked, trying to impart as much love as I could. He nodded his head. "I love you," I cried, but his image had already faded and I found myself standing beside his sleeping body. He called out to me in his sleep. I kept repeating, "I will not leave you. I will not leave you."

What I saw ripped open my heart. He was lying in filth on the bottom deck of a ship out at sea. People were packed together so tightly they could hardly move. Their feet were chained. The heavy rocking of the boat made it almost impossible to lie still. I stood there feeling utterly helpless. I tried to lift him but my arms passed right through him; I realized that I had no physical substance. I couldn't bear it and so I turned to move away, wondering how without a physical form I could rescue him. As I moved through the ship, I saw two men lifting a woman, who looked dead.

"She is still breathing, we shouldn't dump her," said one of the men.

"Captain said there are too many on the ship, we have to get rid of some, and she looks half dead, so over she goes." I saw them throw my sister over the deck into the dark ocean below. I watched in horror as she sank into the sea, but then I saw her spirit rise. She saw me as well and came to me.

Just then Didi appeared. "Go now," she said quietly. "Go into the light." She pointed with her walking stick to where the light was opening. "Don't linger here any longer."

"But Didi, my son . . ." I pleaded. "I can't leave him."

"You can't do anything for him now. His fate will guide him. He is going to another land, and you will follow. But you will not go as a slave," she said quietly but firmly. "Never."

"Didi, my son, how can I leave him?" I cried again.

She stood there firm as a rock, unmoving, without speaking.

I saw the light open and all of the darkness faded away. The ship and its passengers were gone. Even Didi's form was gone. Only her voice remained.

"The Great Mother Spirit will guide you," she said. "Follow her."

With my sister by my side, we stepped into the light and my life as Thema became as a dream.

* * *

It took several months for this vision to unfold fully and for the various episodes of that life to pass before my mind's eye. It was an exhausting experience, but also a tremendously inspiring one. This was my first memory of having a long personal relationship with such a master as Didi, and the fact that she was a woman was very touching to me. Clearly it is no accident that in my current life I promote the work of women spiritual teachers. It made me realize that the memory of her had never fully left me. It had only receded into the substratum of my mind, like unseen currents beneath the surface of the ocean, pulling me forward without any conscious awareness. That life pointed me in the direction of the Divine Mother, which is such a strong theme for me in my life as Dena.

The loss of my son to slavery explained why I was then born in the south—perhaps in search of him—and explained why Joseph's lynching had so traumatized me as the young Elisabeth. That experience stirred the sleeping memory of my African son's capture, and it all now seemed to connect.

I reflected on how moved I had been listening to the young African leaders during the Summit in Senegal. I recalled my feelings for the young woman Barbara, who had shown such spirit and leadership. The older son and young daughter of Thema had survived the attack on the village. Most likely they would have had children, who would have had children, and so on. That means Thema would have many, many descendants now in Africa, my descendants. Some of those young people at the Senegal Summit might trace their ancestry back to Thema. Never before had I understood this level of interconnection. If you consider all the children we have each had, and all of their offspring, this would mean each of us has descendants spread across the globe. If we truly understood this, would there be the possibility of war? Or to put it another way, all wars are but a family squabble. The idea of one global family is not merely an idea, it is a reality. We are all related in one way or another. That is the irony of life.

I was deeply disturbed by the memories of the rape. As a young girl in this life, I had a fear of rape. And still, whenever I read or hear about such a tragedy, I feel it keenly, as if it is happening to me. Now I understood why it awakens such great anger in me.

I also was struck by the lack of freedom I felt as a woman. How ironic that I felt so confined, and yet the one who showed me the way to freedom, the one who was the very epitome of freedom, was a woman, Didi. As these memories returned, at moments I felt her presence very strongly. It was a connection across time and space, and I knew that Didi had never left me. The love I felt for her has never died. Her being continues to vibrate in the universal ethers and at any moment I can tune into her. I can hear her laugh. I can see the sparkle in her eyes. I think now she may be more pleased with me as my understanding of who she is has grown. She came to me at a time when I was wrestling with the issues of coming into my own spiritual life as a woman. The gifts that she gave me in the jungles of Africa were indispensable for my journey onward, and they were to help enormously as Elisabeth was to continue this search, finding ways to deepen her spiritual experience within the social confines of being a woman.

My unconscious memory of Didi became a beacon of what a woman could be, of the spiritual perfection she could achieve; in the modern-day life of Dena, it has been a struggle to keep that beacon before me. There is such a long history of suppressing not only women but also the Divine Feminine, and this history is not easily undone. Didi, my gratitude is inexpressible. That you found me in the wilds of Africa and guided me then has been reason enough to awaken in me an unending dedication to the Mother.

GPIW's work with the young leaders from Africa continued. We brought a number of them to other conferences we organized. Soon after our Summit in Senegal, the tragedy in Darfur, Sudan, began to unfold. The woman delegate from Sudan, who had attended our Summit in Senegal, approached us. Would we help bring together young people from Sudan—Christians, Muslims, and those from traditional African religions, including a delegation from Darfur? We were eager to help.

We brought them to a beautiful nature reserve in Kenya, the perfect setting for a dialogue. The young people sat in a circle under a great tree, as herds of zebras, gazelles, and other animals pranced by. Numerous challenges emerged during this dialogue, as it was the first time so many young people from all over Sudan had come together to talk about the future of their country. What was most apparent was the strength of the women during numerous debates.

As a result of dialogues in Senegal and then Sudan, GPIW began to feel a particular commitment to helping young people cultivate a spiritual vision for the future. Working with the U.N., we went on to organize summits for young people from Asia, Latin America, and the U.S. The U.N. focused on development issues, but our focus was the spiritual foundation for development; thus we sometimes found ourselves at odds with the goals of the U.N. They had a commitment to universal education, but we questioned what type of education, toward what end. Would it be values based? They had a commitment to sustainability, but what interpretation of sustainability? There were many ways to approach that issue. Without a spiritual foundation, would the future be any better than the present? How could the human community truly progress without a shared spiritual framework?

After several years, our work began to shift again and there was a clear connection between the direction of our work and the unfolding of my memories. I was beginning to put together my journey from Africa to the American South, to Russia, and now New York. What a narrative and what a saga! I was both inspired and depleted by these visions and had to admit that at times I found it difficult to attend to the present moment. I could not remain locked in the past. My life was moving too quickly and my work finally was taking me to India.

Despite my deep connection with and love for India, it was not until 2001 that I was to have my first taste of that land, and it was just a taste. I was in Bangkok preparing for the meeting of women religious leaders that was to take place in Geneva in 2002 when I received a call from a dear Swami friend. Would I come open a conference in Delhi that he had organized? It was a last minute invitation and I accepted, eager to set foot on a land I had long loved. But this first experience of India, this tiny taste, was to last only two days, most of which passed in a hotel in New Delhi.

It was not until 2007 that I was to drink deeply from this sacred land. We were preparing a big conference to celebrate the fifth anniversary of the founding of the Global Peace Initiative of Women. The theme we had chosen was the Divine Feminine—the Mother aspect of the Divine. Our work had shifted from creating a global platform for women spiritual teachers to promoting a deeper awareness of the feminine aspect of the Divine and its essential role in the transformation of self and the world.

Since our initial gathering had been held in the West, in Geneva, we decided to hold this second large gathering in the East. We chose Jaipur, India. Many trips to India were needed to organize this, and my work involved meeting with many religious leaders from Delhi, and further to the north, south, east, and west. I touched many parts of India during this huge endeavor. I was very anxious as we had never organized anything in India. My team and I had only been doing this work for about six years, and for each gathering I questioned whether anyone would show up.

Just before the conference was to begin, I made my way up to Rishikesh to visit Swami Dayananda Saraswati, who had issued my first invitation to India in 2001. He had a lovely ashram on the banks of the great River Ganga (as the Ganges River is called). He suggested that I visit the cave of Rishi Vashishta, one of the great sages of ancient India, only a 30-minute drive into the mountains beyond Rishikesh.

I sat for nearly two hours in the cave and had a wonderful meditation and prayed for a sign. It was then that I had the first vision of a golden-haired companion from the higher plane. (More on him in the last chapter.) I couldn't identify him, but I saw him clearly and felt a great blessing, and knew it was a sign that this gathering would be a success, as indeed it was. That Summit in Jaipur was one of the most powerful and uplifting gatherings that we had ever convened or that I had ever attended. Many people told us how it changed their whole worldview. After that, in the interfaith world there was much more focus on the

Divine Feminine. It changed the course of our work, and from that point onward we became more conscious of the fact that it was the Divine Mother guiding our every step.

After meditating in the cave, I went to sit by the Ganga, which was just outside the cave. The spot was deserted. I was alone on my first visit to the Ganga in this life. Without understanding why, I poured my heart out to the river, releasing all my concerns and anxieties about the upcoming conference. I threw my tensions into the river's unfurling curls as it rushed along the rock-strewn riverbed. A great peace came over me as I sat there listening to her lapping sounds, staring into her green waters. I felt her come alive, but her appearance was deceptive. Anyone looking there would see only a river, a beautiful one no doubt, but merely a body of flowing water. I could see that this was only an appearance and, in a subtler form, there she was, Mother Ganga, a beautiful Goddess speaking to me, reassuring me that all would go well with the conference. I was transfixed.

Conceptually I knew about the spirits that dwell in the natural world, but this was only theory, ideas. I had not touched the reality before. But as sure as I was alive, so was She, the essential form of the Ganga; water was an outward manifestation, but She was speaking to me, giving me Her blessing. I gave myself fully to Her, and from that moment on I have never had any care or doubt about the success or failure of any event that GPIW organizes. I was a vehicle, a tool through which the Mother would work.

The Mother assumes many forms, each one serving a different purpose and offering a distinctive glimpse of the infinite cosmic body of the Divine. The forces and forms of the natural world are extensions of this reality and we can tap into the divine powers that enliven them. So the Ganga may be nothing more than a river for many people, but for others She is the physical presence of a divine emanation. She is that to me. It took me many years to understand why I saw her in this way. It is enough to say that in the course of many, many visits to India, I rarely miss the opportunity to pay my respects and offer my love by the side of my dearest Ganga Ma.

The gathering in Jaipur was a huge success and a major turning point for GPIW. Many, many people came, including some of India's greatest women spiritual leaders. Many male religious leaders attended as well, since the subject of the feminine aspect of the Divine is embraced as much by the men of India as the women. We formed deep friendships and for the next several years, we returned frequently to organize additional programs.

Just as GPIW was moving more deeply into spiritual themes, my relationship with my father took a turn. I had remained close with him through all the early years of GPIW, and he was very supportive of my work, always eager to hear about new projects. The United Nations Secretary General with whom he had been close had finished his two terms as Secretary General, and following his departure many of my father's friends at the UN also left. After our projects in Africa, we had drifted away from the U.N., finding their resistance to spirituality an impediment for us.

My father, in his late eighties, became preoccupied with the succession of the company. All three of my siblings were managing the company along with him; they were all exceptionally qualified and capable, but had different visions of management. The matter of succession led to family disagreements and, finally, the division of the company; it pained my father terribly, but ultimately was in everyone's best interest.

I continued to discuss GPIW's various projects with my father, but increasingly he was unable to grasp the real nature of our work as we delved more extensively into spiritual themes. It was becoming clear to me that my father's work in guiding my path was coming to a close. By now I had established extensive networks and was able to more openly steer GPIW in the direction of deeper spiritual engagement. My father could not come that far with me. His interest was peace-building and some aspects of development, but the deeper spiritual themes were beyond his reach. It did not matter to me, as I have always recognized the critical role he played in my life in providing the necessary conditions for me to take up and sustain my work. His continued love and support were all that I needed.

In 2009 we took up an esoteric spiritual theme—the nature of ultimate reality—for a dialogue between Pakistani Sufis and Indian Yogis. After the 2008 gathering in Jaipur, we moved beyond traditional interfaith themes that focused on tolerance and acceptance of each other and initiated a deeper exploration of essential spiritual truths and insights from the different traditions. Much of the interfaith concept was an exclusively Abrahamic dialogue focused on Muslim-Christian relations, with the occasional addition of the Jewish community. The Eastern or Dharma traditions were pretty much left out. Our interest was more in Asia and how the Eastern traditions could help balance what we thought was an over-emphasis on the Abrahamic faiths. It seemed to me that the Muslims in Southeast Asia had a connection to Hinduism: it was their ancestry and therefore part of their collective memory. Could this shared history become a bridge? This was our hope.

We decided to hold the gathering in Rishikesh, which offered a deeply reflective and sacred space for our exchange. It is always challenging to get visas for Pakistanis to enter India, but this difficulty was compounded by the fact that our event was taking place at the same time as a major Hindu religious festival in Haridwar, the Kumbh Mela. Haridwar is very close to Rishikesh, and many tens of millions of Hindus from all over India would be gathering there. Pakistanis would not be welcomed, but we had not realized the mela was happening when we picked our dates. Miraculously, all of our delegates from Pakistan received visas to come to Rishikesh. It was a very positive sign.

The gathering itself was very difficult to organize for logistical reasons, but difficult situations can bring extraordinary results. We had faith that this gathering would be a breakthrough in terms of the reunion of Pakistanis and Indians on a deep spiritual level. It was to be far more than we expected.

As the Pakistanis arrived and I greeted them at the hotel in Rishikesh, I was struck by one of the men. I couldn't take my eyes off him. Later at dinner I was embarrassed to find myself staring at him, as if he was a magnet drawing me to him. Suddenly I blurted out, "Krishna, he is Krishna." I didn't know why I uttered these words.

Krishna is one of the incarnations of the Divine and is greatly loved and worshipped in India. My guru, Paramahansa Yogananda, spoke often about Krishna and inspired love for him in the hearts of his students. Part of Yogananda's mission in coming to the West was to show the similarity between the teachings of Krishna and Christ. So Krishna held a very dear place in my heart, but why did one of the Pakistanis turn my mind towards Krishna?

It was a great surprise and source of satisfaction to find that the Pakistani group felt a deep connection to Indian spirituality. Many had been waiting years for the opportunity to come to India, and they were eager to dialogue with the Indian yogis. They expressed a deep reverence for the teachings of the Vedas, the holiest of the Hindu texts. This confirmed my belief that between Pakistan and India there is one culture, many conversions to Islam to be sure, but a common history and shared roots.

We took the group to the cave of Vashishta outside of Rishikesh, which had become one of my favorite spots. It was a holy day for Lord Rama, another incarnation of the Divine. Sadhus were sitting outside the cave chanting the *Ramayana*, the narrative of the life of Lord Rama. The Sufis went inside to meditate. There is a long narrow passage to the end of the cave, where there is a small platform with a Shiva Linga, the symbol of Lord Shiva, one of the Hindu Trinity. Sitting in front of the Shiva Linga in the dark, one of the Sufis felt an electric current move up his spine and spontaneously began chanting the name of Allah. Outside the sadhus were chanting Rama and inside the Sufis were chanting Allah. It was one of the greatest interfaith experiences I have known, because in that moment it was all one. Rama and Allah were simply different names for the one Divine Reality.

Then the Sufis from Pakistan went down to the banks of the Ganga, by the side of the cave, and blessed themselves in the river. I was deeply touched to see the reverence with which they held the Ganga. "The Ganga is our river, too," said one of the Pakistanis. And I realized how much damage this artificial separation has caused, cutting a people off from their roots and denying them access to the spiritual heritage of their ancestors.

Over the course of the next few days, while the dialogue was taking place, I felt myself drawn as if through suction back into 15th century India. A great pain entered my heart and the tears became living streams, as I had to endure again invasions from foreign lands. I vacillated between joy and sorrow as I saw the coming together of the Pakistanis and Indians in the present, and in between dialogue sessions I witnessed again the hidden past. It was a destruction that I knew all too well—one that had once torn open my heart, and one that has not yet healed in my own or in the collective memory.

PART IV

EARLY 15ᵀᴴ CENTURY INDIA

Never was there a time when I did not exist,
nor you, nor all these kings;
nor in the future shall any of us cease to be.

—Bhagavad Gita 2:12

He saw all these forms and faces in a
thousand relationships become newly born.
Each one was mortal, a passionate,
painful example of all that is transitory.
Yet none of them died,
they only changed, were always reborn,
continually had a new face:
only time stood between one face and another.

—Herman Hesse,
Siddhartha

Chapter 13

"Gita, Gita, how long can you stay there staring at the idol?" I was beckoned out of my reverie by the impatient voice of my brother. "I have been calling you for so long. Didn't you hear me?"

My brother's voice called me back to the outer world. I had been absorbed in the new idol of Sri Krishna that our father had installed in the family temple. "He seems almost alive," I murmured dreamily as I turned to face my brother and then returned my gaze to the idol.

My brother came to sit beside me. He had not much of a religious nature. "You have forgotten all about me," he complained unhappily. It was true. Since the idol had entered our home, I hardly had given my brother a thought, leaving him without a playmate. Something had shifted in me, and the old games didn't seem to matter anymore.

A loud sigh escaped from my brother's lips. Feigning tears, he rolled over onto the hard marble floor, then jumped up and called, "Catch me if you can," as he ran out of the temple. That was enough to bring an end to my musing. A smile crossed my lips and I ran out of the temple, chasing my brother through the paths that led from the temple through the gardens to our residence.

I was born to a *raja* (king) in one of the kingdoms in the northwest of Bharat, now called India. I was the second child and eldest daughter. Our family worshipped Lord Krishna and the divine play of the young Gopal, Krishna's name when he was a cowherd in Vrindavan, filled my childhood. The girls who grew up in the palace with me loved to act out the stories of Krishna's early life. We never tired of playing the Gopis, the cowgirls who were devoted to Krishna, in search of our Lord. We would run through the palace looking everywhere for Krishna, and my mother, who was a great devotee of the Lord, laughed to see our enjoyment. It was a happy childhood.

The day of Krishna's birth was a particularly joyous occasion, with entertainments of songs and dances depicting Sri Krishna's life. At other times of the year, the dancers acted out the story of Lord Rama as he searched for his wife, Sita, after the demon king had stolen her. There was so much joy around us as we lived in our closed paradise, hardly ever leaving the palace grounds, that we were immune to all that was happening outside the palace walls. I took little notice of the affairs of our time, and so attached little importance to the arrival of the foreign armies that were bringing in a new religion.

Then one day I overheard a conversation among my father, one of his ministers, and my eldest brother. I had been looking for my brother and heard he was in my father's quarters. I was about to enter the room when I heard the minister say, "The only way to prevent a war is to arrange a marriage. The Sheikh's eldest son is of marriageable age, and they have offered a pact."

"Must it be so?" sighed my father. "Surely we have much wealth to offer."

"It is not only wealth they seek, but also domination," came the solemn response. "They are trying to impose their religion and way of life. Perhaps we can prevent this. We can make conditions," he said, "although we cannot protect our wealth, as they will impose great taxes. But perhaps we can prevent the destruction of the temples and the forced conversions." His voice broke as he continued. "They have strong armies and are prevailing over one kingdom after another. All of our allies have succumbed."

"But our warriors are brave and will fight," protested my brother in a raised voice.

"We can declare war, if you think that the best course," the minister replied, addressing my father.

My father was silent for what seemed like a long while. I stood outside the door, barely breathing lest they hear me. Finally my father replied in a low voice I could barely hear, "Go see whether an alliance can be made." My brother started to speak, but my father silenced him, telling him he was still too young to understand the full scope of our responsibilities.

When I heard the word "alliance," I could not contain myself and a cry escaped my lips. I knew what that meant. I was coming of age to marry, but there had been no mention of it thus far. I had no desire for an alliance with a Hindu prince, let alone a foreigner.

"Gita, come here," my father commanded. But I turned and ran as fast as my feet would carry me through the rooms of the palace, into the garden, to the feet of my Lord Krishna, where I knew I would be protected.

"Gita, Gita!" He came after me, but I was already gone.

I stayed hidden all that day in the temple, filled with fear at what lay in store for me. It was only as evening approached that my brother found me, curled up beside the statue. "We looked everywhere but the temple," he said. "I should have known you would be here. I won't let this happen," he assured me, clenching his fists. "We will go to war."

I hid my head in his chest. I didn't want war. I sobbed, "That will be even worse than marriage." I knew that I had no choice but to obey my father.

I could feel the tension in my brother's body as he held me tight. "I don't believe this will bring peace," he replied with great bitterness.

Later that night my father came to see me and told me what I already knew. "We don't live only for ourselves, Gita. We have responsibilities to our people. And one of those duties is doing all that we can to maintain peace. Otherwise, many will lose their lives. Do you understand?" I nodded sadly. "If your marriage would bring peace to our kingdom, and save many families from loss, including our own, would you not do it?" I hid my face in my hands to hide my pain. "Would you not do it for Sri Krishna, to preserve the temples we have built for him, to keep him alive with us so that all the young girls can continue to worship him, as you have so lovingly done?"

This touched my heart. The thought that I could serve our Lord by agreeing to this alliance moved me greatly. I took my hands away from my face and looked into his eyes. I saw the struggle there. I nodded my head. For Sri Krishna, I would do anything that was required.

"You must be brave, my daughter, and do this for our God so we will not be forced to abandon Him," he said as he squeezed my hand.

An alliance was struck. I was not more than 13 or 14 years old when I was sent away. My mother mourned terribly on the day of my departure. In the treaty that was signed, there were allowances for the continued worship in our temples, and I was permitted to take several of the girls who grew up with me, as well as Mohini, who had attended me since birth. My father seemed to feel he had received what he needed. My mother consoled me by saying, "Gopal will be with you, Gita. You and the other girls will continue your play as always." I nodded with a feigned smile, but I knew in my heart it was not to be so. It was a solemn day when they came to take me. My father rode with me to the wedding ceremonies. My brother refused to come. I didn't say goodbye to him. I couldn't bear to see the anger on his face, as he made no secret of his opposition to this arrangement.

I thought my life was over until I saw him coming, the one who was to be my husband. As soon as I caught sight of him, my heart trembled. It was as if Gopal himself were standing there, so youthful and radiant and beautiful. A smile crossed my lips, and when he lifted my head covering and saw me, he smiled as well. After that moment, I hardly minded when my father left me to my new life.

My new husband and I were not far apart in age, and he was as playful as I. We made up games. We frolicked, we laughed. The girls who came with me from our kingdom grew fond of him as well. When I was given a new Muslim name, he saw my discomfort and whispered, "Don't mind, Gita, I will not call you Noor. I will call you Gita Noor. It is the joining of our ways. You can give me a name as well."

"Then I will call you Ali Krishna," I replied. We both laughed. "But this must be our secret," he said, and I agreed. From then on, when we alone, he called me Gita Noor, and I called him Ali Krishna.

Three years passed and I had not left the palace all this time. The gardens were beautiful and extensive. I could spend days wandering them with my ladies and never leave the grounds. I was happy. It was a beautiful place to live, and initially I spent most of my time as I had before, sharing stories of Krishna with those around me. But as I grew older things changed. As childhood left me, it seemed that the presence of Lord Krishna also grew dimmer, until the thought of him no longer dominated my mind. I hardly noticed this, as I was so busy with my new life.

I was with child, in the very early months, when I returned home for the first time for my brother's wedding. My husband could not join me, so I went with my ladies. I told no one about the pregnancy because I feared I would not be allowed to travel, and I wanted my mother to be the first to know.

I was excited to see my family after such a long separation. As we got close to the family palace, I asked to stop at the old temple of Lord Vishnu so that I could offer my prayers and ask a blessing for the child growing in my womb. It had been so long since I had been to one of our temples, and suddenly I felt a longing to be in the presence of my Lord. This was a coming home not only to my family but also to our way of life. When we stopped and I stepped down from the palanquin, I was shocked to see that there was no temple there. I looked around. I knew the place; there was no mistake. But instead of a temple, there was construction—a mosque was being built. Impossible, I thought. I am sure this is the place. But then I reasoned that perhaps I had been away so long that I mistook the location for another. I made a mental note to ask my father about it. I would have enough time on this visit for him to take me to the temple.

When I arrived at the palace and met my family, all other thoughts fled. My mother was the first to greet me and I flew into her arms. We hugged and exchanged greetings. In my enthusiasm I blurted out immediately about the child. She smiled, but said nothing. She seemed somewhat demure and failed to demonstrate the happiness one would expect from news about her first grandchild. But I hid my disappointment and asked after my father.

"He is resting," she said. "He has been very tired these days. He will come to meet you later." I rushed off to see the rest of my family, but when my father didn't come the whole day to greet me, I became worried. I went to his quarters and was told he was resting. I called out to him, still feeling the rights of a young daughter, and he granted permission for me to enter. He was sitting up in his bed, looking over some papers. I rushed to him and he gathered me into his arms. I felt like a young girl again, happy to be in her father's arms. He then asked if I was being treated well by my husband's family.

I nodded, with a broad smile. "My living quarters are beautiful. Everything I could possibly want is there. My husband is very attentive and kind. I could ask for nothing more. Yes, I am happy, father. And . . ." I looked shyly at him.

"And . . . And what, Gita? Is there something more to tell?" he inquired with some worry in his voice.

"I am with child."

A serious look came over his face. I pulled back, surprised that neither he nor my mother seemed overly pleased with this news. "Aren't you happy about the child?" I asked.

"Of course I am," he replied, hugging me. "I only want you to be happy."

"Then what? Something is not right here, I can sense it."

After a few minutes he said. "I have often wondered, Gita, if I made the right decision, but if you are happy, that is all I need to hear."

"And you, father, you look tired." He had aged greatly in the three years that I had been gone. His hair, which had been tinged with grey when I left, was now fully turned white, with hardly a black hair to be found. He smiled and brushed away my question.

"Have you met your brothers and sisters yet?"

"All but Govindas," I responded. "He is nowhere to be found." I could not find my elder brother anywhere.

"Ah, he is busy preparing for the wedding. Let us find him."

I dare not press my father further, but I sensed a solemnity in the palace. Something had changed. An uncertain hush had replaced the joyous laughter that I remembered. A wedding was in the planning, and the halls should have been filled with much bustle and fanfare. There were preparations to be sure, but there was also an air of tension that I couldn't understand. The palace looked less lavish than I remembered. But then, I thought, perhaps it was because the place where I now lived was so very grand. How strange that I once thought this place the most beautiful on earth.

When we found my elder brother, I rushed to greet him, but he turned away with just a brief nod, barely acknowledging my presence. I was shocked. We had been so close, and he had so resisted my leaving. Now, after not seeing me for three years, I didn't seem to matter. My father noticed and reprimanded my brother.

"Your sister has come after all this time. Greet her properly."

He stared at my father and then turned away. My father noticed my consternation and put his arm around me.

"Do not mind him. He is overly nervous about the wedding," he whispered in my ear. "After the ceremonies, he will be back to his normal self." But inside I knew this was not the case. "Let us go to the others," he said.

I hardly saw my elder brother over the next few weeks. I was feeling unwell from the pregnancy and so kept to my room a great deal. My other brothers and sisters visited me, and my mother took great care of my every move. But something was amiss. My heart was not at ease, but nobody left any hint of what the trouble could be. I had expected so much from this visit home, but things had changed, and I no longer felt that I belonged there. I couldn't tell whether it was my family or I who had changed.

After the wedding ceremonies, I began preparations for my journey home. I knew that I could not leave without finding out why my brother was so distant. For the first time on this visit home, I went to sit alone before the idol of Sri Krishna that I had once loved so much. I had avoided spending much time at the temple during my stay for reasons that I didn't understand. Something had kept me away, but now something was drawing me there. Perhaps I hadn't wanted to be reminded of what was missing in my new life.

As I sat before the idol, suddenly a well of sorrow rose in my chest and I couldn't stop the tears from overflowing their banks. "How I have missed you," I sobbed. "My Gopal, I miss your presence terribly." It was like a huge release, a dam bursting." I cried and cried and it seemed there was no end to my tears. When they finally exhausted themselves, I realized someone was sitting just behind me. I turned to find the sad face of my elder brother.

"Gita, I am so sorry," he said simply with much emotion.

I quickly wiped my tears and asked, "Why have you turned away from me? You have hardly spoken to me or looked at me. We were so close once."

"I am so sorry, Gita," he repeated. "I didn't realize that you too would be suffering. I didn't mean to hurt you. It is not anything you have done. It is the situation. Everything is different now."

"Until I came here to sit before my Krishna, I hadn't realized how much this separation has hurt me. I can no longer bear to be away from Him. What is my life without him?" My voice was still shaking from the swell of emotions. I recalled the moment when my father asked me if I would form an alliance for the sake of Sri Krishna. It was for him I had married, and yet I seemed to have lost him through the marriage, and the pain of that loss now overwhelmed me.

My brother's lips broke into a faint smile. "You always loved this *murti* (a representation of the divine). Nobody cared for him the way you did."

"And I still do," I said quietly. "Why has everything changed?"

"Do you not see what has happened to us?"

"I see only that everything has changed here in my family, but I don't understand why," I replied. "Until now, I have not left the palace in these three years. I have been locked up in my own paradise where every wish has been granted. Now I come home and everything is so different. I don't understand what has caused this?"

"Gita, do you not know, really?"

"Know what? Please tell me. I cannot bear to have you angry with me."

"Many, many temples have been destroyed. Mosques are being built everywhere. Our young women are being forced to marry and convert. The Sheikh has broken all the agreements. I hate him and his whole family. I want to go to war but father will not let us because of you. You are the enemy now, Gita. You are preventing us from defending ourselves! They are seeking to destroy us, not by killing us but by killing our culture and way of life. It is intolerable." He clenched his fists.

I gasped at his words. Was it true what I was hearing? While I was busying myself in the gardens, passing the days in small trifles, my husband's family was conducting a silent war against my people. I couldn't speak. He saw my consternation.

"Go yourself and see how many temples have been destroyed."

Then I remembered the sacred Vishnu Temple that I had stopped at on the way home. "The ancient Vishnu Temple, I stopped on my way here. I wanted to offer prayers but it was gone. They have destroyed it, haven't they, that beautiful precious Temple?"

"That was the first to go. How much agony it caused Father. He sent a letter of protest but he was told it was old and in need of repair. Then we received a letter saying it was too broken down to repair and needed to be replaced, replaced by a mosque!" My brother could hardly control himself. He stood up and walked to the other side of the room. "I prepared our armies but Father stopped me because he said we must abide by our word, by the agreements, even though they have broken everyone. Why does our word matter when they are bent on destroying us? I know he doesn't want to cause trouble for you. Do you know what it means to destroy that Temple, Gita? It has protected our people for centuries. Our protection is now gone. Slowly our lifeline is being destroyed."

"Has Father not been able to speak reason to the Sheikh, make him honor the agreement?"

"We don't think it is really the Sheikh's doing. He seems helpless. It is his ministers who are in control. They are very clever at finding an excuse for tearing down each temple, saying it is in the way of a new road or a new settlement, or some such thing. There is always some reason to tear them down. But I will die, Gita, before I let them destroy us."

"There must be something I can do," I said in a quiet voice, speaking more to myself than to him. "I cannot just sit by and let this happen. Why didn't someone come and tell me?"

"Father would not let us speak of this to you. Even now, he has forbidden me to tell you, especially in your condition. That is why I have ignored you this whole time. But I cannot pretend that all is well, Gita."

We heard someone coming. It was Father looking for me. "So here I find you, at Gopal's feet," he exclaimed, looking somewhat suspiciously at us.

Neither my brother nor I replied. He saw my eyes still swollen from the tears. He looked at me and then at my brother.

"Am I interrupting something?" he asked in an anxious tone. Again, neither of us responded. "Are you upsetting your sister in her sensitive condition?" he addressed my brother in a stern voice.

"No, it was me inquiring," I said quietly. "On the way home I stopped by the ancient Vishnu Temple to ask a blessing for my child, the Temple we loved so much, but it was no longer there . . . and now I have found out . . ." My voice trailed off and the tears began to flow again.

"There is nothing you can do, my daughter. You are with child, and you must not upset yourself. We have kept our part of the agreement. We can go to war or we can try to live peacefully and make the best of it. I choose the latter. Your brother does not agree with me. But come; let's not speak of this anymore. Let me enjoy my last days with you."

"I will not return," I cried. "I will not go back to that place."

"You must, Gita. There is no choice in this matter. You are married now and with child. Didn't you tell me when you arrived how happy you were there? Don't let your brother's words upset you. We must accept our defeat."

"Why? Why must we accept it?" asked my brother angrily.

My father sighed as if he no longer had the strength for this argument. "I have told you many times," he said looking dejectedly at my brother. "I will not go back on the word that I have given. I will keep our part of the agreement. To break my word is not in keeping with my responsibilities. This is what our sages have taught. I have given my precious daughter. Everything else pales in comparison to that. We can worship our gods with or without temples. They will always reside in our heart. They cannot destroy our Spirit or our faith."

At those words my brother rose and with an angry gesture walked out of the temple. I could not bear to see him like that, yet I was torn between the positions of my father and my brother, to say nothing of my responsibilities to the father of my child.

I looked with great sadness at my father. "How can I return," I asked, "when our family and our people are treated thus? How can I act as if nothing has happened?"

"I no longer know how to guide you, my Gita. At the time of your marriage, I felt a great responsibility to prevent war, but perhaps I was not right. I no longer know. It is too late now to change course. We no longer have the means to battle. Your brother is overly eager, without realizing the harm that would be done if we were to go into battle and lose. So we must make the best of the situation, as you must."

This was the first time my father was speaking to me not as a child, but as an adult, not seeking to hide from me the reality of the situation, but almost seeking my support for his decision. To see him in his weakest moment, the one who had always appeared to me to be invincible, was almost more than I could bear. It broke my heart to see his dejected state, his struggle to uphold his word and his questioning of the choices he had made. I had only seen my father, the raja, in his glory as a strong leader, always abiding by what he thought was right, never one to submit to injustice. But seeing his weakened state awakened something in me, a strength and conviction that I didn't know I had.

I could not enjoy the rest of my visit. I spent much of the remaining days sitting in front of the idol of Sri Krishna, begging Him to help me find a way to undo the damage that had been done. I hadn't realized how much I missed His presence. I found myself looking up into his joyous eyes, once again addressing Him as if He was the dearest of friends, as indeed He was.

Before leaving, my father took me aside and asked me to put out of my mind the conversation with my brother. "There is nothing you can do, my daughter. You are soon to have a child and you must keep your mind on that."

But this was impossible for me. Being home had made me realize how much I missed my deities. In addition to seeing the pain inflicted on my family, the very thought of idols being destroyed struck a deep wound in my heart. How was I to accept this?

On the journey home, my sadness slowly turned to anger, to a fiery resistance to what was taking place. I pulled aside the curtains of the palanquin so that I could see the towns and villages on the road back to the palace. The whole region was being transformed. Yes, the new buildings being erected were beautiful, but the world I loved so much was being destroyed bit by bit.

Chapter 14

B y the time I reached the palace, I could not contain my anger. I went straight to my quarters and into bed. Word spread that I was unwell, and my husband rushed to my side. I told him what I had heard and seen, with great anger in my voice.

"But Gita, you do not understand. We have brought in the best artisans and craftsman from far away to make improvements, to rebuild the towns and to make everything new. Your father's kingdom was in decline. We will bring new life to it. You will see what beautiful buildings we will create. We will transform the region. It is better for everyone."

"But the Vishnu Temple . . ."

"It was old and falling down. It had to be replaced. I am sorry about that."

"We don't want our towns to be transformed," I replied bitterly. "For centuries, and more, we have worshipped in our temples. They are very dear to us. By destroying them, you are tearing out our heart. Is that what you and your father want—to tear out my heart? I saw what this is doing to my father. Your people are slowly killing him. I think that death on the battlefield would have been better."

He was silent. Then he added, "I don't know what to say. I have no control over these matters. If it were up to me, I would leave your temples."

I don't know what came over me, how I found the strength to utter these words, but then I said, "Your father has broken the agreement. I am with child, with his heir. I will take no food or water until he rectifies this and signs a decree declaring that no more temples will be destroyed, no more forced conversions. If he doesn't abide by the agreements, than what honor does he have? None. I cannot allow my child to grow up in such a setting, where there is no honor, no respect for one's word. This goes against everything I have been taught." What I didn't tell him was that the very thought of idols being destroyed was like an arrow piercing my heart, that I couldn't bear to see this insult to the deity that I so loved, an injury that was all the greater because we were left with no defense. At least on the battlefield one would die, if one had to, defending one's beliefs and one's God. There was honor in that.

"You are with child, my Gita," he said joyously, ignoring the rest of my words. "Why didn't you tell me earlier? How wonderful!" He reached to hug me but I drew back.

"I mean every word of what I just said," I replied firmly, pushing him away.

"But you can't be serious. You don't know what you are saying. You can't make this demand of the Sheikh, and you can't go without food, for the child's sake!"

"I can and I will. And if he does not agree, your child and I will perish."

"You would do this, Gita Noor?"

"He leaves me no choice. I cannot bear to see the pain it has caused my father and brother. What your father has done is wrong. It is you who do not understand. What your father is doing will kill my father. I cannot let that be. Would you not do the same if it were your people who were being destroyed? This is worse than war, for it is killing our spirit." I began to cry as I spoke of the harm being inflicted on my father. He didn't know what to make of it and, without consoling me, he withdrew from my room. It was my first disappointment in him, my awakening to the fact that our spirits were not one, that he didn't fully accept who I was. This added to my burden.

A physician came to see me the next day to persuade me to eat and drink, telling me I would hurt the child if I did not take nourishment. My heart ached at the thought of harming the little one growing inside of me, but I had no choice. I knew the only power I had was through the child in my womb. My husband was beside himself. After several days of pleading with me and with his father, he decided to join me in the fast. At a certain moment, he looked at me, growing faint and rising only with difficulty from my bed. He must have seen the conviction in my eyes, and he seemed to understand. I had not expected to have him choose me over his father; it was the last thing I thought possible. And so more pressure was placed on the household.

After several more days, I was quite unwell. It was a tremendous struggle for me. I could hardly get out of bed. Finally his father relented. He came to see us and in front of us signed the decree, declaring from that day forward no temples would be destroyed without the consent of the Hindu raja, my father.

I wondered what had given me the strength to take such a stand. It was not in keeping with my character, which was of a gentler more acquiescing nature. Under normal circumstances, I found it very difficult to be contrary, but these were not normal circumstances. After the visit home I had begun to feel that my love for Sri Krishna itself was being challenged, and it was He giving me the strength. It was not only for my father or brother that I persisted, but also for my Lord. I realized through this experience how deep was that love.

I had been praying to Sri Krishna throughout my ordeal, imploring him to nourish the child. As I gained strength and the weeks passed, I worried that my action might have had some ill effect on the growing baby. Soon the baby became a more visible presence in my womb, my love for the child increased, and my prayers intensified. "Please, Lord Krishna, let the child be healthy and not suffer from my lack of food," I pleaded. After many weeks of such pleading, a response came.

"Gita, a holy man has been here to see you," cried Mohini with excitement, rushing into my chamber one day. Mohini had a way of finding out all the news of the palace.

"Where is he?" I asked, startled but pleased.

"He has been sent away."

"Sent away? I must see him." I went to the palace guard and demanded they go find the holy man who had been turned away. Three days later, Mohini beckoned me. "They have found him," she said. "He is waiting." She took me to him. Guards surrounded him. I greeted him warmly and offered him food and drink, but he politely declined.

"I have come only to give you a message, but I would like to speak with you alone," he said in a quiet voice. I motioned for the guards to leave. Mohini also began to go, but he stopped her. "You may stay to witness what I have to say."

As soon as the guards left, I started to bend down to touch his feet in a mark of respect but he stopped me. "Nay, Rani, not in your condition." I was quite far along in the pregnancy, but the desire to show respect to

him was strong. I obeyed and did not bow down. Instead I gazed at him.
I didn't recall ever seeing him before. He was not among the many holy
men who had visited my father over the years, although there may have
been many who came that I never saw. He motioned for me to sit down
and he seated himself beside me.

He was of middle stature and in the early years of old age. His hair
and beard were a mix of black and grey, with most of his hair being tied
in a knot on top of his head, as was the custom for wandering sadhus. He
was dressed simply in an orange cloth or *dhoti*. His kind but piercing eyes
were his most notable feature.

"You have been concerned about the child that will soon be born to
you. I have come to tell you that your child will be fine. Your fast has done
the child no harm." I was relieved to hear his words, but wondered how
he knew about my ordeal. He paused for a few minutes and then said,
"You have felt the pain caused by the destruction of the temples. The
effects of this violence will reach far into the future and cause suffering
for many, on both sides." He was quiet for a few minutes and then
continued. "But you must also know that we are not blameless in this
matter." I looked at him inquiringly. "We have sacrificed truth for ritual."
He repeated these words, looking at me intensely but also looking right
through me. He paused as if wanting me to digest these words and then
said, "The true temple, the only one that matters to the Lord, is in the
heart. Do you understand?"

I shook my head, indicating that I didn't understand. What did he
mean about sacrificing truth for ritual? Wasn't truth found in the Vedic
rituals? That is what I had been taught. If you performed all the rituals,
the gods would bless you.

"You will understand in time." We were quiet for a few minutes. I
again asked the sadhu if he would take food, but he again declined. After
a few minutes, he continued. "You will give birth to a son. He will have a
kind heart, and he will love his mother, but he will be taken from you to
be raised in the Koranic teachings."

I frowned at his words and placed my hands protectively on my
stomach. "My son taken from me?"

"You will have no choice, but you can make a condition."

"What condition?" I asked.

"Ask that the idol of Sri Krishna that you so love be brought to the palace in exchange for the gift of your son. When you turn your mind to Sri Krishna, the pain of separation will ease."

"An idol in the palace? You know that can never be. The Sheikh's ministers would never permit it."

"You have the strength and the will within you to insist." A slight chuckle crossed his lips, and then he peered at me with his piercing gaze. "It will be done. He will consent."

"But, if by some miracle I do manage to bring the idol here, it will have to be done in secret. I would need to have a Brahmin priest to perform the daily rituals. How would I manage this?" I mused half to myself and half out loud. The idea of bringing Sri Krishna to the palace pleased me greatly.

He smiled, "Nay, Rani. You do not need a priest. Have I not already told you that we have sacrificed truth for ritual, and that is why we are now suffering? You can perform the needed prayers."

"But this is against the Vedic injunctions!" I exclaimed, shocked that a holy man would advise me to go against the prescribed laws. "I cannot do this. I am a woman and a Kshatriya. How can I perform the required prayers and ceremonies? How can I care for an idol? Surely this would bring some ill effect?"

"Did Sri Krishna need a priest to feed him or did he take from Radha's hand?" He smiled and again said, very slowly enunciating each word, "We have sacrificed truth for ritual." He let these words sink in. This was the third time he said that phrase and I took note. Then he added, "Your fast showed your inner resolve, and your love for the Vedic way of life. You must devote yourself to Sri Krishna as you did when you were a child, before you came here. I ask this not only for your own benefit, but also for the protection of our people and the preservation of our way of life. You do not realize what the effects will be of your prayers here in the middle of this Islamic fortress. Do not get distracted by the pleasures of the palace. Through your son you will have great power." Then he said in a booming voice that seemed to echo from above and beyond, from all of space. I heard it descend like a thunder and it rang in my head for years after. "Use the position that has been given to you, Rani, to uphold Dharma!" My whole body shook at his words. He rose to leave but I couldn't move. I couldn't rise from my seat to offer him the respect that was due. All I could do was stare at his face, which had turned from a gentle mien to a stern one and now was gentle once more.

"How do I do this?" I asked urgently in barely more than a whisper, fearful of the great responsibility he seemed to be placing upon me.

"You will know," he said simply in a gentler tone.

As he left I heard his parting words, "Keep watch, Rani, on what goes on within these palace walls, and beyond. Keep watch." He raised his hand in blessing and then was gone.

I sat motionless for a few minutes and then was overcome with an urge to see him again, and so I made my way to the palace tower, climbing the steps with great difficulty, clinging to Mohini's arm. After reaching the top, I stood and watched him as he faded in the distance, wending his way along the dirt roads into the forest. My husband found me there, my eyes still fixed on the departing sadhu.

"You should not be up here," he said, putting his arm around me as Mohini slipped away. "I heard that a man was here to see you. What did he want?"

I barely heard his question and didn't answer, still watching for the disappearing trace of the sadhu. Then he asked again and I said in a voice barely above a whisper, "He said we will have a son, and that the child will be fine, and kind-hearted."

As I came nearer to the birth date, I trembled at the thought of what lay ahead. I did not want to challenge the Sheikh again. One encounter had been enough. But I knew I had no choice. Soon after my son was born, my husband came to say that the child had to be raised in the Koranic way, as he would be the heir. I protested, but as the sadhu had predicted there was no choice. So I made my condition. I would return home with the child unless my idol was brought to the palace.

"The Sheikh will never let you or our son leave the palace," he protested.

"Then there will be war," I threatened. "If I attempt to leave but am prevented, my brother will surely come to take me," I insisted.

There was much protest and back and forth negotiations, but in the end Sri Krishna was secretly carried into my private quarters. The very idol that I so loved was now kept locked behind a closet door. He was here with me in the palace.

At first I sat before the murti with the ladies who attended me, trying to remember all the stories and songs I had heard as a child. As the stories returned to me, I began to experience the joy I had known then. I spent more and more time in the quiet of my chamber, and Lord Krishna again became a living presence for me.

My brother came to see me one day after the idol had been installed.

"You will need a Brahmin priest, Gita, to perform the rituals and ceremonies. I will make the arrangements."

I shook my head. "That will cause a disturbance here," I replied. "Not many here know about the idol and it is better to keep it that way." I had not told anyone about the visit from the sadhu. For some reason, I felt to keep the visit with him buried in my heart.

"But how will you care for it?" he asked in surprise. The shadow of a frown crossed his face. My brother was not a religious man, but he kept to the letter of the law and did what was required of him. According to tradition, Brahmin priests were needed to perform the proper ceremonies to maintain the idols.

"I think my love with reach him with or without rituals. Did the Gopis need ceremonies to please him?" My brother didn't answer. "Do you remember how I loved this idol?" I asked.

He smiled, nodding. "You would speak to him as if he were alive. I never quite understood your devotion. But I fear, Gita, that some ill will befall us if you fail to provide the proper care for this deity."

I smiled. "Do you think there is anyone who could care for him better than I can? He was alive to me and will again be," I replied. "My life will be complete here now that Sri Krishna has arrived." I spoke with determination and my brother, still not convinced, had to acquiesce.

"Well, we won't tell the priests about this arrangement."

"Shhh," I said. "Nobody must know about the idol."

At first I didn't see any need to perform rituals or ceremonies. It was enough just to sit in front of Sri Krishna and sing my love for him. But over time I felt the need to do more, so I would invite scholars and pundits to the palace to teach me. There were times when I longed to hear the Vedic mantras and see the rituals performed, but whenever this desire entered my thoughts, I would hear the sadhu's words, "We have sacrificed truth for ritual." Then I would hear him say, "Build a temple in your heart. That is where the Lord dwells."

One day when my eldest was about six years old, he came to visit me while I was at my prayers. I got up to greet him. After hugs and sweet exchanges, he asked, "Why do you pray to a statue?" It hurt me deeply to realize that my world was foreign to my son. I replied, "I am praying to Sri Krishna, not to a piece of stone. The idol is just a reminder of the Lord. Sri Krishna is no different than Allah. They are one and the same." He thought for a while and then asked, "But Allah has no face and no body. How can they be the same?" I started to explain, but his mind was already elsewhere and he pulled me away to play. After this, I began to worry how I would instill in my children the love of Dharma. How would I protect Dharma as the sadhu had proclaimed? It was a questioned that haunted me.

I had six children in all, three sons and three daughters. My sons were raised in the Koranic teachings, but my daughters were left with me and they learned to love Lord Krishna. They acted out scenes from his boyhood and sang the songs of the cow maids who were his playmates. I became more and more engrossed in my devotions. My husband had taken another wife, a princess from one of the Muslim lines, and then a third wife, much younger. He hardly visited me, but I didn't mind because it left me free to spend my time with the Lord. There were few people in the palace that I could trust or grow close to. I was ever watchful that nobody would know of my devotions and religious practices. A sense of loneliness and isolation grew over the years, especially after my husband took the second wife. I compensated for this by engrossing myself more and more in the care of my Lord Krishna, feeding the idol, dressing him, speaking to him, seeing in him my dearest friend.

Over the years my husband rarely commented on my devotional life, but as he and the children grew older, after he had taken two other wives, he began to make hurtful remarks. One day he found me locked in my closet as I was performing my devotions. He knocked, but when I didn't answer he called out to me in an annoyed tone. I opened the door and emerged from my secret hideaway.

"Gita Noor, you are spending more time in there, and people are beginning to talk. Perhaps it is time for you to forsake this idol, or at least spend less time locked away. Increasingly you are absent from the palace functions and it looks like something is amiss."

"What are you saying?" I asked in alarm. He knew what Sri Krishna meant to me.

"It was fine when you were young and had just come from your father's palace. But you have been here a long time. When will you adopt our ways?"

At that moment I knew it was his other wives who were instilling these thoughts in him. From the moment they had entered the palace, they had no liking for me, although as much as possible I tried to keep out of their way. I looked at my husband with hurtful eyes.

"I don't understand how you can sit before that stone stature and think it is God," he continued. A deep pain entered me as he spoke these words. It was bad enough that I was so isolated and alone, but for him to deride me was too much. I had never heard such harsh words from my husband.

At first I thought to explain once more that I was not worshipping a stone statue, but the Lord himself, but I stopped myself. If he didn't understand after all these years, there was no use in explaining once again. Besides, what did it matter?

"You seem to forget your promise of long ago, after I gave birth—the promise that you would not interfere with my devotions."

"That was long ago and I have not interfered all these years."

"A promise is a promise," I replied coolly. "It cannot be withdrawn."

"Gita, all I ask is that you spend less time locked away."

Something came over me that I didn't expect. I nodded as if in agreement. From that moment on I began to hide the extent of my devotions even from my husband. I would find other excuses to stay away from palace functions, as they were unbearable for me. I fought my desire to retreat and live in my own world, but I was not happy in doing so.

Chapter 15

O ne day a Muslim scholar appeared at the palace, requesting to speak with the Hindu Rani. He expressed a great interest in learning the deeper truths of the Vedic religion and approached me with a proposal to hold a scholarly discussion on various religious topics.

"Why do you approach me?" I asked. "Surely my husband's ministers would be better able to organize such a lofty event." I was pleased at the idea of a religious exchange. Such an event had not taken place before, at least in our kingdom.

"You will have far better access to the true knowers of the Veda," he replied respectfully. I looked at the man before me. He had such a humble appearance, yet had a great reputation as a man of knowledge and wisdom. "This exchange is vital," he added quietly. "Please assist me."

"You seem to be one of the few here to believe so," I responded in a surprised tone. We were both quiet for a few minutes. "I will speak to my husband about this matter. I am sure he will see the value in this, and I will do my best to convince him."

The scholar hesitated before speaking. "I am telling you in confidence that his ministers will choose the least able among the Vedic scholars. It is essential for you to select them. The ministers will try to turn this into a debate; it is not a debate I am seeking, but rather a deep exchange of knowledge. Do you understand?"

I nodded. Indeed I did understand what he was saying through veiled language. This would turn into another attempt on the part of the palace to undermine the Hindu community, without my husband even realizing it. I gazed at him curiously and responded, "I am extremely grateful that you have come to me," I replied. "Our conversation has only increased my respect for you." He bowed and departed, leaving me to wonder how I was to achieve what he had requested.

My husband agreed but informed me that the exchange would have to be positioned as a debate. That was the only way the ministers would permit it. When I requested to find the Vedic scholars, he hesitantly agreed but made one condition: if the Muslim scholars were to win the debate, I would give up the idol.

"And if they lose?" I asked.

"Then let us publicly declare that you have had an idol of your Lord in the palace all these years. No more praying in secret."

I reluctantly agreed. I could not at all be sure that our scholars would win the debate, and I knew that I couldn't live without Sri Krishna. In my mind it was life or death for me.

I had several weeks to prepare for the event, but how on earth was I to find the great minds of our tradition? My father was very ill and so could not be of much help, and my brother knew little of religious matters. I searched the kingdom, seeking out every holy man and scholar I could find. There were many who were quite competent, but I was not satisfied. The day for the debate arrived and I was beside myself with anxiety. One by one the scholars that I had invited entered the hall. Just as they were being seated, along with the Koranic scholars, I was told that another one of my guests had arrived. I asked that he be ushered in, wondering whom it might be. Everyone I had invited was already seated. When I saw him, all care and anxiety fled. It was he, the sadhu who had come to me years earlier during my first pregnancy. I rushed to greet him, my eyes brimming with tears of gratitude.

"The Lord thought you might need some assistance," he said simply.

Needless to say it was the sadhu who countered every argument posed by the Koranic scholars. Again and again he exclaimed that it is human arrogance to limit the limitless Lord to either form or the formless. The unfathomable One, who is beyond human concept, is both. If he is in every bit of creation, then he can be worshipped in everything—a stone, a leaf, a handful of water. Where was he not?

At the height of the debate, I saw that suddenly the whole exchange had turned into a deep conversation between the sadhu and the Muslim scholar who had approached me. The rest of the participants became silent as few could follow the intricacies of their discussion. When the allotted time was over, everyone had to agree that there was no winner or loser. As the participants were leaving the hall, the Muslim scholar who had befriended me came over to thank me for organizing the event.

"I was much impressed by the sadhu you brought. I would like further exchange with him. Let us go greet him."

Happily I agreed, but as we searched the hall and surrounding rooms, we could not find him anywhere. I sent the palace guards to search the area, but he had disappeared.

I was able to keep my murti, but the secrecy was to be maintained. This was to be the first of numerous religious discussions that the palace organized. My husband had to concede that such exchanges would help to create better relations between the religious communities, and ironically both the Hindu and Muslim scholars looked to me to help organize the discussions. It was this effort that brought me out of my seclusion. Finally I had found a place in the palace, a position that I believed to be useful.

My husband's attitude softened after that. He was of a more intellectual nature and respected the arguments put forth by the Vedic scholars, as well as the sadhu. But he was ever careful not to show too much sympathy for my people or me. He had enemies within the palace and there were continual efforts to discredit him. I understood this and never blamed him for keeping his distance from me. It had long ago become clear to me that, despite our youthful love for each other, we had different obligations and duties, and in some ways I had become a liability for him. His duty was to advance Muslim rule and mine was to protect Vedic culture to the degree that I could. I had to be ever watchful and work to keep negative forces at bay. When they would grow too strong I would find the arguments to appeal to my husband. He learned to walk two paths, to keep his ministers satisfied and to appease me.

One evening, after tending to my Lord Krishna for most of the afternoon and evening, my husband approached me as I was preparing to recline for the night. It had been a long time since he had come to me in that way, and my desire for him had long ago dimmed. But for some reason that night he was filled with passion for me. There was nothing I could say or do to dissuade him. I looked at him with tenderness. My passion for him had long ago been transformed into a longing for the Lord, but I still had much affection. As I wavered, I glanced at Sri Krishna, wondering what to do, and then in the dim shadows of the night, I saw a blue light emerge from the murti and take the form of Lord Krishna. I watched in amazement as he entered the body of my husband. It was

Krishna, Krishna himself, who had come to me. I was beside myself with joy and I gave myself fully to him. After that night, every time I saw my husband, it was Krishna's form I saw. Every time I heard his voice, I heard behind Krishna's flute calling me. The Lord had made me his own.

For my father's kingdom these were difficult times, despite the many promises that were made by those who had come uninvited to our land. The destruction of temples had temporarily halted, but the building of mosques continued. Women were still forced into marriage and conversions multiplied. Hindu culture was threatened, but there were also pockets of flowering and a continual flow of sages. The Islamic culture provided an infusion of beauty in many ways. Gardens sprouted up as well as elegant buildings. The integration of cultures brought benefit, but the execution of this new mixing also brought much pain and destruction. It was a pain that was to remain for many centuries, tucked into the hearts of many. The Muslim rulers, with few exceptions, failed to see the beauty and depth of Hindu civilization. After all, they had come for our wealth, not for our knowledge. My husband tried to walk the middle path, but even during his rule there were powerful ministers in the court who were bent on the destruction or at least the weakening of the Hindu way of life.

Eventually rumors spread that the Rani had a secret murti of Sri Krishna in the palace, which created much controversy. As the sadhu had urged me, I kept watch on what was taking place within the palace walls, and to the extent that I could, what was happening in the outer world, but this was more difficult as I rarely ventured out. I heard reports and I spoke my peace. The ascendency of Muslim rule and the loss of Hindu culture weighed heavily on me. No matter how hard I tried to protect our way of life, it seemed I had hardly any impact at all. On occasion I would remember the words of the sadhu, when he said that I didn't realize the impact of my devotions in the midst of this Islamic fortress. What did he mean? What could I, one simple devotee, accomplish?

I tried at times to find the sadhu so I could ask him about the meaning of his words, to no avail. His whereabouts remained a mystery. I gradually came to understand that as long as our deities remained alive for us, our culture would survive. We would not succumb to destruction, although we would pass through difficult times. There would be an ascendency at some time in the future. This is what the sadhu must have meant: keep up the devotions so that Sri Krishna would be more real than anything else. This would ensure our survival.

We are taught that the Lord cannot help but respond to his devotees. This is a universal law that he himself has set in place. In fact, the only thing that brings a response is our intense longing. If the desire for him is there, we are under his protection, come what may. Perhaps our struggles would in the end strengthen our devotion. Perhaps this was why the sadhu had impressed upon me the need to remain steady, ever focused on the Lord. It was not only for my own spiritual well-being, but also for the well-being of my people. Without understanding his meaning, I had done the best I could to abide by this commandment, and yet all that I had done seemed so inadequate. It pained me that I had to pray in secret, that I could not share my love for my Lord with the world. This was a difficulty I had to endure, and I often thought that if I had more courage, if I had been stronger, perhaps it would not have had to be so.

Thus the years passed. One day I learned that there was a holy sage waiting to see me. I thought nothing of it, since many such men passed through our kingdom and came to greet the Rani. But when I entered the room and saw the sadhu who had come to me so many years ago during my pregnancy and then again during the scholarly debate, a strange tremor came over me, a premonition of the message to come. This time, I bowed at his feet. He was very aged now, bent over, with wisps of white hair tied in a knot above his head. I was no longer a young woman. I started to express my deep gratitude, but he only smiled. I credited him with turning the direction of my life, and guiding me into a deeper understanding of the role I could play in the kingdom. I had not seen him since he had mysteriously appeared for the debate. I had long wanted to thank him for ensuring that my murti would stay, but it seemed that words were not necessary. He had come and gone at that time with hardly a word to me. Although he had made such a deep impression on me, our verbal exchanges had been very limited.

After we were seated, I offered him food and drink, and this time he accepted. After eating, he said approvingly, "You have made your heart a temple, and a fine temple it is. Sri Krishna abides there."

I smiled and replied, "My life has had no other meaning or purpose but to worship Him. For many years I wondered whether my service was adequate, with no priest to care for my idol." I stopped and laughed. "Had you not given me the authority that day, I would have been beset with guilt and fear that I, a woman . . ." The smile left my face and I did not finish the sentence. I had not fully eradicated my qualms about this matter.

He responded in a reassuring voice, "Are not the wives of the rishis as highly regarded as the rishis themselves? What would Krishna be without Radha, Narayan without Lakshmi, Shiva without Parvati, Brahma without Saraswati? That is the divine play. There are no spiritual limitations for women. The laws are prescribed for the maintenance of society, but those who know are able to supersede these laws. The performance of rituals and ceremonies are necessary for society but not required for those who are naturally filled with the love of God. For them rituals are superfluous, unless they choose to abide by them for an outer purpose."

Now I understood something of his words. I began to realize that love was supreme. "Sadly, I could not prevent the destruction of temples, but I tried to be a bridge, to build understanding between our people and the followers of Islam."

He nodded again, then said, "You do not know the power of your prayers and actions. Bringing Sri Krishna into the heart of this palace was a deed of great courage and significance."

"I did only what you instructed me to do," I smiled. 'But I could not spare our people." I turned thoughtful. "I have often looked back and thought I should have pressured my husband more, but despite all that we have lost, love for the Lord still runs deep among our people. Sri Krishna is yet alive for us."

"As he will be for many centuries to come," replied the sadhu with a smile. He continued, "It is hard to understand the ways of the world. What we set in motion through the law of cause and effect must run its course. There was a cause for theses invasions, and there will be an outcome, a reaction, and so the cycle continues. The timing and nature of the reaction is yet to be determined, but be sure of this, no action goes unnoticed by the great universal law of justice. We are all accountable for our actions, individually and collectively. In due time we will regain what we have lost. Eternal truths cannot die. Even when time ceases, they remain. We need not worry. Despite what appears to be, the wisdom of the rishis will continue to vibrate throughout the universe. What they have given to humanity, no man or nation can undo."

"And the suffering of our people?"

"All life is suffering until we awaken to the true reality," he said quietly. "Is there not suffering within this palace? The conquered and the conquerors alike suffer. This is the nature of life. No one is spared." He looked off into the distance, as if peering into the future. "You must think beyond one lifetime." He was silent for a few minutes and then said in a low voice. "Your work here is almost done. I have come to tell you this." I took in his words and understood their meaning. The tremor that I had felt when he entered the room returned, but then gave way to a feeling of peace.

"I pray that in my future lives, I may continue to worship and serve my Lord Krishna," I said quietly.

"Your journey now takes you in a different direction. Free yourself from the attachment to the luxuries you have known here. You cannot carry them with you. Your desire to bridge the two cultures has planted seeds, but such efforts will take a long time and will only yield fruit in the future. In your next life, you will be born into a Muslim family, and your husband will be born among the Hindus." He must have seen the surprise on my face, because he smiled and said, "You have loved the Lord in form. Now you must learn to love the formless. It is the same God you will serve." He may have sensed my resistance because he added, "Have no worries. You are in the hands of the Lord. All are equally his children, Hindu and Muslim alike." He grew quiet and then added, "Half of your descendants will be Hindu, and half will be Muslim." I looked at him questioning, wondering how this would be. But the answer came immediately to my mind: my daughters would carry the Hindu lineage. He nodded, reading my thoughts, "Yes, your daughters, who you have taught well, will carry on what you have so lovingly preserved."

We sat in silence for quite a while. I closed my eyes and took in his words. The thought of my death did not disturb me. When I opened my eyes, he was gazing at me with great care. "I must go now," he said. I nodded. But still we sat a while longer. Then he bestowed on me a parting blessing. The rays streaming from his eyes seemed to penetrate my very being. His last words echoed in my soul, "You have upheld Dharma and will be blessed for this."

I could not follow him. I could not move. I felt the power of his words and stood there for a long time before retreating to my quarters.

The months passed. A marriage was arranged for my elder son, but I was not involved in the affair. All decisions were made without me. When it was done, my son came for my approval and I nodded my blessing. A year passed, and the marriage for my second son was arranged. Again, I allowed my husband full control. Increasingly, it was the fate of my daughters that occupied my mind.

One morning I arose at the first rays of sun and quietly set out to see my brother. My father had passed some years earlier and my brother now ruled. He greeted me warmly. No longer did he regard me as the enemy, despite the difficulties that still arose. After exchanging family news, I informed him of the reason for my visit. I knew that I didn't have much more time and I wanted to secure my daughters' marriages with Hindu princes. He hesitated. He was not on the best terms with my husband.

"How can I give you my word, Gita? Their marriages are not in my control," he said.

"I will make Ali promise," I replied. "It is most important to me. I cannot have peace until I know you have agreed to arrange their marriages." Still he hesitated. I knew it was a most unusual request.

"Surely, he will want to make alliances that suit his needs," he said with an echo of bitterness.

"I have given my sons for this. But my daughters are of our line. I have brought them up with the love of Sri Krishna in their heart. I will not have done to them what was done to me," I said firmly. "I will not see them sacrificed."

He seemed surprised by my conviction and my words had their desired effect. "If Ali agrees, I will take this responsibility. I give you my word."

It was a huge relief, as if a great weight had been lifted from me. Like my father before him, my brother was a man of his word. He did not give it lightly. My daughters had assumed a place of great importance to me. It was as if all I had strived for would find its fulfillment through them. When I returned home some weeks later, I called my daughters to me and felt inspired to speak to them of Lord Krishna. They laughed, for they knew all the stories. They were steady in their devotion.

"Remember," I said to them, "always keep Sri Krishna in your heart. Pray to him day and night and he will protect you and ever guide you." They nodded in agreement, surprised by the serious tone of my voice. This brought me great ease. When they left my quarters I sat for a long time at the feet of the murti of Sri Krishna. How I yearned to see the Lord come alive for me as he had some years ago when he entered the form of my husband!

"Sri Krishna, Sri Krishna, may I never forget you," I whispered, "no matter where I go. Let me rest eternally at your feet." My yearning increased. I felt a warm current rising through my body as if all my yearning was now expressing itself in a tremendous heat, the heat of desire for my Lord. I was ready to leave this world behind and know only him, only him.

In my fervor I must have lost consciousness, because the next thing I knew I was lying in bed with my husband seated by my side. My fever was such that I could hardly speak.

"You have taken ill," he said. "Just rest. You must rest and recover for the wedding is just days away."

I nodded, remembering it was soon to be the marriage day for my second son. "Promise me something," I whispered faintly.

"Shh, just rest."

"Promise me, our daughters . . ."

"Rest."

"Promise me, you will let my brother arrange their marriages. I want them to marry Hindu princes."

He squeezed my hand. "You must get better now and then you will decide who they will marry. They have been in your care."

"Give me your word and I will rest easy."

"You have my word, my dear, now rest and get well for our son's wedding."

My husband sat a while by my bedside. I could see the worried look on his face. He seemed agitated. After some time, he slipped away. I didn't fault him for anything that had happened over the years. He did the best he could for me. I smiled to think he would be reborn a Hindu. Perhaps then he could experience something of what I felt. And I, where would I go? I couldn't worry about that. As long as the Lord was with me, I would be fine. I called one of my attendants and asked to have a note sent to my brother indicating Ali's agreement with our arrangement. This was the last thing I needed to do.

With a sense of having fulfilled all my duties, I drifted into a quiet sleep, only to be awakened a few hours later by the presence of my elder daughter, sitting silently by my bed. Of all my children, she had been the closest to me because of her natural spiritual inclination. I loved her dearly, and she had been a bridge between her father and me; she knew how to speak with him to allow me the seclusion I needed. Through the dim light I could see tears slowly carving small streams along her checks. I wanted to comfort her, but the words wouldn't come. I wanted to tell her that all would be okay, but I couldn't speak. She saw my efforts.

"What is it, Ma?" she asked in a tearful voice.

Again I tried to speak but couldn't, and so with my eyes clinging to the door that hid my murti of Sri Krishna, I smiled the faintest smile. It was all I could do. She seemed to understand. Nodding her head, she whispered, "I won't forget, Ma. I won't forget all that you have taught me," and she started to sing quietly one of my favorite songs to Sri Krishna.

Her singing brought me a great sense of peace. I was happy now. Everything was taken care of. My daughters would be provided for. They would remember me in their devotions. Knowing this brought a warm feeling to my heart. I closed my eyes and turned my mind to the wedding a few days off. I didn't need to be there. There was pain for me in seeing my son married off to a woman with whom I would have little connection. It Ali's second wife who would be a mother to her, not me. I would have no role in this, no place in her heart. She would keep distance from me, the discarded Hindu mother of her husband, the mother who converted only outwardly to make an alliance. My sons were long gone. They knew all the Koranic texts, but not one prayer to Lord Krishna. But what did it matter? Their minds were more on ruling than on spiritual matters. It was my daughters, my daughters who had the spiritual inclination. When they married Hindu princes, would my sons cut them off? Already my family was divided. What would the future bring? I did not want to think of the future. It was enough now that I had done my best. The future would have to take care of itself.

I turned my mind to the sadhu. What did he mean that I must learn to love the formless? Wasn't my love for Sri Krishna enough? As I thought of the sadhu's parting blessing, his face appeared before me, smiling and beckoning me. The sight of him made me so happy. Where was he calling me? He was beckoning me somewhere. Then I saw a light. Ah, he was calling me there. I didn't know what lay ahead. All I knew was that I was ready and my heart was at peace, and so with a mind at rest I entered the light.

Chapter 16

An exchange between one of the Muslims and one of the Hindu participants in the Sufi-Yogi Dialogue pulled me back to the present. Suddenly I interrupted.

"I want to explain about the idols," I said insistently. I began by stating that they were entry points into the higher reality. We weren't worshipping the marble or wood figures. They were a way for us to connect to the one reality behind everything. I spoke passionately, as this was an issue that had followed me into my present life. Being born into a Jewish family, into a religion which eschewed any representation of the divine, I had had to keep secret the many pictures of my guru and of my lineage of Masters that lined the walls of my home. For years I had taken them down whenever my parents visited to avoid my mother's anger, and re-installed them as soon as they left. Now I realized the karmic source of this behavior. I had grown used to praying in secret many centuries ago, and it was a pattern that I easily picked up again as a young woman in this life. Rather than encounter my mother's disdain, I chose to hide my religious practices. It was not a course of action of which I was proud. I often chided myself for hiding my love of the many images, paintings, and statues of the divine manifestations I had in my home. It took me many years before I could overcome this old karmic pattern and bring my murtis out of the closet, so to speak.

After giving a passionate defense of the murtis, I fell silent, and then looked with surprise into the smiling faces of the Pakistani Sufis.

"We know this," one of them exclaimed. "This is not an issue for us."

"Another point that must be made," I continued, "is that the essence of the Vedas is the ultimate monotheism. There is only One. Everything—all the divine forms and all that is manifest—comes out of that One." I had to make this point. So much of interfaith dialogue was centered on what people call the "monotheistic" religions. This was a way of delegating the other religions to a lesser position, but it was a complete misunderstanding of the Vedic worldview.

"Yes, we know that as well," another of the Pakistanis responded. I sighed in relief.

It was the last day of our dialogue. I had been in and out of the past, seeing scenes and hearing conversations from five centuries ago, and then trying to be attentive to what was happening in the here and now. For the most part the dialogue had gone well. There was an unspoken but very real bond between the Pakistanis and Indians that only needed to be uncovered. They were of one culture. Many of the Pakistanis had only to trace a few generations back before finding their Hindu ancestors. They knew they had common roots. There was a political divide but not a spiritual one. I sat there wondering if any of them were my descendants.

Half of my descendants were Muslim and half Hindu, I thought. And how odd that here I sat bringing the Hindus and Muslims together in dialogue. Was my life as a Rani in north India the beginning of my interfaith interest and work? Were the seeds planted then, and did it take five centuries for those seeds to bear fruit? Was the work I was now doing through the Global Peace Initiative of Women an outcome of my efforts during that time? We think of action and reaction, the unfolding of karma, as immediate. But most often it does not work that way. Karmic law is extraordinarily complex and the logical mind can't organize it into a neat sequential package. Only the intuitive mind can see into its deep mysteries to understood the patterns that are uncovered. It is a most intricate weaving, a mosaic masterpiece, where each thought and action links to another. It is wondrous to realize that we are the makers of our own destiny. If only we could become more conscious of this fact.

Over the few days of the dialogue a tenderness had grown between one of the Pakistani men and me. He was the one about whom on the first day I had exclaimed, "He is Krishna." I soon realized that he felt a deep link to the Vedic tradition and coming to India had meant a great deal to him. It was his first trip there, and in a sense it was a coming home. Perhaps he had been my husband in that life, or perhaps there was something about him that awakened my memories. I could not say.

At first I was confused. What did my attraction mean? Was I to be with him again? One of the dangers in awakening memories is that it can lead you to mix up what was true in the past for what is appropriate right now. It has happened to me again and again— through my interactions with Jay, and then Clyde, and now this man. It is a special treat to meet loved ones from the past again, but we must have the discernment to know the proper relationship for the current life. It is not always easy when emotions are stirred, and we can never be sure that this person is not simply the means for awakening a memory. It has been one of my cardinal rules that I never impose my memories on another, so I have never shared my memories with those I believe I have identified from the past. Even with Jay. I accept that they may just be the factor that awakens me. The past of other people has remained hidden to me. It is best that way, as I believe that whatever has not been realized through one's own efforts should remain at rest.

A friendship formed between this Pakistani Sufi and me that was to last several years. We spoke by phone and exchanged emails for some time, but gradually the busyness of everyday life took over, whatever karma we had together had been fulfilled, and we drifted apart. The river of life keeps moving.

It was no surprise for me to learn of my past love for Lord Krishna. That love had never died, only retreated to a quiet corner of my subconscious mind until the time was ripe for it to re-emerge. It was this unremembered love that inspired Elisabeth and then Sonya to seek refuge in the Bhagavad Gita, although neither had recaptured the story of this relationship with Sri Krishna. It was not until this life that the recovery of that love was to flourish fully, so many centuries later.

The dialogue in Rishikesh was the first of what was to become a series of Sufi-Yogi Dialogues bringing together the Muslim and Hindu traditions. We met next in Nepal, and then in New Delhi, then in the state of Kashmir in India, and finally in Japan. Through these recurring meetings, the dialogue deepened and a profound connection grew among the participants.

After the awakening of the memories, I understood why I felt this particular Hindu-Muslim calling. It was an area all but ignored by most interreligious and peace organizations, which has been so focused on healing the conflicts within the Abrahamic family. The wounds suffered by Vedic culture as a result of the Islamic invasions, which have lasted centuries, were deep and even now are not fully healed. The invading forces dominated on so many levels: political, economic, artistic, religious, and most importantly, spiritual. It is quite a tribute to the

Rishis, the seers of old, that the Vedic wisdom not only survived but also is thriving today and finding its way into every corner of the world. The wounds are personal ones for me as I remember being helpless while all this came to pass. I have not been able to erase from my subconscious mind the memories of beloved temples being trampled on and divine forms desecrated.

Some months after this dialogue, Marianne and I were at a conference in San Francisco where I was speaking at one of the sessions, describing the work of GPIW. I mentioned the recent Sufi-Yogi Dialogue that we had organized in Rishikesh, and as I was discussing it, I suddenly blurted out with great feeling, "Even now, 500 years later, we have not recovered from the desecration caused by the Muslim invasions." After the session, Marianne took me aside and laughingly pointed out that I had said "we." My identification with that life was still strong and so for me it was a very real experience. But others in the audience may have found this more than a bit odd!

One must conquer the feelings that arise from past experiences. The way to do this is to understand that there is a greater purpose to all that unfolds, and that it is all the play of karma. A universal truth states that loss and gain and conquest and defeat should be regarded with an equal eye. The wheels of time vacillate between success and failure and each must have its turn. The wise know not to be troubled or elated by the vicissitudes of time.

There are periods in history when cultures are thrown together for new energies to emerge, and there are times when cultures are ripped apart for reasons that are less apparent—perhaps to find again their essence and to recover what has been lost in the interchange. Much human suffering has resulted from both the coming together and the pulling apart. What are we humans to learn from this?

The partition of India into two countries is an example of such a tearing apart. It was meant to heal the underlying tensions that resided in the communities after the years of invasions and domination, but it has not served this purpose. Instead, outside forces have intervened, pulling Pakistan away from its cultural roots, its unity with India, and forcing it into a new orbit of influence. In time the situation will stabilize as Pakistan finds its own course, separate from India but free from the hardening fundamentalist forces seeking to gain control. The true hope for the region is for Pakistan to find its identity in its Sufi heritage, the mystical path that has much in common with the yogic tradition. Then Pakistan and India will live in peace, supporting and reinforcing the spiritual foundations they share.

The human story thus far has been one of dominance: one group seeking power over another. That narrative has led us to a very dangerous point in our collective history. Can we as a human community choose a totally different path now and leave behind the old failed patterns of patriarchal dominance? I say failed because they have not led to happiness, even for those who exercised power. Eventually, humankind must awaken to embrace all cultures and traditions as equal paths to truth, but how will this shift occur? Perhaps the feminine wisdom, which is less about power and domination and more about integration and inclusivity, can lead now in a new direction. Perhaps the human community has advanced enough to put aside the worldview that separated people into different boxes and adopt a worldview, rooted in the divine feminine, that sees us all as one integrated whole. My work was guiding me toward these conclusions.

In the months after my return from India, I spent much time reflecting on the memories that had emerged. I had finally found my life in India and now understood my deep connection to and love for Vedic culture. Since finding my guru at the age of 20, I have identified strongly with Hinduism, although most western followers of my guru did not have this feeling. I knew that for me it was a far older connection, one hidden in the past. I was once again surprised by the memories, as I did not imagine myself in such a position, but had always thought I must have been simply a yogi in some mountain setting. But then again, it all made sense. My work in the interfaith arena had begun centuries ago. I was now nourishing the seeds that had been planted so long ago. It was also of great significance that as the Rani Gita, my focus was to pass on the knowledge to my daughters and to give great care to the female line, something unheard of at that time. Was this the beginning of my concern for the role of women in spiritual life? It was a concern that led me in Africa to Didi, and then to start a school for girls in the American South, and that inspired the founding of The Global Peace Initiative of Women in this life. As Gita, I felt myself unfit to perform the Vedic rituals, but it was the sadhu who encouraged me to break these thought patterns, patterns set and reinforced so deeply by society, then and to this day—a theme that has woven itself through many lives.

As I relived the scenes from 15th century India again and again, experiencing the feelings evoked by the various episodes, I began to see patterns emerge that shaped my future lives: the feeling of being helpless as a woman, even a Rani, to protect my people and culture; the desire to defend my deity and to help others understand and respect my culture. To this day when I find myself in an interfaith setting where little respect is shown to Hinduism and the philosophy of yoga, where there is little understanding of this great ancient religious tradition, I find myself pained beyond words and angered. To me, it is as if the destruction of temples is happening all over again. I did not understand these strong feelings in me until these memories returned. Once they emerged, I was able identify the source of my current emotions.

When I began meditating in the early 1970s, meditation was not mainstream. My mother thought I had been brainwashed by a cult, so I would take the phone off the hook when I meditated. It caused me much pain to have to hide and sometimes lie about my spiritual practice, but it was the only way to pacify my mother and to keep my father from getting caught in the middle, having to choose between his wife and daughter. As I remembered my life in India, I thought how odd that I had to repeat this pattern of secrecy. Was the practice so embedded in my subconscious mind that I naturally fell once again into the pattern of hiding my spiritual life, centuries later? I am only beginning to understand how subconscious patterns work at a subtle level, intruding themselves into subsequent lives. We give little thought to our behavioral patterns, which most often have been set in the past. The subconscious mind has great influence over one's life until one becomes more conscious and determined to take control. Meditation and spiritual practice enhance the ability to perceive patterns and eventually to break those that are not useful to our progress.

This is the teaching that comes with past life recall. It is not the memories themselves that are so important, but the resolution of old thought patterns and emotional responses that are no longer helpful for the soul's evolution. Neutralizing or burning the karmic seeds or tendencies, *samsara*, is what helps to shape the future. We cannot change the past, but we can consciously work to change the thought patterns our past actions have produced so that we can determine the future. Our present moment-to-moment thoughts and actions create the blueprint for what will be, and we can learn to take control of this process.

I remembered the sadhu's parting words to me: I would be reborn in a Muslim family. I wondered at his meaning. Islam was the religion with which I felt the least affinity. By now I was working extensively with a number of advanced Buddhist teachers and had begun to feel a strong connection with Buddhism. I was also close to a number of very special Christian teachers who were mentors in my interfaith work, and because of my own background I felt a love for Judaism. But I had no emotional connection with Islam, although increasingly my work was leading me toward deeper engagement with the Sufi community.

Marianne, who was in charge of much of the organization of The Global Peace Initiative of Women and who was a long time Buddhist, found a Sufi teacher and soon became a practicing Sufi. This came as a real surprise. I also met this teacher and soon became a regular visitor to his home outside of San Francisco. His spiritual influence was weaving itself into the work of GPIW as I found myself increasingly surrounded by Sufis.

I don't remember in what setting the memories began to emerge, but it was a few years after the first Sufi-Yogi Dialogue when I found myself back in the past. The process is always the same: a suction cup pulls me back and there is little I can do to resist. I find myself increasingly internalized, tumbling back through the vortex of time, and the external world fades away. I begin to see scenes as though a movie is passing before my inner eye, and I hear conversations. I know who I am as I begin to experience all that I see through that person's perception. It becomes clear that I am she, and she is me. As I relive the scenes again and again, it is only by watching as closely as a detective that I know where and when it is all taking place.

The memories were no longer returning through a vision in the pre-dawn hours, as they had the first two times. Now they were coming in meditation, although there still was an awakening factor, someone I met or some experience.

Early in my interfaith work I had been invited to a United Nations sponsored conference in Iran on religion and ecology. In many ways it was a difficult visit and there was much unease and discomfort, but on a deeper level I felt an old connection, more with the culture and the people than anything else. Some years later I became friends with the wife of the ambassador to the UN from Iran. A deep spiritual friendship developed, a closeness that resulted from a shared spiritual understanding. I introduced her to many of the Hindu and Buddhist teachers with whom I was working and she quietly expressed gratitude for these novel experiences. She, like I, saw the Oneness. We both knew the Divine is One, experienced through different forms and narratives. Then she and her husband were recalled to Tehran and I didn't see her for a number of years, but my connection to Iran continued.

One day I found myself back in old Persia, in a very humble setting, far different from the royal life I knew in India.

When I recalled my life in India as a Rani I knew not to get carried away by those memories of grandeur, as through the course of the soul's journey one experiences many, many different stations in life. I remembered the sadhu's words when he cautioned me to free myself from attachment to luxury. When I was subsequently born in Persia, I remembered none of this. The joy that came to me in that life was not from material comforts but from the simple teachings of my Sufi father. I was to learn in this life to go inside for joy, to seek things not of this world. The memories that now returned were of a time that I have come to treasure. It was perhaps my most humble birth, but also the most joyous.

PART V

LATE 15ᵀᴴ CENTURY PERSIA

As the air carries fragrance from place to place,
so does the embodied soul carry
the mind and senses with it,
when it leaves an old body
and enters a new one.

—Bhagavad Gita 15:8

I died as a mineral and became a plant,
I died as a plant and rose to animal,
I died as animal and I was man. Why should I fear?
When was I less by dying?

—Jalal al-Din Rumi

Chapter 17

O ur time between births when we rest in the subtle world, or world of light, can vary greatly. The demarcation of time is different in between births. What may seem like a few days in the subtle world can be years of Earth time. Some say that one day in the astral world is equivalent to one year on earth. We take birth when the conditions are right for the soul to continue its journey toward full awakening. I was not long in the world of light when conditions called me again to Earth.

I was born in humble surroundings in a small village somewhere in the Persian Empire. My mother died in childbirth; I was her parting gift to my father, their only child. He treated me as his greatest treasure, and despite the pleading of his sister, my aunt, to let her raise me, he refused to part with me. He said that the very sight of me brought him closer to Paradise, so he called me *Minoo*, meaning heaven. He felt the Lord had sent me to be his comforter; I tried to be that for him from an early age.

My father was a tradesman, although I don't remember what his trade was. He cared very little for money or worldly comforts. Our simple two-room abode had few furnishings, but love there was in plenty. Never for a moment did I feel want.

I carried with me from my previous birth a vague and subtle remembrance of my blue-hued God, Lord Krishna. My father recounted how as a small child I would wander outside our little hut and play in the dry soil, seeking to make a statue of sorts. Inevitably it would crumble and I would dissolve into tears. My father would run out to see what was wrong, but I couldn't express what it was I sought to create. As I got older, the desire for this statue did not desert me, and I continued my efforts. My father found this quite amusing and he loved to tell the story of how one day I was successful in creating a form.

He emerged from the hut to find me all smiles. "Very good, Minoo," he exclaimed. "My child has become an artist. But what is it, dear?"

"It is God," I exclaimed, as if he of all people should know.

He laughed heartily and pulled me onto his lap. "But you know, my child, that God has no form."

"He does," I replied with conviction.

"And how do you know that?" he asked, playing along with me.

"I have seen him."

"Oh, have you?" laughed my father again. "And what does the Lord look like?"

"He is blue and he has long, dark curly hair, and he wears jewels of so many colors. He has the most beautiful eyes . . ." I replied dreamily.

"A blue God?" He smiled. "That must have been an angel you saw. You know that Allah has no form."

I frowned. I didn't care what he said. I knew that I had seen God. And so I carried my little earthen shape to a corner behind our hut and there I played with my image of God, speaking with him, although he had no name, and sometimes bringing him food from the little that we had. He was my playmate in childhood, and he brought me comfort, security, and happiness.

One day a great rain came and washed away my rudimentary attempt at a statue. Baba saw the sad expression on my face. He sat me down and said. "If you want to see God, my little one, you mustn't look outside. You must look inside," and he pointed to my chest. "Here is where you will find the One you seek."

Baba was to tease me about this for years. As I got older, the form imprinted as a memory in my mind began to fade, but that spot where I had placed him became my private place where I could always retreat for quiet discourse with my Lord.

We had very little material comfort as I was growing up, before Baba's students came. We hardly had enough food. Often hunger pains haunted me in the night, and I was awakened by the cries emerging from my stomach. Baba denied himself in order to make sure that I had something to eat. When I pointed out to him at night that there was nothing for tomorrow, he smiled and said, "Don't worry, little one, the angels will provide."

In the early years the angels provided only love, and I had to make do with that, feeding my empty stomach with the joy and laughter Baba provided. But later, things changed. In the mornings there would often be a basket of food at our door. This happened on many occasions, and one day I decided to catch sight of the angels who were leaving the baskets. I woke in the early hours, wondering what they looked like. Would I be afraid of them? Would they have wings as the stories told? Would they have human faces? At dawn I crept out of bed. It was cold, as Baba had not yet started the fire, but I braved the cold to wait. As soon as I heard a sound, I opened the door. To my consternation, it was not angels at all, but some women from the village who had baked us fresh bread and other foodstuff.

I ran to him. "Baba, it is not angels. It is the women of the village who are leaving the food." I was quite disappointed.

He simply laughed and said, "My little one, who do you think sent the women? Angels work through human hearts and hands, always remember that. They don't come themselves lest little girls discover them." Years later I found out that the women left the food so secretly out of respect for Baba. He did not like to accept gifts or help from others, so they preferred to leave their offerings in the hidden hours of the dawn.

My favorite memories from those early years were the evenings when we sat by the stove and he told me stories of Sufi saints in the simplest language so that I could understand. These saints became my friends. The stories always had a moral, some teaching for me, but Baba could not stay serious for too long. After the story, he would say something so amusing that both of us ended up laughing, sometimes laughing so hard that my chest hurt. "Laughter," he said, "draws the angels near. They love the sound of human laughter." And so we made a habit of laughing before bed in the hopes that the angels would come to us in sleep. They never came to me. The blue form that I had imagined when I was younger no longer visited my imagination. In the morning Baba asked me if I had seen the angels. When I shook my head no, he said, "Minoo, you must learn to see as I do, with the eyes of the heart."

"Don't be silly, Baba, how can you have eyes in your heart?" Surely he was making another joke.

But he was serious. "Ah, you must discover them. They are there; I can assure you of that."

There were times when things were difficult for us and I knew that I was a burden to him, although he never admitted it. During those times he looked at me and said, "Perhaps I have been selfish to keep you near. It may have been better for you to go your aunt so that you could have been properly raised."

I shook my head vigorously. "Never say that, Baba." I knew I would never have such fun with my aunt.

"But you are getting older, child, and a girl needs a mother. "

"Why do I need a mother when I have you?" I broke out laughing, "I am sure the angels don't visit Aunt Maryam's house!"

"Allah has sent me a child with wit."

Baba was greatly loved in the village. That was why the women took turns caring for us with their food offering. They understood his humility and never wanted to make us ashamed of our need. I grew up feeling very protected and loved.

There were other presences that graced out house, particularly Baba's Sheikh, who had died before I was born. Often in the night I heard Baba speaking to an invisible presence. "Baba, who are you speaking with?" I asked one night when I overhead him from my bed. "Who is there with you?"

"Are you not asleep, Minoo? It is only my Sheikh who is here. Go to sleep now. He is showing me many beautiful things."

I slipped out of bed and crept quietly to the next room in hopes of catching sight of this mysterious figure that was such a presence in our lives. But there was no one in the other room; it seemed like Baba was talking to himself. I went back to bed, wondering why Baba had this habit of speaking to an empty room. The next morning I asked him, "There was nobody here last night. I came out of bed to check."

"How many times must I tell you, my little one, that these things can only be seen with the eyes of the heart."

I thought for a minute and then asked him, "You said he was showing you something beautiful. Was he showing you Paradise, Baba?"

"Indeed he was."

"What did it look like?" I was intrigued.

"More beautiful than words can say."

I ran to the door to open it, and looked up into the sky. "Where is Paradise?" I asked.

He smiled and came to stand beside me. "Surely you don't think it is on a cloud somewhere in the sky."

"Then where is it?"

"It is right here, my child, with us now, but you must have the eyes to see it. You cannot see it with these human eyes."

"I know," I repeated, "only with the eyes of the heart." By now I had learned this refrain.

After our evening meal, Baba would retreat quietly to his corner to say his evening prayers before sending me off to bed and reciting a bedtime story. On one such occasion, I sat quietly by his side. When he was finished, I asked him, "Baba, if God has no form, then what does He look like?" He simply smiled, but I pressed him, "How can you pray to someone who has no form?"

"That is a difficult question to answer." Then he added, "Close your eyes, Minoo." I shut my eyes tightly closed. "You cannot see me now, but you know I am here, right?" I nodded. "Just because you can't see the Lord doesn't mean He is not there. There are other ways to know the Lord, which you will learn when you get older. It is not a matter of what the Lord looks like, it is a matter of what He is."

"But how can you pray to something you can't see?" I persisted.

"Suppose I were to tell you that the Lord is love itself, that very feeling of love that warms your heart is the Lord's presence. Without him there is no love. When I pray I accept that overwhelming love into my heart and send it to you, to the people in our village, and to the whole world."

I still wasn't satisfied, but I didn't press him. When the blue face of my childhood God faded away, nothing had taken its place. It was still a mystery to me how one could love what one couldn't see.

Baba loved his Sheikh more than anyone, except me perhaps. Before the Sheikh's passing, he had lived in a faraway town and Baba had spent many years with him before returning to the village to marry my mother. Often Baba would give me hints about the training he had received, but then he would look at me with pretend sternness and say, "Don't try it, my Minoo. This training is not for you. Your path is only love and service. That is all you need to know. Love all who cross your path and serve them, then you will be a true Sufi. Service will bring you to Paradise."

"Must I love even the donkeys?" I asked with a smile.

"Especially the donkeys. Look how they serve us."

"And the thieves?"

"The thieves too, for they need it the most."

"And the rocks and the mountains?"

"Of course. What do you think keeps them in place? It is Allah's love that keeps everything just as it should be. Our love is but an extension of that. In this way we are helping the Lord in his work. Remember that always, Minoo. We are servants of the Lord, doing his work. We have no other task."

Despite his words, I often thought that I should follow in his footsteps and receive the same training he had gotten from his Sheikh; I thought in the back of my mind that had I been a son, that is how it would have been.

As I grew older, Baba would increasingly enter ecstatic states. Sometimes when he would return to his normal awareness, he would hold his finger to his mouth, indicating that I should not speak. I learned to wait until he was ready. Then he would speak to me.

"Who was here, Baba?" I asked, knowing that some divine presence had been with him. Sometimes it was one of the angels, sometimes a Sufi saint. They appeared to him and I watched as he went in and out of ecstatic states. I learned how to care for him during those times; I knew when simply to sit and wait. Although I could not see or hear what he saw and heard, I did feel the presence in the room. There would be a very subtle shift that I could sense, and Baba taught me how to feel it through my heart.

Once a year Baba's sister would come from a distant village to stay with us. It was a time of great fun for me as she always brought many gifts and articles of clothing that she had made. But it also disturbed our daily life because she knew nothing of Baba's states. Her visits were always a bit too long. We would be glad when she arrived and even happier when it was time for her to leave. It was from her that I learned to cook and care for Baba. By the time I was twelve I could take care of most of the household chores, but Baba never ceased to help. Before his students came, we would prepare all the meals together, and even take the clothes to the river for washing. He made everything into a game, so that none of the chores seemed burdensome.

It was on one such visit from my aunt that she raised with Baba the issue of my marriage. "Minoo is almost reaching that age," she said. "You must begin to think of a husband." Baba was quiet. I was in the other room and not meant to hear, so I didn't say anything, but her words disturbed me. I decided not to mention it to him, hoping that he would forget the subject.

It was a festival day and the women from the village had brought us very special foods. I spent the day preparing them, very pleased with my work, and hungrily eyeing the feast I had laid out. I went to fetch Baba. As was his habit, he was sitting on the floor propped up with pillows in an ecstatic state. I sat beside him and waited, as I so often did. After a time I realized the food was getting cold and I was getting hungrier. My day's work would soon spoil. Rarely did we have the opportunity to have such a variety of food, and I could not bear the thought that it would go to waste, that I would not be able to enjoy the meal so generously gifted to us. I didn't know what to do. Baba had told me never to disturb him when he was in such a state, but he didn't usually stay away this long.

One hour passed and then two. Darkness set in. Baba usually lit the lamps, as he cautioned me about the danger, but with trembling hands I now lit them. Suddenly the thought occurred to me that perhaps he had died. He was as still as stone. I felt his hands but they were still warm. He had not moved since I had first entered the room hours ago. Perhaps Baba had gone to Paradise and couldn't find his way back. I tapped him lightly on the shoulder, calling his name and then began to cry. I don't know what possessed me but I couldn't stop crying. I shook him, calling him loudly.

After a few minutes his body shifted and then he slowly opened his eyes. Joy was pouring out of them, like streams of sunlight. I suddenly felt ashamed. "What is it, child," he asked in not more than a whisper.

I reached over and hugged him, so glad to hear his voice. "I thought you had left me for good. I don't know what I would do without you," I replied in a still tearful voice.

He patted my head with his hand. "Allah would not take me from you, not now," he said, "when you are still young. Never fear that." He chuckled and then began to sing so sweetly. My heart was relieved. After a while he got up and said, "I see you have prepared a feast for us, Minoo. What a happy surprise!"

"It is spoiled now, Baba. It has been sitting there for hours. The fire has long gone out."

"Nonsense," he said with chuckle. "I am sure it is quite delicious."

I began to serve the food. With sadness I leaned over to taste the dishes I had prepared with such care, thinking that my great surprise for him had been ruined. But to my amazement, the food was steaming hot and was as delicious as when I first took it off the fire. I looked at Baba in astonishment. There was a twinkle in his eye, but he didn't say a word.

Winter set in and it was very cold. Some days the fire barely warmed the room. We both slept as close as we could to the flames. It was during a very bitter spell that I fell ill. Baba did not think I would remain with him. In my feverish state I faintly heard his urgent prayers. I heard him begging for my life and then at the end I heard him surrender and say, "Take her if you will. She is dearer to me than life, but she was given by you and can be taken by you." I thought at that moment I would die, but instead I came back to life. Over the next days my fever subsided and within weeks I had my energy back. He embraced me, holding me close to his chest. It is the only time I ever saw my Baba cry. It had been my time to die, he said, but his sheikh had come to intervene. He said that was Allah's second gift to him: my return from the clutches of death.

Everything changed after that. Soon after, his students began to come. At first there were only a few. One of his early students was a young man from the village. He loved to play music and often brought his instrument to our home to play for Baba. Baba listened politely and did not encourage him, but I loved the sound of his voice. I would quietly leave my work and sit in a corner listening as he played his stringed instrument. The music carried me away; I was entranced. Without exchanging a word with Baba, I knew that he didn't approve, but I couldn't understand why.

There was a garden by this man's house and he would pick flowers for us. He would give them to me and I would set them around the house, but one day Baba asked him, with unusual directness, whether he came for the teachings or to visit Minoo. The boy looked down at his feet and said, "Of course the teachings, Master."

"I wonder," replied Baba. I was embarrassed by my father's tone but said nothing.

In truth this young man did take every opportunity to speak with me, but I mostly kept in the other room when the students were there. One day this man caught me as I was serving tea. Baba was outside speaking with another student. We were alone. "Minoo," he said quietly. "I am going to ask the Master for your hand in marriage. Will you agree?"

I was completely startled. He was a few years older than me, and I thought him very good looking. I loved his music, and most importantly he was a student of Baba. I could not deny that I had taken a liking to him. I nodded. Just then Baba entered the room. In my nervousness I spilled the tea as I poured it and then ran from the room. Nothing escaped Baba's attention.

That night he was unusually quiet at the evening meal. He didn't speak with me at all before bed except to say, "Goodnight, Minoo." There was no story, no laughter that night.

The next morning, he called me to him. "Did you receive a proposal yesterday?" He asked sternly. He rarely spoke to me in such a tone.

I didn't reply. I didn't know what to say.

"I see," he said, "And did you encourage him?"

"I like him, Baba. He brings us flowers and he plays such beautiful music."

"And I have not been able to give you such things . . ."

"I didn't mean that."

"Don't be deceived. Beauty is not only in flowers, child, or in music. There is a greater beauty you must come to know."

"Baba, he said he was going to approach you."

"He should not have spoken to you before getting my approval, and you should not have encouraged him. I will not give my approval. You watch, this young man will be gone shortly and he won't be back to this village again. He is not serious about the path, and you cannot be given to such a one."

In my stubbornness, I did not believe Baba. But not long after, the man found a moment to speak with me alone again. He was going on a journey to a larger town where he could have more success with his music, but he would come back and speak with Baba then about our marriage. He asked if I would wait for him, and again I nodded.

Baba did not raise the subject of this man again, but secretly I hoped he would return and that Baba would find it in his heart to forgive him. But Baba was right. The young man never came back. I had given my word to wait, and this weighed on me for many years to come. I was never quite sure whether it was the boy, or his music and his gift of flowers that

I missed. It was perhaps that he had given me my first taste of a beauty that our meager means could not provide, but I never hinted of this again to Baba.

With each passing year, more students came. It was not long before we were unable to accommodate them in our small abode. One of his students approached him about building a larger home, but Baba refused. "We have done quite well here all these years. There is no need for anything larger." This student then approached me to prevail upon him.

"Baba," I said one evening. "Your students desire this. They can no longer fit in this small room. In the evening so many are sitting outside because there is no space."

"Aren't you happy with what we have, Minoo? Haven't I taught you to be content with what the Lord has given?"

"But it's not for us, it's for them. Of course I am content. I love our little home. We have no need for anything more, but many are being turned away because there is no place here. Haven't you also taught me not to refuse a gift from the Lord?"

"So now it is my daughter who is giving the teaching." He smiled and relented. A new home was built with a large room to accommodate the students and small living quarters for the two of us. After this, many came, not only from the neighboring villages but also from faraway towns. I didn't know how the word had spread. How did so many people come to know about Baba, my simple Baba, who was a man of few words? I think they came for his joy, because it was not sermons they received. He would smile and laugh with them, tell stories and then laugh some more. He was an endless fount of joy and one could not be in his presence without feeling some of his happiness.

Sometimes a student asked him to tell a story from the Prophet's life. He said you can read all of that in the holy books, so I will tell you what the Prophet did today, here in our village. He related a story of kindness or faith, or some other quality he wanted to cultivate in them, and he always came to the same conclusion: to live in, feel, and see with the heart, to become one with the great universal love. This was his only teaching.

"All of the stories in all of the holy books do not amount to much if you have not become love," he said. "That is the only teaching there is. Love is not a feeling; it is a state of being. You must love so that you become love itself; then, and only then, every act of yours, every deed, every word, will uplift the whole of creation. That is the work Allah has entrusted to us. Become love, Allah says, and then you will know what I am."

Sometimes Baba turned students away, saying, "I am a simple man, not a learned one, and if you are seeking learning you have come to the wrong place. If you want love and joy, there is plenty of that here." Sometimes the prospective students left and I asked Baba why he turned them away.

"They want what I can't give them," he said. "There are others who can provide what they are seeking. You know, my child, we have no use here for scholarly debate. Only love, that is all we need."

Rumors began to spread that Baba was a man of miracles and a different sort of student began to appear, students who sought material rather than spiritual gain. Again Baba turned them away, saying that the only miracle he knew was love, the greatest miracle of all. That he could give them. One day a very well dressed couple came from the city, seeking Baba's blessing for a child. They came to our home several times and each time the woman was more beautifully dressed than before. I could not help but stare at her clothes, woven of such fine material. I stood by the door of the room where Baba received students, observing her the whole time they were there. On one occasion she came in a beautiful shawl of such intricate design that I could not help but openly admire it.

Although married for many years, the woman could not bear children. "Can you help her?" I asked, when Baba explained their situation to me.

"I told her I am a simple village man. What could I do? Only Allah can help. She must pray to Allah."

"But surely your prayers can help as well," I replied.

"Minoo, we must be content with what Allah provides. I have told you that many times. I will pray for her, but if Allah chooses not to send children, she must accept that and not yearn for what has not been given." He eyed me carefully as he spoke these words.

"Why are you looking at me like that?" I asked cautiously.

"Since this couple has been visiting, I have caught in your eyes something I had not seen before, Minoo. Do you desire beautiful clothing like that woman wears?"

I shifted uncomfortably, embarrassed by his question. "Why does nothing escape you?" I asked, in an annoyed tone. "Must you take note of every thought that enters my mind?"

"Indeed I must."

"Is it wrong, Baba, to love beauty? I cannot help but be drawn to beautiful things. Is that wrong?"

"Of course not, my child. Beauty comes from the Lord, and He has created it for our enjoyment. What is harmful is the desire for something that does not belong to you, that has not been given by the Lord. This creates discontentment and this takes one further away from the Lord. I hope that is not the case."

"No, Baba, I don't have discontentment. I am merely drawn to beauty."

"The greatest enjoyments of this world cannot compare to the beauty of God. Always remember that, Minoo. Don't be satisfied with the lesser beauty, with material objects that come and go. Material objects can't give happiness."

I couldn't deny that I had a strong attraction to beautiful things, but it was an attraction that I tried to suppress because it couldn't be fulfilled, and because Baba kept trying to turn my mind in a different direction.

About a year later, the couple returned with their newborn son. They thanked Baba profusely, but he refused to take any credit. "I have done nothing," he replied, "except to put you in the hands of the Lord. It is he you must thank."

The man took out a large bundle of money and offered it to Baba. "At least let us return your kindness," he said. But Baba refused the money. The man insisted. "Compared with the joy you have given us, this money means nothing."

"The Lord's work is not a business," Baba replied quietly, refusing the offer. "It is kind of you to offer, but we have no need for anything here."

I stood by without saying a word. We were now feeding many of his students and our costs had increased greatly. We could have well used the money, but I knew to keep quiet. Baba was a man of principle and it was impossible to convince him of something that went against his beliefs.

The woman then took off her shawl, the beautiful shawl that I had so admired on a previous visit. "Let me at least make a gift of this to your daughter." She said, placing the shawl around my shoulders. I ran my fingers along the fine fabric, which was softer than anything I had ever touched. How beautiful it was! I looked at Baba in anticipation, hoping he wouldn't ask me to refuse it.

"That you may do," replied Baba with a twinkle in his eyes. "I cannot prevent you from making a gift to my daughter, if she chooses to accept it."

I looked at Baba for some indication of disapproval but I found none, so I gladly accepted the gift, thanking the woman profusely.

When we were alone, I expressed my joy to Baba. "Baba, feel how soft it is. I have never felt anything so warm and soft. This will keep me warm now in the coldest nights," I said wrapping myself tightly in the new gift.

"You have been dreaming of this for a whole year. I thought best for you to have it and be done with this desire that has been chasing you here and there."

"So do you now see my dreams as well?" I asked in surprise, none too pleased.

He only smiled, without responding.

"Just look, Baba, how beautiful it is," I said twirling around in my new garment.

"Don't get carried away," he cautioned. "It is merely a piece of cloth that in time will fray."

"But I feel like a princess in this," I continued.

"You have always been a princess in my eyes and in the eyes of the Lord. It is not fancy dress that makes you so."

I now felt embarrassed at my enthusiasm so I took the shawl off and wrapped it neatly, putting it aside. "I won't wear it then," I said sullenly.

"That is not the way either, my child. It is for your enjoyment. I want you to put it into perspective: enjoy the gift, but don't hanker after more. We are simple village people and should not be seeking the luxuries of the world, which will distract us from the greater goal."

"I know that, Baba."

"Do you see now, Minoo, how the Lord watches and waits? He provides for our desires when the time in right. You must learn patience. Patience is the greatest friend one can have."

It was around this time, as word of Baba was spreading, that a group of scholarly officials came to visit him. At first I thought they came to pay their respects, as so many others did, but it soon became clear that their intention was to expose him, to prove him a fraud. They had come to test and to ridicule him. They appeared at our door when Baba was busy with one of his students, counseling him on an important personal matter.

When I saw the official look of the group, I ran to fetch Baba, but he motioned me not to disturb him. I invited the scholars in and served them tea. Time passed and still Baba did not emerge. I went to him again. His student was gone but Baba was immersed in spiritual joy. I couldn't disturb him and so asked them to wait a bit longer. After a while, I began to get nervous and so went and quietly reminded Baba that his guests were waiting. Baba opened his eyes and smiled. "I will come, Minoo, to meet them although there is no good purpose to their visit."

I stood by the door nervously as I watched Baba engage with the official looking group. They coldly began to inquire of Baba about his knowledge of the sacred texts.

"I am not a learned man," replied Baba simply.

"Then how can you teach?" asked one of them disrespectfully.

Baba was quiet for a few minutes, looking intensely at the man. Finally he asked, "Who determines the qualifications of a teacher? Only the Lord himself. We are his servants and he decides who is best fit to transmit his message."

"That is blasphemy!" exclaimed the man. Then another stated with equal disrespect, "We have heard that you do not observe the required prayer five times each day. How can you set an example for the people if you yourself do not observe what is required?" The dismissive tone of his voice stung me, but I remained quiet.

"Only five times?" Baba responded. "That is not nearly enough. One must always be in prayer, in communion with the Lord. That is what I teach."

The man shifted uncomfortably, clearly angry at Baba's response. He quickly changed the subject. "We have heard that you do not observe the required fasts. How can one be regarded as a teacher if all the rituals are not followed to the letter? This sets a bad example for the people."

Baba burst out laughing. "You may ask my daughter about all the fasts we have observed. We have excelled in that these many years. No one can accuse us of refraining from fasts."

I could not help but smile as I saw how cleverly Baba was responding to these men. But I was also angry, furious that they would speak to him in such a condescending tone. On and on their examination went, their rude questions and Baba's skillful answers. Their last words were threatening, letting Baba know that he was under watch. When they finally left, I asked nervously, "Why did they come? What do they want from you, Baba?"

"They have chased the Lord away with all their debates and rituals," Baba sighed. "If only they knew that none of that is necessary. The only thing the Lord asks for is our love, and that is the one thing they don't know how to give."

"Will they cause us trouble?" I asked fearfully.

Baba shook his head. "What trouble can they cause us? If they speak ill of me perhaps fewer student will come, and you will have less work. That won't be so bad," he chuckled.

Soon after, it came to our attention that these men were spreading rumors about Baba, telling people to beware of him, that he was a charlatan, but that didn't stop the students from coming. Those who sought scholarly knowledge were not the ones drawn to him in the first place. Those who came recognized his gifts and no amount of demeaning talk could dissuade them.

Some years after this incident, another proposal of marriage came my way, only it went straight to Baba. A very devoted student of his named Anoush approached him for my hand in marriage. Baba spoke to me about this.

"Anoush is a good man," he said, "and a very devoted student. He will make a fine husband, Minoo."

I shook my head. "I don't want to marry, Baba. Who will look after you?"

"The same One who has looked after me all these years."

"Baba, no. I don't want to marry. I don't want to leave you. I am happy here the way things are."

"I hope it is not that other boy you are still thinking of and waiting for?" he asked with a frown. I shook my head, although the thought of him still lurked in the corner of my mind, the remembrance of his music and my entrancement. I still held onto the hope that one day he would return and Baba would find him acceptable. "Don't you want your own family, Minoo? One day I will be gone from here. It is my duty to make sure you are cared for. Anoush can provide for you and he is dear to me, just like a son."

When he spoke those words, a wound that had long been hidden opened. I moved away from him, turning aside so that he would not see the pain in my eyes. Baba was silent, but then he asked again slowly, looking at me with a steady gaze, "Are you sure, Minoo? Such an offer may not come again."

The tears began to form. He would not be pressing me so if I were not a daughter. "You say that Anoush is like a son to you. Is it that you want a son, Baba?" I asked in a quivering voice. "Someone you could properly train."

"Minoo!" he reprimanded me, taken aback. "Have I not properly trained you?"

"Not as you would a son, Baba."

He was shocked to have me challenge him like this. I had never done so before and it pained me to speak this way, but I had to say what I felt. I turned to glance at him and saw a hurt expression cross his face. Then I turned away, unable to bear it. "I see," he said quietly. "You are expecting austerities."

"Isn't that how you were trained?"

"Didn't you have enough of austerity as a child, when we didn't have enough food to eat, when all of your clothes had holes and I had no stockings for you? Do you want those days again?" he asked sternly. "Yes, I was trained that way so that my students wouldn't have to be," he said firmly. "Many people fast and don't find God. I would treat a son no differently, Minoo. You are wrong in thinking that." Then he added in a slightly gentler tone, "I have tried to show you that the only training a Sufi needs is the path of love. It is love that Allah seeks, not fasting and other deprivations, my child. Love and service, that is the training I have tried to give you, and I am sorry if I have failed to teach you this. I would be no different with a son." He left the room and then I heard him leave the house, the door swinging shut behind him. He did not return the whole day.

The tears were streaming down my face. I sat alone in the room that day, pondering his words, feeling terrible that I had spoken to him in this manner. He had never given me any indication that he wished I had been a son, why did I think this? In his presence I felt so close to God, how could

I question his teaching? He was joy itself, and wasn't that what I wanted to attain?

As the day's light grew weaker, I set about to prepare the evening meal. His students would be coming and I needed to have things ready for them. Even if he didn't return, I would be ready. As I prepared the evening food, the heaviness I had felt that day began to leave me. Why had I challenged him? I knew full well that the love he gave me was worth a hundredfold any other training I could receive. I knew that a son could be no dearer to him than I was. I was wrong, completely wrong, and I felt ashamed. As this feeling came over me, I heard his gentle chuckle. It grew louder. I looked around and in the other room but he was nowhere in sight.

"Baba." I called. There was no answer, only his chuckle. It seemed to come from all directions, from the right and the left, in front and behind, above and below.

"Baba," I whispered as I sank to the floor. "I am so sorry, please forgive me." And then his laughter took hold of me. I realized it was coming from inside, not from anywhere in the house. My body shook with laughter and I realized it was coming from my heart. It was the laughter of the heart. This was what he had been trying to teach me all these years—to see and hear and know with the heart. The heart is the way to Allah. I could not stop the laughter from bubbling up from within. My whole body shook with such joy that I thought it would burst. And in between my gasps, as I tried to catch my breath, I heard the heavenly voices singing their approval.

I looked up. He was standing before me, his eyes lit with confirmation.

"Now my daughter has become a true Sufi."

I learned more that day than years of austerity could have taught me. Never again did I doubt his training. After that day he assumed a different role for me, more the Sheikh and less the father. After that, rarely did I have time alone with him and rarely did we get to speak as father and daughter. The subject of marriage never came up again. His students began to see me in a different light. Baba found a suitable woman for Anoush to marry; he told me that she would be like a sister and look after me in my old age. I did not pay attention at the time, but many years later, after he had passed, I realized his foresight then and understood why he had chosen her.

Chapter 18

B aba was careful to keep the customs of the day, and in those times women did not often leave their homes freely or unattended. But Baba did have women students and he took great care of them. He loved them as much as his male students. He was perhaps more discrete with them, but the training was the same. When the wife or daughter of one of the Sufi students would show an interest, Baba would send them to assist me with my duties. Occasionally he would show up in the kitchen and say to one of them, "You may serve me the meal tonight," or "Come and sit beside me after the evening meal. I have some words for you." What it meant to them to have some special time with the Master, I can only surmise.

Although Baba had traveled before he settled down and married my mother, he had not left the village since I was born. When his students asked him to visit a certain place, he responded that he had no need to go anywhere. I smiled because I understood that the saints came to him. So I was very surprised when one day he announced that we were going on a journey. I was excited. It was the first time that I would be seeing the world outside of our village.

"Allah will show the way," he said simply. And so we started on the road along with a few students. We rode all day, passing villages, and then by nightfall we came to a rather large town. The students arranged for us to stay at a guesthouse. It was a tremendous adventure for me. We continued the next day and the next.

"Baba, where are we headed?" I finally asked.

"Allah will show us."

The adventure was losing some of its appeal. I was unaccustomed to traveling and was beginning to long for home. The students were also getting a bit anxious, as Baba didn't seem to have any particular destination in mind.

"Master," one asked. "Do you know the name of the place we are seeking? Perhaps we should ask directions? The road we are on is getting more and more deserted. We may not find a village by nightfall."

Baba laughed. "Do you know a better guide than Allah?" The student fell silent.

After five days of travel, when we had long left towns and villages behind, and there seemed only mountains and endless desert before us, Baba paused. "He is near," he said.

"Who," I asked.

"You will see."

"But, Baba, there is nothing here. Nobody."

He smiled. "Your heart, Minoo, that is what will guide you."

"Yes, Baba, I know, but sometimes the heart can't see which way to go."

"That is because your mind is not still enough. When the mind is still, the heart sees clearly."

Suddenly I saw a clearing in the distance. "There, Baba!" I shouted, pointing ahead. "There's a small hut. Let's go and ask." It seemed to appear out of nowhere.

"Now, my child, you are learning."

He got down from the horse and ran ahead of us. The door was open, as if we were expected. A tall, thin man suddenly appeared in the doorway. I could see him from a distance. Baba reached him first. Even from afar I could feel the intense love between them, their eyes fixed on one another. They did not speak for a long time. The rest of us stood there, waiting, thinking we would be introduced. But the introductions never came. Baba and the man went off into another room, while a woman appeared and brought us into a room for tea and food.

"I should bring some food to Baba," I said to her, feeling very awkward because I never ate before him.

"Oh, don't you worry," she replied. "He is being fed plenty." She then showed the students to their place of rest and brought me to her room. "You will stay with me," she said. She didn't speak after that, retreating to a corner of the room. I couldn't sleep much that night. Every now and then I would peer over to where the woman was. She remained sitting upright all night it seemed, hardly moving. I must have fallen asleep sometime close to dawn, and when I awoke the sun was streaming into the room through a small window. I found her smiling face greeting me. I asked for Baba.

"He is being well cared for," she replied. Then she went about her duties. I assisted as we prepared food for the students. After eating, the woman called me to come down to the river with her. We gathered all of the dirty clothes from our long journey and washed them in the little stream that ran behind the house.

"I should get Baba's clothes, as well," I said to her. "Oh, that has been taken care of," she replied. She didn't speak after that. As we lay the clothes on the rocks to dry, I sat down by the stream and looked up at the sun, now nearly midway in the sky. The light was blinding, so I turned my eyes away. I had so many questions but no one to answer them for me. Who was that man? I had never seen him before and yet Baba seemed to know him so well. Why had we come here and what was Baba doing with him behind closed doors?

I glanced over at the woman. She sat silently a few feet from me with closed eyes, her face beaming like the sun. And who was she, this mysterious woman, with a majestic air about her and an aura of silence and self-containment? We sat for some time, taking in the sun. Gradually my mind settled down and the questions departed. What did I really need to know anyhow, I thought, as I listened to the quiet babbling of the river beside us? As my breathing seemed to synchronize with the ripples of the water, a wave of peace swept over me and I could no longer distinguish between myself, the flow of the river, and the beaming light of the sun. As my thoughts ceased, a sense of oneness, of unity, naturally arose, and with it came a fountain of joy, bubbling up from within. I don't know how long we sat there, but I was gradually brought back to outer awareness by the voices of Baba's students who had come to find me. When I opened my eyes to greet them, the woman was gone. As I looked around at the faces of the students eager for some information about Baba, I thought, so this is what Baba has been trying to teach me all these years.

The days passed. We didn't see Baba at all. The students were becoming restless, but whenever they asked about Baba, I would simply shake my head and say, "No questions, and no answers. We must wait." We all had to sit silently and wait, without knowing what our next move would be.

Many days passed, and then as suddenly as he had disappeared, Baba re-emerged. He was radiant, with such joy on his face. "We can be on our way now," he said. And with those simple words we prepared for our journey home. The man reappeared at the doorway as we took our leave.

He gave me a loving glance and said to Baba, "So this is the one you nearly lost."

Baba smiled. "She is my joy. I don't know what I would have done without her all these years." The man's smile broadened and I looked up into his face. I could find no words to say to him. Could this be Baba's Sheikh?

As we walked away, I realized that I had not said goodbye to the woman who had looked after us with such kindness and care.

"Wait, Baba," I said. "I have not thanked the woman who cared for us. I must go back." I ran to the house. The door was open. I walked through the rooms but neither the man nor the woman could be found. I looked outside around the house, but it was deserted. I walked back slowly to Baba, confused. Where could they have gone? "She is not there," I said in a perplexed voice. It could not have been more than a few minutes since we left the house, where could they have gone?

He nodded as if he knew she would not be there, and then he said simply, "Let us be on our way."

As we journeyed home, the experience became more and more like a dream, as if we had stepped into another realm, another reality. When we reached our village I began to wonder whether or not we had imagined the whole scene—the man and the house, the woman who took care of us. Baba had hardly spoken on the journey home. An aura of silence accompanied us the whole way, but once we reached our village, his laughter began to flow again. I was glad to have him back.

I couldn't get the image of the man or the woman out of my mind. Day and night I thought of them, so I finally summoned my courage and asked Baba. He didn't reply.

"Was that man your Sheikh?" I asked quietly one evening as we sat together. He nodded. "But I don't understand. When I was a child he came to you in an invisible form, why did he come this way now, in a physical body? And why did he not come here? Why did we have to travel so far? And what were you doing with him all those days? I don't understand why . . ." The questions poured out of me.

"So many questions," he interrupted, shaking his head with a coy smile. And then he added, "Even to you, my child, there are things I cannot reveal."

But I pressed him. "He came in a body to teach you certain things. Is that right, Baba?"

He nodded again, "Now no more questions. You will know all you need to know in time."

"One more question." He nodded his ascent. "The woman, was she also a sheikh?"

He nodded again. "That was his saintly wife, a woman of high spiritual stature. I never made any distinction between them, although in all the time I knew her, she spoke little. I treated them with equal reverence. I wanted you to learn once and for all, my child, that I would treat you no differently if you were a son. Get rid of those doubts quietly lurking in your mind. The Lord makes no distinction. You received many blessings by being in her presence. Now you know that a woman can achieve the same spiritual stature as a man. Never forget this, Minoo. Never."

Something shifted after this journey. Many, many students came to Baba and our quiet life came to an end. Some traveled great distances to see him. Our house was always full. I don't know how I managed, but somehow we always had enough food for everyone. Some of the students traveled too far to return to their villages at night, and we always found a place for them to rest. On that journey to see his Sheikh, Baba had attained an elevated state and I never saw him come down from that state afterwards.

One morning found us alone. It was rare these days. After serving him the morning meal, I seated myself on the floor beside him and leaned over the many pillows that propped him up. Suddenly I had an impulse to hug him, just as I had when I was young. It had been many years since I had related to him in that way, and I refrained. But he knew my thoughts and reached over and drew me to him, stroking my hair.

"What good times we have had, the two of us," he said. Then after a few minutes he added, "The days left to me are few. You must promise me not to let anything disturb the joy that is now settled in your heart. Never let go of it. It is the most precious gift from Allah." His words would return to me many times in the months and years ahead.

A few weeks later Anoush and I were at the door saying goodnight to the students who had visited with Baba that evening. As Anoush prepared to depart, Baba called him back and asked him to spend the night with us. He did that often so I took no note of it. It was a lovely evening and as I stood outside alone under the dark canopy of sky, taking in the last few minutes before going inside to prepare Anoush's bed, I felt a presence beside me. It was Anoush. We stood in silence looking up at the starry night. It was a warm clear evening.

I broke the silence, "When Baba is gone, Anoush, you will have to assume the role of teaching the others. He has great faith in you."

"Don't speak of that, Minoo. Hopefully he will be with us for a long time still. But when that day comes, it is you who will have to lead us then."

I smiled and shook my head. 'No, Anoush, it is not meant to be. I will support you, but you will be the strength for the others."

"Then we will do it together," he said with conviction.

There was great respect and affection between the two of us. "At one time, Baba had wanted us to marry," I said. "He told me that you were like a son to him, and I got angry."

"You got angry with him?" Anoush asked in amazement.

I nodded. "I accused him of wishing I was a son. I don't know what came over me, but that day I learned the true extent of his love. I realized that his greatest love for me was not that of a father, but that of my Sheikh. He loved me so intensely because he saw Allah in me, just as he sees Allah in everyone. It is Allah that he loves, and he has tried to awaken that same love in me, but I have not been able to attain it." I sighed. It was the first time I had spoken so intimately to Anoush.

"Which one of us can attain that, Minoo? I also feel that I have not fully appreciated the gifts he has given us, but he would not want us to fault ourselves for this. We are still students. He alone is the Master."

A chill set in and we moved inside. As usual Baba was sitting very straight, propped up with pillows, in a quiet meditative state. I went to get the bedding for Anoush, when suddenly he called me back into the room in an urgent tone.

"Something is wrong, Minoo," Anoush said with panic in his voice. "He doesn't seem to be breathing."

"That happens sometimes," I said "Don't worry, he will come back. He always does." I went about the preparations, but I could see that Anoush was anxious so I went over to Baba and touched his hand. It was stiff and cold. I touched his chest to see if his heart was beating. It was still. I shook him gently, but he was stiff and I could see that life had left his body. That heart, which was filled to the brim for so many years, had now ceased to beat. I looked at Anoush. "He is gone," I said in an anguished voice. "He is not coming back this time." Despite my pain, the tears wouldn't come. There was a joyful presence in the room. I could feel him still. There was joy even in the sadness.

Anoush sat paralyzed, not knowing what to do. He broke down and cried. Both of us sat there for some time, and then I said to him, "He is with us still, but we must wash the body and prepare it for burial. You must go get some of the others to help." Anoush nodded and went off. I sat alone with Baba, remembering his words of a few weeks earlier: I should not let anything disturb my joy. I wanted this time alone with him, one last time to sit by his side.

"How can I have joy without you, my Sheikh?" I asked. Immediately I heard his response. "You are not without me. Where have I gone? Was not my Sheikh with me all these years?"

"You are right, Baba. There is no separation."

Some weeks later I had a dream, or rather a vision. Every day the students continued to pour in. I cared for them as I had in the past, but Baba's seat was empty. They sat around the piled cushions where he used to recline, sharing stories. One evening the students pressed me for some stories of their Sheikh. I was better at serving than speaking. I could think of nothing to say and so declined to speak. Later that night, I had a dream. I found myself in a most beautiful garden. It was filled with flowers of every possible color and size. The garden was abundant, overflowing with beauty. Most unusual was the light that illumined the place. It was unlike the day's sunlight, unlike any light I had seen before. Then I caught sight of Baba. I was so happy to see him. I said to him, "Baba your students are still coming. They have asked me for stories but I don't know what to tell them. What should I say?"

He didn't answer but his face radiated. Then I saw the Prophet standing next to him. Baba beamed at me, still not answering. He was basking in the joy of the Prophet. The Prophet looked at me with such loving eyes and replied, "Just give them love." At that moment the floodgates of my heart opened as never before, and I felt myself expanding and expanding. There was no end to this expansion and no end to the joy. It seemed to keep increasing, and then I awoke.

And so I began to recite stories of my childhood, when we had no food and the angels would deliver baskets by our door through the hands of the village women. I remembered many other tales of my youth with Baba. They never tired of these stories. I could not bring myself to feel comfortable in this role and was more often serving food and drink to the many who continued to come. After some time Anoush began to take the role of storytelling. He knew Baba almost as well as I did, but Anoush never failed to have me by his side when he spoke of Baba. The closest he could come to Baba, he said, was when I was there with him. Ironically, the deep friendship that Baba had envisioned for us ultimately came to be.

In my later years it was Anoush's wife who looked after me, exactly as Baba had predicted. She became the sister I never had.

I had no dreams of Baba but that one dream soon after his passing. Anoush began to see him more regularly as he was the one destined to share Baba's teachings. I accepted this, but in my heart there was a still that subtle feeling that had I been a son perhaps it would have been different. Try as he might, Baba had not been able to erase fully that feeling, which continued to lurk quietly in the crevices of my mind.

The years passed and I advanced in age. Baba remained an invisible presence for me and over the years I heard his voice inside giving me guidance. But I longed to see him again, as he had seen his Sheikh. Every time that Anoush shared with me one of his dreams of Baba, I felt as if I had failed him in some way. Why did he never come to me, only to Anoush?

I was sitting in the garden on a warm spring day. The sun was bright but not too hot. There was a lulling breeze in the air and I closed my eyes to appreciate its caresses against my check. The thought of Baba came to me, and a smile crossed my lips. But the smile faded as I began to wonder why in all these years he had never appeared to me. After that one dream, no more had come. The thought entered my mind that perhaps I did not have the ability to see him, that I was not advanced enough to have this vision. Throughout my life I had experienced this lack of confidence, only I knew how to cover it up. Baba knew this about me and when I was a child he would quickly reprimand me if he saw the slightest self-doubt sneak into my mind. I had certainly improved over the years, especially since the episode when I accused him of wanting a son, but still I had not fully overcome this failing.

Suddenly the wind ceased and the air fell totally still. I heard his voice, "By doubting yourself, you are doubting me." The words came through the surrounding silence. I opened my eyes, startled that this subtle thought had become almost audible. Then I heard him laugh. Through the sunlight I could see his form. He stood before me. I closed my eyes and then opened them again. He was still there, looking as he always had, although younger and more radiant. I didn't speak, only gazed at him, feeling the joy of his presence.

"There is nothing that I have given to Anoush that I have not also given to you." Spoken without sound, these words entered my mind. We were conversing in an interior space.

"But am I worthy, Baba?" I asked silently, looking up at him, "Am I worthy of your love and care for me? I have so wanted to achieve what you set out for me, but I fear I have failed you."

He smiled. "It is only such thoughts that keep you away. You must rid yourself of this doubt, which you have long carried with you. Let it go. You are as capable as anyone, my child. You would not have been born to me were it not so. It is not visions that matter, but rather the depth of your love, and that you have in abundance, my child."

"Baba . . ." I began to speak out loud. But as I spoke his name, his form began to fade into the sunlight and I saw him no longer.

The vision of Baba stayed with me for all the years that were left to me. I never spoke of it to anyone. It was too precious a memory. Baba had come to erase my self-doubt, to help me see that I was as capable as anyone of reaching the highest spiritual states if that was my deepest desire. Finally, the feeling that had haunted me since childhood of being inadequate as a woman seeker was erased.

It was time for me to move on. The world of beauty was calling me, and so my life as a simple Sufi village woman came to an end.

Chapter 19

The memories of my Baba touched me deeply. I was very close to my father in this life, but I also knew that I idealized this relationship to some extent. Since childhood I had held my father in high esteem, more than my siblings had, and I often failed to acknowledge his human foibles and failings. Perhaps it was the memory of this other more perfect relationship that inspired me to seek its duplication in my current life. For many years I sought to have spiritual conversations with my father and was continually surprised by his agnostic worldview. When I began meditating and cultivating an interior life, he wanted to learn what I was up to and so read *The Autobiography of a Yogi*. To my dismay he dismissed it, and that ended our spiritual exchanges.

My tenderness and love for my father continued and ironically he played a key role in bringing me to my life's work in the interfaith world, but I learned that I would not gain from him the kind of spiritual knowledge I was seeking. For years I continued to hope that our relationship would take a more spiritual turn, but it remained centered on our shared love of beauty and on his desire to help me find a way to contribute to the betterment of society. Perhaps it was the memory of my other father, the Sufi, which initially led me to hope for a deeper spiritual exchange. Such memories, even when unconscious or unacknowledged, color the relationships of our current life.

From my life in India and most likely even earlier, in my subconscious mind I carried the feeling of being inadequate as a woman seeker. It was my Sufi father who helped me to counter that undercurrent. As the Rani Gita, I had been hampered by these thoughts, and they had to be worked out in the life of Minoo. Such sentiments can linger in the subconscious for a long, long time, carried over from one birth to the next, hindering the progress of the soul. Most women hold imprints of this feeling of inadequacy, stamped on their mind by society, sometimes in the subtlest way. In my life as Dena, I have always felt fortunate not to be burdened with this misperception. After my Sufi life, in my onward journey as Thema, Elisabeth, and Sonya, those feelings had not been present. To the contrary, I had felt a pride in being a woman and a commitment to advancing the status of women. Now I realized that I had been set free by my Baba. That was one of the purposes of my life in Persia.

I also hold dear the memory of how joyful a simple life can be, without the material luxuries to which we become addicted. It is true that Minoo could not shake her dormant desire for things of beauty, but from her Sufi father she learned that true beauty resides in the soul. This is a lesson that needed repeating, as you will see in a later chapter.

In the course of my work at the Global Peace Initiative of Women, I have met many extraordinary religious and spiritual teachers, both women and men. Some have tried to make me their disciple, but I have been clear in my commitment to my own guru, Yogananda. I have seen many people flirt with different spiritual teachers and paths. In our time it is not uncommon to follow multiple paths, but I have known since a young age that my course was set and all I had to do was follow it to the best of my ability. However, my closeness with a few of the spiritual teachers I have met in this life has given me some comfort, making up for the physical absence of my own guru. I have always envied those who were able to spend years by their master's side. Even though my spiritual understanding matured and I understood the benefit of learning early in life that the true guru is inside, not outside, still the longing for physical contact was there.

Remembering my days by my Baba's side helped ease this longing. I, too, have known what it is like to live in the presence of a master, to hear wisdom expressed in the most natural of settings, and to know divinity through the simplest acts of daily life. When you can see your experiences over many lives, you realize that at different times you have experienced it all. Each life offers a different teaching, and the sooner you accept your current situation and see what the hidden lessons are for this particular life, the quicker you will advance. Who receives everything in one life—wealth, a happy family, health, peace, and spiritual attainment? These gifts are normally spread out over the course of time, so each life brings the fulfillment of a different desire. How can we then be jealous of another person's gifts, when we realize that we have experienced the same?

Even before beginning my work at GPIW, I had a love for many of the religious traditions. As a graduate student at Columbia University after my divorce, in addition to my study of the Vedic tradition, I studied the mystics of many of the great religious traditions. I eagerly read the Hasidic masters and learned that their teachings were no different from what I had learned from my own Master. I read the lives of many Christian mystics and saw that their teachings were the same as well. I learned through my Master to see the oneness in the teachings of Christ and Krishna. I became close to many great Buddhist teachers in my interfaith work and began to see that the Ultimate Reality in the Buddhist and Vedic traditions was one and the same, only expressed differently. Islam was the last to reveal itself. As my memories of my Sufi life stirred, I saw that the teachings of this tradition were also the same. There was only one truth, albeit many languages and metaphors to express this Reality, according to different times and cultures. If we strip away the cultural imprints, that One Reality shines forth as the ultimate truth underpinning the entire manifest and unmanifest worlds.

After several years of exploring the shared views of the Sufi and yogic traditions, we also began to explore the commonality between Hinduism and Buddhism. The Hindus or yogis talk about the *atman*, the Self, one's true nature, as being a manifest expression of the unmanifest *Brahman*, the ever-existing primordial consciousness out of which all emerges. The Buddhists talk about non-atman, non-Self, expressing the view that there is no permanence, no constant in a universe that is always in flux. According to this view, the atman has no ultimate reality. As I grew close to Buddhist teachers, an internal yogic-Buddhist dialogue began. How could we reconcile these two views? Where they really the same, only seen from different perspectives? I had to explore this further, so we organized a dialogue in Japan with support from a lay Buddhist organization on the theme of Self and Non-Self, Permanence and Impermanence.

I had long known that Japan held a special place in my spiritual journey, but for many years I didn't understand what it was. On my thirtieth birthday, I bought an antique kimono; one day I looked into the mirror and saw the face of a Japanese woman staring back at me. That was my first inkling of a Japanese life. About fifteen years later I took my first trip to Japan with my father when we began working with the spiritual organization that had founded a museum. As soon as I came to know this spiritual organization, which had Shinto roots, something stirred in me. I had not encountered thus far a spiritual group that saw beauty and art as a spiritual pursuit and a spiritual goal. According to their philosophy, divine light radiates through a great work of art, uplifting us momentarily into a heavenly realm where we can taste a higher state of consciousness. This resonated with my own belief and experience, and so Japan began to represent for me the world of beauty and harmony. The more I got to know Japanese culture, the more I saw this harmony manifested in so many aspects of their way of life—how the food is prepared and displayed, the tea is served, and flowers arranged. Every act is a microcosmic representation of a universal harmony and balance. That is the beauty and wisdom of old Japan, the remnants of which still remain. I had vague recollections of a past life in Japan. When my father and I had gone to the Sanjusangendo Temple, I had seen images of a betrayal and a fire, but I had pulled myself back to the present and had never pressed to uncover any more.

GPIW was now working extensively with a number of Japanese organizations, some of which were funding our work. I was traveling to Japan as often as two and three times a year. I felt that Japan, in addition to India, was one of my spiritual homes, so I greatly appreciated all the opportunities to travel there for some project. First the visits were for the Shinto-based spiritual organization and then for the Buddhist community. More than a decade passed and still no more information about my Japanese past had been revealed to me. By now I had seen a number of other lives, but nothing from Japan, only vague images of fire and flight, and I made no serious effort to penetrate further. In fact, I never called forth the visions and memories. I merely accepted what came and integrated the realizations into my life's work.

Now I was in Japan again in a beautiful retreat spot, wrestling to reconcile concepts of Self and Non-Self. The dialogue was taking place in a restored 19th century villa in Kyoto, with beautiful paintings on the shojis and the evocative smell of tatami mats, and an exquisite garden with a lake, surrounded by overarching trees and moss-covered walkways. It was entry into old-world Japan, one that I greatly loved. During the course of the dialogue I felt myself being beckoned by the past. I knew there was hidden in my subconscious mind a story to remember, a story of great importance for my onward journey, but the images would not emerge. No scenes unfolded before my inner eye.

Two years later, I was in New York when I received a call from an official of a Japanese peace foundation informing me that they were granting me an interfaith peace prize for the work of the Global Peace Initiative of Women, with a significant sum of money attached to the prize. It came completely out of the blue and was truly a great honor. GPIW had never sought recognition for its work, as many of the other interfaith organizations had, but rather we had remained always focused on what we needed to do to achieve gender and East-West balance. As our work evolved we also began to realize that spiritual communities had a responsibility, given the multiple crises facing the Earth community, to work together for a transformation in consciousness. Only such a shift enables us to perceive our human unity and our unity with the natural world, and this realization is then the foundation for a radical change in behavior.

As we began to work more for this spiritual transformation, we began to see a new energy emerging. We formed the Contemplative Alliance, which we hoped to build as a movement that would bring together those committed to some form of meditation or contemplative practice. This Alliance is based on the belief that a collective inner spiritual shift is a prerequisite for any significant outward change in society. It is this inner spiritual work—through prayer, *japa* (reciting the name of the Divine), *mantra* (sacred syllables or words), *pranayama* (breathing practices), etc.—that brings inner transformation, understanding, and a broader worldview. As we change, one by one, we will see a global response. To address the world problems of violence, environmental degradation, climate change, economic and gender inequality, etc. we must change our consciousness, our understanding of the nature and purpose of life. We must shift from a focus on outer consumption to the pursuit of inner contentment. In other words, outer development must be balanced by inner development.

For so many years, we at GPIW had been trying to listen for spiritual direction. What should we do that would be most effective? To which part of the world should we travel next with our growing spiritual entourage? We had become, in fact, like a troupe of wandering spiritual minstrels responding to calls from different points of crises. The last thing on my mind was that our work would ever be recognized for an award, and so I was stunned by the news, but also thrilled.

I went to Japan to receive the prize and to give a speech. When selecting me for this award, the foundation may have thought they were simply supporting the work of women in the interfaith world, but GPIW had grown into much more than this, as my speech would reveal. In addition to feeling greatly honored and grateful, I was deeply moved because the prize came from Japan. As I stood there in Tokyo, addressing the audience, I wondered who it was receiving the prize. Was it Dena or was it someone else who truly deserved this honor?

As I made my way from function to function, speaking with the media, expressing my gratitude for the award, finally the memories of old Japan began to emerge. It was there that my love for beauty and the arts found its fullest expression. It was there that I had my encounter with the female form of the divine. It was there that my Shinto and Buddhist paths converged.

PART VI

16ᵀᴴ CENTURY JAPAN

The soul is unbreakable and incombustible;
it can neither be dampened nor dried.
It is everlasting, in all places, unalterable,
immutable, and primordial.
The soul is spoken of as invisible, inconceivable,
and unchangeable.
Knowing this, you should not grieve for the body.

—Bhagavad Gita 2:24-
25

Though the flame be put out, the wick remains.

—Japanese Proverb

Chapter 20

It was a time of strife when I was born in Japan, but when I came of age there was a brief period of peace between the rival ruling families. My father married me off at a young age to a man from the opposing clan in the hope that this would strengthen the ties between our two families, and for a while it did. My husband had great charm and a most attractive appearance, so initially I was pleased by the arrangement. But his charm turned out to be his fatal flaw and eventually led to the downfall of both our clans. His fine looks were not matched by an inner nobility. To the contrary, his character was weak and lacking in integrity, and soon this began to eat away at my peace and happiness.

Declines are also said to be times of ascent, and the tragic course of my marriage turned me to the spiritual life by a most unexpected twist of fate. The first hint of awakening emerged several years after my marriage when I began to realize my husband's love for women and for spending.

As my father lay dying, he called me to him. "You are not happy in this marriage, Matsu. I see it every time I look into your eyes," he said quietly as we sat alone. "What has happened, my little flower? It is as if something in you has died." He was frail and I did not want to add to the sorrow of the moment, so I didn't answer. I tried my best to put on a cheerful face every time I met my father, but his discerning eye caught the sorrow hidden deep in my heart. "I am sorry, my little flower, that I imposed this marriage on you," he sighed. "I didn't mean to sacrifice your happiness even for the sake of furthering peace." I looked away, not wanting him to see the struggle that my eyes would reveal.

"I am happy to be a bridge between the two clans," I responded. "It is my duty."

He was thoughtful for a few minutes, and then continued. "You must find your happiness elsewhere, and it can be done. There are ways that you can still work to build peace, Matsu. You have a special gift, an unusual sense of beauty and a most discerning eye. Ever since you were a child you were drawn to beautiful objects. We must put this gift to use. You must take charge of organizing a festival of the arts each spring, during *sakura* season, bringing together artists from all the clans. This will help secure the peace. The arts can help our people move beyond their clan loyalty, and no one has greater sensitivity than you, my little flower. Promise me you will take on this responsibility."

I looked at him questioningly. He alone knew my love for beauty, the care I took of every aspect of my life and household. This went unnoticed by my husband, but my father, with his observant eye, perceived this quality. Although the idea was appealing, what power had I? How could I take on such a grand endeavor?

"I must see to this before I leave this world," he mused. "I will write to the Prince, and make this last request. He cannot refuse me."

"You mustn't," I interjected hastily, trying to restrain him from rising from his bed. "You are weak. Besides I don't want to bother the Prince with my personal matters. Father, you should not be concerned about me. It is I who must look after you now."

"No, Matsu. This is something I must do. I fear for the future if we don't find some way to strengthen the ties. I thought your marriage would serve this purpose, but I had no way of knowing that Okimoto-san would be so profligate in his ways." He called for writing implements and proceeded to write to the Prince. He handed me the note but I did not reach to take it. I was as if frozen until he spoke to me in a stern voice, as stern as he could in his weakened condition. "It's not just for your happiness that I am making this request of the Prince, but also for the good of our clan. You must carry this note to him. Promise me this."

I looked up into my father's face and my eyes became watery. Still I did not reach for the letter. His concern touched me deeply: that he should have my welfare on his mind in his last days.

"Matsu, will you not obey my request?" He gazed at me with both love and insistence. It was this determination that was the hallmark of his character, an unrelenting will that I found in few others. How often I was to remember this quality in the years to come. Unwillingly, I took the note. His face broke into a faint smile. "Now I can rest," he said. "I can rest, knowing that you will continue my efforts for peace."

This was my last conversation with my father. He passed away a few days later. I held onto the note for several weeks before I finally summoned the courage to take it to the household of the Prince. The Prince received me. I bowed low before him before passing on to him the note from my father. "This was his last request," I said shyly. "He was insistent that I bring it to you, otherwise I would not have disturbed you with this matter."

"I was very sorry to hear about his death. It is a great loss for all of us. I have always admired your father and his efforts to end the fighting between clans." He opened the note and read it without any expression on his face. I could not see any reaction. Then he put it down and gazed ahead thoughtfully, as if absorbed in some inner reflection. The minutes passed; when he didn't respond, I was sure that I had made a mistake in coming there. Finally he looked at me kindly and said, "I cannot refuse any request from your father, especially a dying request. He has asked that you organize an annual arts festival to bring the clans together. There is growing tension again. I don't know if this will be useful, but I have no objection. You are the perfect one for this, Matsu-san, since you have relationships through your marriage, so you will have my full support." Then after a few minutes of silence, he added, "I will make an official decree so there will be no opposition to you. And whatever is needed from our side, finances or other assistance, you shall have. It is the least I can do for your father, who gave so much for the sake of peace."

My heart burst open at his words. "I will do my best to fulfill my father's wishes and his expectations of me," I replied, trying to control my enthusiasm. "On my father's behalf I am most grateful to you. He would be so very pleased."

He nodded. "I wish you well, Matsu-san. If you have even a portion of your father's wisdom and determination, you will succeed."

Bowing low, I took my leave.

My father in his dying days had given me new life. I didn't realize then quite what he had done for me. It was to be discovered in the years ahead as the arts festival became a beloved event for so many people and was a vehicle for keeping the peace for a number of years. As I began to engage in the process of organizing the first arts festival, my attention turned from sorrow over my father's death and my husband's infidelities to joy in meeting all the artists of our region from all the clans. We included the fields of painting, poetry, calligraphy, pottery, and textiles—all the things that I loved most. There could be no greater parting gift from my father. In his wisdom, he knew that this would bring a blossoming within my soul, and so it did.

The arts festivals were well received and attended. It was a time of great flourishing of the arts in our region and this effort to bring all the artists together was much appreciated. I gained a deeper understanding of each of the arts as I met personally with some of the best artists and artisans of our day. It was a great education for me; I learned to discern the finest quality in painting, textiles, pottery, and poetry. I gained a particular love for landscape painting and acquired many of the finest scrolls over the years. I also developed a keen love for textiles and received gifts of the finest kimonos, among so many other objects.

Each year the festival grew. It kept me fully engaged, so much so that I paid little attention to the comings and goings of my husband. Many years passed and my life became one dedicated to beauty, to elevating society through the appreciation of the arts. I had discovered new purpose. During those years, I found myself living in an extraordinary world, a near celestial realm into which none of the ills of the mundane world could enter. I was quite happy, and as time passed, my interactions with my husband grew fewer and fewer. I had three children from the early years of our marriage and they were the only concern that we shared. I was present for official functions when society demanded, and so I imagined that people saw us as the happy couple that he presented us to be. I thought this would continue until our old age, but it was not to be. It was inevitable that my bubble would one day burst.

We were nearing the end of winter when I received a visit from my sister. She seemed agitated, but my mind was elsewhere as the annual festival was only weeks away. We spoke of trivial matters over tea but after a while she fell silent. I looked away, instinctively feeling there was some unpleasant matter she wanted to discuss, most likely to do with my husband. She had no liking for him. On occasion she would report to me about an affair of his, and I would dismiss it as mere gossip, trying my best to hide the pain that still lurked in my heart but which emerged now and then when my sister brought such talk to my attention. Over time, I had became accustomed to hearing such things and no longer even brought these rumors to my husband's attention. I dreaded the angry words of denial that would flow from him. As long as I denied the rumors,

I could maintain my honor and public face. His free spending ways were also troublesome, but he managed to make excuses for his extensive journeys and exorbitant habits.

"Do you not see what is going on?" my sister asked me in a quiet but urgent tone. "His affairs were bad enough, but now this public disgrace, it is not to be tolerated, Matsu. You must put an end to it."

I didn't respond.

"Matsu, can you not see the danger . . ."

She must have noticed the confused look that crossed my face because her voice became calmer. "Don't tell me that you don't know."

"I am very busy with the festival. It is only weeks away," I replied, turning my eyes downward. My heart was racing.

"The festival! He is about to ruin it all for you! You have become blind because of that festival and you don't see what is happening before your very eyes."

I didn't know what to say. I didn't know what he could have done that would be worse than what he had been doing all of these years.

"Everyone is speaking of it, Matsu." She said, again lowering her voice.

"Speaking of what?" I asked fearfully, turning my eyes to meet hers. "I really don't know what you are referring to. Another affair?" My eyes must have shown my ignorance because she took my hand caringly and shook her head in disbelief.

"You really don't know, do you?"

I shook my head.

"Matsu, how naive you are. I hate to be the one to have to tell you that your husband is having an affair with the consort of the Prince, and he seems to be flaunting it. At least he could be discrete. Everyone fears the day when the Prince will discover this," she said with obvious disgust.

"It can't be true," I replied in a trembling voice, withdrawing my hand from hers. "He would not be so foolish." My mind ran over the events of the last few months. Yes, the consort of the Prince was making regular visits to our home, but my husband had said it was official business. She was carrying messages from the Prince. Naively I believed him, but would he be so foolish as to challenge the Prince in this way?

"You must speak to him," she insisted. "You must make him end this affair immediately. His reckless behavior will cause much suffering for all of us, and especially for you and the children."

"My words carry no weight with him," I replied in a quivering voice, still in a state of disbelief.

"You must try. Otherwise all of your efforts through the arts festival will be lost. Everything father worked for . . . it will all be lost." Then she added more gently. "I fear for you, Matsu, and the children. You are the only one who may be able to get through to him."

I nodded as if it were all a dream. Everything I had dedicated my life to these last ten years was now threatened. I could not stand by idly and let it all be destroyed.

Several days passed before I gathered the courage to approach my husband. He had been away a good deal these last few months; he had just returned from a journey and was in high spirits. I waited until the right moment when we were alone. I began by discussing some matters relating to the children. He nodded absentmindedly. This was routine for us. He would simply nod when I informed him of the children's doings, without asking any questions or making comments, as if it were no concern of his. I was used to this. Then I mentioned there was something important I needed to discuss with him.

"I have never interfered in your personal matters," I began. "Although there has always been much talk, I have ignored it." He shifted uncomfortably. "You know what these art festivals have meant to me. They have allowed me to have a life outside of my duties to you."

"Yes, yes," he said hastily. "They have been very good for you. I have always supported you in this."

"But now, all of my efforts are threatened." My tone turned grave.

His expression changed. "What do you mean?"

"My sister was here. She said everyone is talking about your affair with the consort of the Prince." I spoke slowly in an effort to hide the shaking in my voice, but I could not prevent a trembling from overtaking me.

"Nonsense," he laughed it off in an unconvincing manner. "Mariko loves to spread gossip." I was watching him carefully. His face turned pale when I mentioned the consort of the prince, and his voice was now clearly agitated. I had learned to read my husband's body language, which often revealed the falsity of his words.

"This is complete recklessness," I cried angrily. My eyes were glaring. "Don't you realize what you are doing? You can have any woman, why must you carry on with her? I am pleading with you not to put us all in danger."

"Matsu, I give you my word, there is no truth to this rumor." He regained his composure and now spoke to me sternly. "It is your duty to refute such gossip. Mariko has always been jealous of you. She is trying to turn you against me. Why do you fall for it? How crude of her. I expect you to go to her and refute this baseless talk. This year, I will participate in the arts festival and we will preside over it together. I have been absent for too long. Yes, we need to be seen together so everyone will know there is no truth to this talk!"

Summoning my courage, I replied, "This time, I don't believe you. Why can you not end this before word gets to the Prince? There is no telling what this will mean, but it certainly will end what little peace is left."

"I have told you the rumors are untrue. My word should be enough for you." He got up abruptly and left the room.

I sank to the floor in tears, knowing in my heart that he had betrayed not only me but also the truce among the clans that my father and I had worked so hard to maintain. I didn't know what more I could do. A few weeks later, days before the arts festival was to begin, I received a notice from the Prince cancelling the festival. Notices of the cancellation were being posted everywhere. I immediately went to his residence, but he would not receive me.

"The Prince has asked me to convey to you his deep regrets," the attendant told me. "He knows how hard you have worked for the festival, and he has great respect for your efforts, but it cannot proceed."

I understood the meaning of these words. I could not return home. I didn't know where to go. I sent my attendant on ahead of me, and once alone, my feet led me down to a quiet spot by the river. Signs for the festival had been posted on every street and now they were all being taken down. I could not bear to see this. I stood on one of the bridges overlooking the river, staring into the rushing water. So much work had gone into the festival and the artisans all had such confidence in me. What would they think now? All the world would know of my husband's betrayal. Who could I unburden my heart to, where could I find any comfort? My honor lay shattered before me.

All seemed lost. What would my life be without the arts festival? I had no marriage to speak of and now I was losing what was most dear to me, and I could do nothing. Tears began to trickle from my eyes. For a moment, I thought perhaps the best thing would be to end it all. Even the image of my children did not prevent this thought from entering into my mind. My honor was gone, and their honor as well. I could not show my face to the world again.

As I was thinking thus I felt a presence by my side, but I didn't look up. I kept my eyes fixed on the water. Then I heard a voice speaking gently, "The sakura will come into bloom in a few days. It is the most beautiful season. Can there be sadness at such a time?"

I wiped my tears and looked up to find a Buddhist monk standing beside me, watching me thoughtfully.

"Ah," he continued. "This sakura season is different. We won't have the arts festival," he said softly. "I too am very sorry for that, but we mustn't let this disturb our peace of mind." His voice was melodic, calming, and I could not help but be affected by the gentle tones in which he spoke.

"It is a shame, a great shame," I said in barely more than a whisper.

"I know," he said. "I have attended every one. I have watched you each year as you have called the poets forward. What you have accomplished is noble. I have admired you for it. The festivals were the only time when everyone forgot their station in life, forgot the differences that define us, when all of society could come together in celebration of beauty. It was a wonderful thing that you accomplished, Matsu-hime. But you mustn't mourn its loss. The only constant in life is change. When something is taken, let it go, as the trees let go of their blossoms when the breezes lift them away. Something new will come."

I was struck that he knew my name and now looked at him curiously. He appeared quite some years older than me and had a rather ordinary appearance; his eyes were compelling, soft yet firm, smiling yet serious in their depth. I didn't remember ever seeing him before.

"Have we met?" I asked him in a steadier voice. "I don't remember seeing you at the festivals."

He chuckled. "I have been to every one and even read some of my poetry. You never noticed me because I didn't wish to be seen. But now things have changed. You have need of my assistance."

I sighed. "The festival has been cancelled this year and I don't know about the future. I don't know what will happen but I can't imagine my life without the arts festival." I looked off into the wandering water and thought once more of merging with it, to release my life into the life of the river.

"It's not the festival itself that gave you so much joy, but the beauty you found through the arts. That beauty is still there, all around you. Nobody can take that away. But you must know there is a greater beauty. That which we love in painting, in poetry, is only a reflection of a far greater beauty, which cannot be seen with the visible eye, but it can be known. That is the real goal to seek."

There was something so calming in the cadence of his voice, and for a moment I forgot my pain. I look at him perplexed. Was this a chance meeting or was there a deeper purpose? "I fear for the future," I said with sadness and anxiety. "The festival was a way of putting aside anger and hatred."

"Yes, I also am concerned. For a few days we were able to put aside our differences and rivalries. It didn't matter which clan an artist belonged to; after all, no one can own beauty. It belongs equally to all."

"Everyone will inquire about the cause of the cancellation, won't they?" I asked, the pain returning to my voice.

"Matsu-hime, you have done no wrong."

"But my husband . . ." my voice began to crack. "It will be known. Any honor left to my family will be destroyed."

"Honor? Your honor is untouched. Your husband's deeds have no true bearing on you. They reflect his character, not yours."

"I wonder how much is known about my husband's doings," I sighed, half to myself, and half out loud. He didn't respond but looked at me with compassion. Words were not needed. The expression on his face suggested he was aware of my husband's misdeeds. I sighed again. If this Buddhist monk knew, then how many others would also know the truth? "What will happen now, I don't know," I murmured.

"Fighting could break out any time," he said quietly. His smile disappeared and was replaced by a solemn expression. "There may be difficult times ahead. You stand between two powerful clans, born into one, married into another. You may need to take refuge, and it would be an honor for me to assist you." I was silent, not understanding his meaning, but there was something about him that made me take him seriously. I looked into his face and found a sincerity that made me instinctively trust him. "Consider my words, if not for yourself than for your children's safety." I was startled at the mention of my children. How did he know so much about me? "I urge you to come to the monastery and see whether it is a place where you could take refuge for a time," he said simply.

"Sensei, I don't know how to respond. I am Shinto."

"As am I."

"You?" I looked at his dress. It was that of a Buddhist monk.

"I was born into a Shinto family, but my parents died when I was young. We were very poor and a Buddhist monk took me in. He taught me all that I know. That is why I am who I am today." I was still perplexed by his interest in me. "I am not asking you to become Buddhist," he continued with a knowing smile. "I am only concerned for your safety and that of your children." There was a pained look on his face as he spoke these words. "There is the danger of war now. Your husband has crossed all boundaries, and I'm afraid there is no return."

At the mention of my husband, tears again flooded my eyes. Despite the monk's kind words, I felt the pain of being bereft of my family honor. Surely this would not end well for my husband, for me, or the children. They would forever be known as the children of the man who betrayed the Prince and broke the peace.

"There is not much time. Things may move quickly now. Please give serious thought to my invitation. You can send for me at any time, day or night. He handed me a piece of paper with his name and the name of the monastery written on it. I stared at the paper in disbelief.

"But Sensei . . ."

"Matsu-hime, I will await your arrival." With those words, he bowed low and disappeared among the rush of people crossing the bridge in the coolness of the early spring air.

I walked the streets in a daze. Could it be that this world I knew and loved, the world of beauty that I had created for myself, was crashing down around me? How did the monk know what was about to unfold, and was I foolish to trust him? When I reached home, I shut myself away and mulled over the monk's words. My mind rebelled but my heart conceded. There was nobody else to guide me, but despite his kindness and the wisdom of his words, I couldn't see clearly what my course of action should be. My mind was clouded and confused, and I had no one to whom I could turn.

Chapter 21

The next morning, I rose early and took one of my attendants along to the Shinto shrine that our family frequented. The shrine was tucked away in a forest outside the city. My father had often taken me there as a child, but I hardly visited it any more. Beauty had taken the place of the gods for me, but now I needed them. I needed Her, the Goddess of the Sun, the ancestor of our people, to show me the way.

The path to the shrine was lined with tall trees on either side. Although my heart was heavy, I stopped to gaze at them, wondering why I had stayed away for so long. The trees were beautiful, ancient and stately, and stood erect with a knowing air, witness to all that had passed over the centuries. We humans are born and die, but the trees remain. I drew close to one of the large elder pines and touched its bark, running my fingers along its skin, and then rested my cheek against it, releasing all my anguish as if the tree could take it from me and provide some solace.

Over these many years I had become such an admirer of man's artistic achievements that I had drifted away from the beauty of the natural world, the beauty of the majestic trunks as they reached for the sky, the beauty in the sound of streams that curved over rocks and bramble. My mind had sought this beauty in paintings and in the words of poets, but those were only imitations. Even the most refined artistic achievements were only an imitation of what the gods had created for us, their children, to enjoy. Now, in my moment of sorrow, the healing power of the natural world hit me with great force and provided comfort as no human or art form could have done.

When I recovered my composure, I felt strengthened by the presence of the nature spirits. It was a lovely spot, this Shinto shrine. It was here in this forest of old that our Shinto gods dwelled. I approached the shrine and performed the appropriate ritual, praying with all my strength to

Amaterasu, the Sun Goddess, that she would somehow shelter me. I stood for quite some time before the shrine, pleading with her to hide me as she had once hidden herself. When the gods were giving birth to all that is, Goddess Amaterasu hid herself in a cave and darkness fell over the earth. The gods were in a quandary as to how to bring her back into the world, so they convened nearby, knowing there could be no life without the sun's light. It seemed to me now that darkness was once more enveloping the earth, and I wanted to hide somewhere as she had, but my mind was too confused and could think of nowhere to go, nowhere to hide myself. Only death will receive me, I thought, only death.

As I finished my prayers, I heard his voice. "There is not much time. Not much time. Not much time. I will await your arrival." The words of the monk rang again and again in my mind. I tried to shut them out, but they wouldn't depart. Was it days or months? I didn't know. And why did the monk care so much for my safety? I had no enemies. Who would want to harm my children and me? The questions flooded me all morning. I spent a few hours walking among the trees, wandering about, reluctant to return home, hoping for some clarity, but even Goddess Amaterasu deserted me that day. She provided no clear answers as to what I should do. I had nobody but the monk. He was the only one who had come to my aid.

When I returned home, I sent a note to my sister, seeking her assistance, but when my attendant came back from my sister's home, she returned with no reply. "Was Mariko-san home?" I asked surprised that she had sent no response to my request. "Did she receive the note?" My attendant nodded. "And she sent no reply?" She shook her head. Although my marriage had created some distance between us, I did not think her capable of deserting me. I had to acknowledge sadly that she was distancing herself from me.

That afternoon I learned my husband had departed for a journey, in a hurry, with no explanation of where he was going or any indication of when he would return. That seemed an ill omen. Perhaps he was preparing for the worst, but surely he would not abandon me and the children to face dishonor alone. I did not think him capable of that, but for so long I had refused to see the scope of his weaknesses. I held on to the belief that somehow, someday, he would correct himself.

I spent the next few days mulling over the monk's words. His image stood between death and me. It was as if his arms were around me, preventing me from doing what the loss of my honor bid me to do. The more I thought over the incident on the bridge, the more I realized there was a deeper purpose to the meeting. It could not be an accidental occurrence. Something more was intended, so I decided to visit the monastery and learn more about the monk. There was something about him that drew me, but it was not an ordinary attraction. Nobility, not of birth but of character, shone in his face and his voice.

Over the next few days I walked through the rooms of my home as if saying goodbye to all of the beautiful objects I had collected over the years, standing before each painting and scroll, each piece of pottery, before each and every one of the beautiful objects that I had so lovingly assembled. I went repeatedly to my dressing table and picked up my beautiful jeweled combs and ornaments for my hair. How I had loved to wear them. And my kimonos . . . the pride I had taken in them. Each day during the festival I made sure to look my best, wearing the new kimonos gifted to me by the best weavers. I took out the ones that long ago my mother had given me for my wedding. I never wore them anymore but I treasured them.

One evening as I was sorting through these kimonos from my mother, I decided to put one on. I rang for my attendant. "Help me dress," I said to her, motioning to an elaborate kimono my mother had handed down to me from her mother.

"This one?" she asked in surprise. I nodded. "My lady, it is so beautiful, but I have not seen you wear it in so many, many years. What is the occasion now?" It was a kimono only worn on the most formal occasion.

I smiled. "No occasion, I just want to remember my mother this day." She had died soon after my marriage and was spared the grief of knowing about my unhappy union. Once, only once, I saw her wear this, and I told her she looked like a celestial being. My attendant helped me put on the many layers and then drew up my hair with my most precious hair ornaments. When we were done, I asked her to bring in the children. "I want them to see me dressed like this," I said.

My two sons and my daughter were brought in. "How beautiful you are," exclaimed my daughter, the youngest of the children. My sons, who were just coming into manhood, concurred, gazing at me proudly.

"I do feel like a heavenly being," I sighed with a mix of joy and sadness. "But I think the days of wearing these kimonos are now in the past for me."

The children stayed with me for some time, and then suddenly I felt very weary. I asked the attendant to take them to bed, saying that I would undress on my own. I was left alone, and slowly took off my intricate dress and ornaments. The sadness I had felt these last few days was departing, leaving numbness in its place.

My attendant returned. Bowing low, she said there was someone to see me. I looked up startled, wondering who would come at this late hour.

"Is it my sister?" I asked in a hopeful voice.

She shook her head. "A Buddhist nun," she replied. "She said it was urgent that she see you now."

I nodded, thinking to myself how strange that she would come at this hour. I knew immediately that she must have come from the Sensei, and I assumed that since he seemed to know so much about me, he must also know that I had made up my mind. I would take up his offer of going to the monastery at least for a short while, until I could see more clearly what the future held.

When the nun entered, I realized that something was amiss. "The Master has sent me to bring you," she said with a great sense of urgency.

"Now, at this hour?" I asked in surprise. "I have decided to come for a visit but I will need a few days to prepare, to gather my belongings."

She shook her head. "He said it must be this very night and that you were not to take anything. There is no time." Bowing low again she added, "Lady, he has said that you must trust him and come with me, the children as well."

"How can that be?" I asked. "I need some time. Tomorrow perhaps. You can spend the night here."

She shook her head. "What is to be done must be done under the cover of night and nobody must know. He has insisted on this. Three monks are in the garden, just outside, waiting to carry the children with us."

"But my belongings, how will I gather them so quickly. I have many things."

"Take nothing, my lady. There is no need."

"Surely, I must make arrangements for the household..."

She bowed low and then in a pleading voice said, "Sensei is

sometimes hard to understand, but I have learned to trust him, as you will also learn. If he has said it must be so, there is a reason. I plead with you to come as he has requested. He has instructed us not to leave without you and the children."

"Wait here," I requested. "I will check on the children." I moved through the rooms as if in a dream until I came to where the children were sleeping. I was not by any means mentally prepared to leave my beautiful home and all my treasured objects. As I entered the room, I smelled smoke. Opening the shoji that led to the room next to where my children slept, I was met by leaping flames engulfing the room. I stood for a moment paralyzed and then ran back to the children. Waking my sons and lifting my daughter into my arms, I ran back with them to my room where the nun was waiting.

"There is a fire! Let us go quickly," I cried. She followed me out into the garden, but then I paused. "I must alert the others," I murmured. The nun was quick to respond.

"I will go back. You continue on with the monks." She cautioned, "You must hurry now before anyone sees you."

"My attendant, she will not leave without me. She will look for me," I whispered hoarsely. My heart was racing and I could barely speak.

"Hurry, before it is too late. I will find her." She returned to the villa while the monks took the children from me and helped us over the garden enclosure into the neighboring forest. It all happened so fast that I was barely aware of what was transpiring.

I did not look back to see the flames consuming my home and all the beautiful things that I held so dear.

Horses were waiting by the edge of the forest to carry us to the monastery, which we reached shortly before the first hint of dawn. Sensei was at the gate to receive us. A look of great relief crossed his face when he saw us. Throughout our flight I had not the clarity of mind to consider the cause or the implications of the fire. My only thought was that we had narrowly escaped death, and that we owed our life to Sensei. I didn't know whether it was purely coincidental that he had sent the nun that night or whether he had some foreknowledge of what was about to unfold.

Without a word he led us to a room where the children and I could rest. I turned to thank him but no words would come from my mouth. I was in a state of shock and could not speak. My only thought was that miraculously the children and I were safe. I slept through most of the next day. When I awoke I was alone in the room. For a few moments I didn't remember where I was and wondered if the whole experience had been a dream. But when I fully came to and saw the simple nature of the room, I realized this was no dream. I had come to the monastery. The children were gone and I became fearful. Perhaps something had happened to them. I walked outside and saw that the sun was well past its peak. I suddenly felt hungry. I retreated to the room and was debating whether to wait or go in search of somebody, when the door slide open and a nun entered with a tray of food.

"Where are the children?" I asked anxiously.

"They have eaten and are with Sensei," she said. "You have slept a long time and must have some food now. They will come soon."

I took the food and thanked her. When I was done, I slid open the shoji door and walked into the garden. I sat on a stone and simply stared ahead. My mind was empty. I could think of nothing. I could not even take in the beauty of the garden. I don't know how long I sat thus, but after some time I heard the children and looked up to find them running down the path to me. The nun who had served me food had brought them to find me. I hugged them and then went back to my staring out into space.

"It is time for their evening meal," the nun said quietly. "Will you join them?" I didn't answer. I am not sure I even heard. I simply turned my head and stared out at the emptiness before me.

As darkness was falling, another nun came to lead me back to my room. I don't remember whether the children were there or not. I simply lay down on the mat and drifted into a deep sleep. Several days passed in this way. I was somewhere between waking and sleeping, engulfed only by empty space, the darkness of the void. I had no fear, no emotion. I had detached from my body and was unable to bring myself back to my surroundings. I could not grasp what had happened, where I was, what I was to do. The safest thing for me seemed to be simply to disappear. And so I disappeared for a time, hiding in very still places where nobody could find me, where I could be unknown even to myself. But this could not last forever. One day I awoke to find the shoji door open to the outside air and the sun streaming in. I rose and walked outside. Spring was in its full glory and the sun was streaming down on me.

The garden was beautiful. I smiled to see the artistic placement of the flowers—so many colors, so many shapes. The sakura had long faded, but other trees were flowering. It was as beautiful as my garden at home, but different. Yes, this place had a very different feel. It was quiet, silent except for the birds, of which there were many, flying to and fro, settling on one branch and then another. I watched them for some time and slowly the numbness that had engulfed me since I fled my home departed, leaving in its place a gentle acceptance of my plight. The peace of the garden filled my heart with a welcome calm. I sat there drinking in the silence and then it was as if my mind suddenly awoke. The children! Where were they? How long had I been asleep? Who had cared for them? What had happened to my home? Was it all gone? The Goddess had surely deserted me. The Goddess. I had prayed to her and she had not responded. These thoughts crowded my mind.

"Matsu-hime." I heard his gentle voice behind me. "It is good to see that you have recovered." I turned to find the welcoming face of Sensei. A faint smile crept over my lips at the sight of him, but he must have caught the confusion of my mind. "You have been in a state of shock. It is understandable. We have been waiting for you to return to us, and the children are very eager to see you. We have moved them to another room so that you could rest."

My initial smile turned into a frown. "How is it that I am here? I don't remember. Was it a dream or reality? That night, the fire, did that really happen?" I asked hesitantly.

Seating himself beside me, he replied in a gentle voice, "I am afraid so. It was as real as you and I are here speaking. It seems that the Prince discovered your husband's affair and sought to kill him. He didn't know that your husband had left on a journey. The fire was meant to look like an accident."

"But had the Prince no thought of me and the children?" I exclaimed in disbelief.

"There are no boundaries to jealously and rage. I am sure he wanted to make your husband pay a price for what he did."

"But my husband must now think we are dead. I must get word to him that the children are safe." He didn't respond, but his expression changed. "Despite his recklessness, they are still his children. He must be concerned." My voice was almost defiant. Still he was silent. By the serious look on his face, I sensed that something was wrong. "Has something happened to him?" I asked after a few minutes in a shaking voice.

He nodded. "He has been killed," he said gently, his eyes full of compassion. "When word got to the Prince that he was on a journey, assassins tracked him down and killed him. I received word this morning."

I was silent, struggling to comprehend his words. My husband, dead, how could that be? Whatever had taken place between us somehow didn't matter any more. He was still my husband and the father of my children. I could not hide the sadness and fear that overtook me. "It may be a pretense."

He shook his head. "Word is on the street and I have confirmed it. Everyone is expecting retribution, and then more retribution. There will be war now."

The tears began to flow. My children were now fatherless, without a protector, their lineage stained. Who would care for them? Who would receive them? And to think war would begin again. Nothing could be worse. I struggled to compose myself. "The Goddess Amaterasu. I went to the shrine to pray to her, to seek her help. Even she has deserted me," I whispered. The depth of my grief could not find outward expression.

"Who do you think sent me to you, if not the Goddess?" he asked in the gentlest of voices. "Did she not respond to your prayers? Has she not provided you with a place to hide?" There was such kindness and care in his manner. I looked up at him inquiringly. It was true. I had prayed for Her to show me a way to hide myself, and that is exactly what She had done. "Your children are safe here," he continued. "You are welcome to stay and make this your home. Nobody will know of your presence here."

"What happened to the rest of my household?" I asked, afraid to hear the answer.

"I am afraid we couldn't save all the members of your household. Some of the bodies were very burned and the word is that you were found dead, and that the children somehow escaped."

"My attendant . . ."

"She also died."

"And the nun?"

"I'm afraid she didn't get out. She did her best to retrieve your attendant but it was too late. The whole building collapsed."

"She sacrificed herself for me. Why?" I murmured, realizing the full extent of the tragedy.

"I am sure she felt it her duty and her honor to do so," he replied quietly.

I was overcome by this news and fell silent. After a few minutes I murmured, "My sister. We could take shelter with her."

He shook his head. "Your husband's deeds have placed you in a very precarious situation. It is better not to think of leaving here until we see the end of this. Nobody will know that you and the children are here. You will be hidden. Let the world think you are gone so that you can have new life."

"New life," I repeated quietly. It seemed my life was over, not beginning.

Some days later Sensei came to tell me that an assassin had murdered the Prince's elder son. Now full out war was to be expected. "Matsu-hime, they may look for your sons. Revenge knows no limit. I suggest we shave their heads and give them ordination as monks. They will be safer that way. There are other novices here their age." I nodded my approval. I had no alternative now but to place my life and the lives of my children fully in his hands. "They will receive training here and a good education. It is best for them."

"And my daughter?"

"I have been considering her situation. I have a sister with a family. Her children are not much older than your daughter. She lives not far from here. I suggest she stay with them. You can see her as often as you like. It will be better for her to be with other children."

I could not bear the thought of separating my children, but I had to trust his counsel. There was wisdom in Sensei's words. Far worse than separation would my children's death, and I understood how bitter things would become.

"Until things settle down we must keep you all out of sight. We do not know if the monasteries will be checked." And then he added gently, "It will be better also for you to take the appearance of a nun."

I didn't respond right away but after a few minutes I replied, "Why just the appearance? I will become a nun. There is nothing left for me in this world, so I should begin to seek another."

The shaving of my hair caused me more grief than I imagined it would. Looking at my reflection in the pond that morning, I thought sorrowfully that I was now burying the last bit of beauty I possessed. Sensei came to see me after it was done. I turned my face away in shame.

"Mayu. That will be your new name, your Dharma name, because you are now, even more than before, as lovely as a flower.

Still looking away I replied with a sad sigh, "Like a faded flower. I have devoted my life to beauty and now all beauty has fled, as if it wants no part of me. Why? I don't understand why I have come to this state."

He chuckled and said gently, "Mayu, your Buddha Nature shines forth like a brilliant diamond. It is far more beautiful and captivating than anything you have seen or sought thus far. You have been living in the world of shadows, mistaking those shadows for reality, mistaking darkness for light. The beauty that you seek is yet to be revealed to you." I turned to face him, gazing into his eyes. I had never before seen eyes that were so steady and unwavering, so untroubled by the currents of emotion, so kind and caring. They had a strong effect on me. "You have put aside your ornaments, Mayu, now seek the inner jewels, the real treasure that you possess."

I did not fully comprehend his words, but deep inside I knew he was speaking truth. Although I hardly knew him, in some ways he seemed like an old friend.

"You must now undergo training. There is no other way. It may be difficult at first considering the life of comfort you are accustomed to, but you will learn."

"I owe my life and the lives of my children to you. I will do whatever you request of me. I will be the best student that I can be." Then as he stood up to leave, without thinking I inquired, "May I ask you a question?" He nodded. "Why did you seek me out and find me on the bridge that day? Why did you send for me that night when the fire broke out? Why this concern for me?"

This time he turned his eyes away. I perhaps imagined there was a flicker of emotion, a feeling he did not wish me to know. "Perhaps one day you will find the answer to these questions. Nobody can escape the past, Mayu, nobody. We are all at its mercy until the last *samsara* is burned and the last desire fulfilled or nullified."

I didn't understand his meaning until many years later, but by then it was too late to return the love he had shown me. As I sat in the garden for a long time that day, I realized that indeed my Goddess Amaterasu had responded. It was she who had sent Sensei to me. It was she who had rescued me from the fire. It was she who had found me a place to hide, just as I had requested in the shrine that day. In the years ahead, the Goddess was never to leave me, but over time my understanding of her transformed. The brilliant mind, the clear mind that shines, ever present every moment in the symbol of sun, was to become for me the awakened mind of the Buddha. They were one and the same. There was no distinction. This was the work that lay before me: to bring together once and for all the form and the formless, that ever-existing consciousness beyond language and concept and the appearances that this undivided One takes as the knowable Divinity expressing itself as Buddha Nature.

Chapter 22

I did not see Jakucho Sensei much in the next few months. I was left on my own. I had been given a room that was quite spare but still more comfortable that the accommodations for the other monastics. I did not eat with the others but was served in my room. I felt isolated and would spend my days in the garden thinking over my life, wandering through the monastery, which to my surprise had some art treasures of its own. I began to feel restless and one day stopped a monk who was on his way with a tray of food for the Master. "May I bring this to him?" I asked. He hesitated. But when I insisted that I wanted to be of some service, he acquiesced.

I slid open the shoji door and entered the room with the tray. He was busy at his writing table and did not notice me. I remained on my knees by the shoji door, waiting for some sign from him. Finally he looked up. "Mayu, it is you," he smiled. "What a surprise."

I had been thinking much of him these last weeks, wondering why he had not called me to him. Since the day in the garden some months after I took ordination, I had had no time with him. Now for the first time, seated before him, I felt a nervousness that I had not felt before. "I have not seen you, Sensei, since the day of my ordination. I have had much time to think and reflect, and now I am ready for my training to begin."

"Ah," he replied. "I have been waiting for this. I did not want to rush you, since your arrival here was somewhat against your will," he chuckled. "You had to be ready and come to this decision on your own accord." We were quiet for a few minutes, and then he asked. "Are you really ready now, Mayu? Is this the life you choose? When I last saw you, you were bemoaning the loss of your hair. That is the least of what will be taken away. Every part of you that you hold dear will be crushed. Every thought you think will be shown to be illusion. Your feelings, your likes, your dislikes, they will all be shattered. There will be nothing left except the jewel that is your Buddha Nature, but it will shine so and you will understand there is no loss, only gain. But until that time it will be difficult. There is no other way."

He sat gazing at me intensely, as if to discern whether I was truly ready. Then he continued. "If you are uncertain, you can stay here as a guest for as long as need be. I have taken you and your children under my care. There is no need for you to go further." War was still raging and I knew there was no place for me outside the monastery walls. But even when the war ceased, would I want to leave? The thought of Sensei had begun to dominate my life. He had assumed a place of great importance. Whatever I did now, I considered what he would say, how he would regard my thoughts and actions. I looked into his steady eyes and did not respond right away. "You may take more time if you need to," he advised, continuing to examine me as if surveying my thought and feelings.

"I have already taken ordination," I replied.

"But you took it under pressure. Your heart must be fully committed before the true training can begin. You must know for sure." I hesitated. He continued, "I see change in you, Mayu. These days alone have benefitted you. I have tried to keep my distance so as not to influence you. I want you to be free to leave here when the war is over."

"Where would I go?" I asked.

"That is not a good enough reason to proceed. You must want what the training has to offer. The monastery cannot be merely an escape for you. It must be a chosen path."

"My life in the world is over, I have no doubt about that," I responded with newborn certainty. "I have been happy here, happier than I thought possible. I have wondered how it can be, to be happy with no possessions at all, no objects of beauty to engross me. Everything has been taken from me, except my children, and yet I am coming to a place of contentment."

"And what is it that has made you happy, Mayu?"

I felt my checks grow flush. What could I say? The truth was that he was becoming a guiding presence for me. The fact that he was nearby, even if I did not see him, gave me comfort and peace. He waited for me to respond.

"I want to know the peace of Lord Buddha," I replied firmly. "I have had a taste now, but only a taste. The inner treasures you spoke to me about, I have a sense of what you mean but I don't know them. I want to find those treasures, and I know the only way is through Lord Buddha." I was quiet for a few minutes, surprised by my words. It had taken me some months to come to this conclusion, and it was the first time I allowed myself to accept the Buddha. Then I added, "I also know that it is the Goddess Amaterasu who has led me here, led me to you. I see no contradiction now between my Shinto faith and the teachings of Lord Buddha. I have reconciled them in my heart."

He nodded with a smile. "It was important for you to come to this realization on your own. It was necessary before you could go any further. But now you must consider whether you want to proceed," he said. "You have had a life of comfort, I have wondered how you might bear this training. That is why I have not insisted. And your children are still young. Your situation is an unusual one and I have debated what to do."

I had seen my children on a regular basis over the past few months. My daughter was doing well with the family of Sensei's sister and, although I missed her, I was grateful that she now had a family. My older son took quite well to the monastic training. My younger son less so, but both of them were becoming quite independent of me. It was better for them to seek a new life, one where they could be free from the stain on our family honor.

"Have you really left your world behind, Mayu?" I nodded with certainty. There was no going back. He continued to eye me carefully. "I see that you are stronger now, and I see a conviction in you that was not there before. Yes, Mayu, we can begin your training. I have been waiting for you to come to this understanding on your own. I am most pleased."

I did not know at that time what the training would entail for me, and I mistakenly thought it would allow me more time with Sensei. I wanted to learn from him. He was the incentive for me, but I was moved to the nuns' quarters and hardly saw much of Sensei in those days. The training was difficult, with rising before the sun, hours of study and chanting, and service. I was treated no differently than the others. This disturbed me a great deal at first, but gradually I came to see the benefit. It took years to chip away at habits and preferences, but I did not waver in my decision. After that conversation with Sensei, never did I wish for my old life. There were times of great peace and contentment, a quiet joy that flowered inside, but also times of struggle and lack of inspiration. I took these all in and tried to attain that equanimity that had so impressed me about

Sensei. I realized that enduring the fluctuations of life was the path to equanimity. There was no other.

Several years passed. I continued to see my children on occasion but saw very little of Sensei. Finally one day he appeared and invited me for a walk in the garden. "It is good to see you, Mayu," he said. "I have come to check on your progress." After asking me a few questions about my response to the training, we fell silent. It was a beautiful early summer day and we were surrounded by an array of flowers.

"It has been only a few years since I came here," I remarked. "But it feels like a long time, a lifetime. The world has become a dream to me. I feel so distant from the life I once lived."

"You have found peace here, and joy I hope."

I nodded. "I hardly think about my old life now. I have buried the past."

"Fighting has become more sporadic. There may be some accord soon," he said.

I had heard nothing of the outside world and didn't want any news. I didn't want the thought of that world to enter my peaceful abode. "It is better for me not to know anything of it," I said. "There is no point for me."

"You are right," he smiled. He glanced at me as if there was more to say, but he kept quiet for a while. Then he said, "You have been serving in the kitchen, is that right?" I nodded. "I have another task for you. There is no need for you to serve there anymore. I would like you to help me with some work."

"What work is that Sensei?" I asked with surprise.

"You will see," he responded with a twinkle in his eye.

A gift of many art works had been left to the monastery and Sensei wanted me to oversee their care. I knew he was seeking a way to please me and to keep me near him. Later he asked me to help organize his writings. Through one means or another, he found a way for me to be near. This did not interfere with my training because I kept to the monastery schedule, rising early, joining the chanting, studying the sutras and learning to cultivate the inner life. And so the years passed.

One day Sensei asked me to do an errand in the city. After the war had ended, I had on occasion left the monastery for one purpose or another. I always hurried back as soon as possible, not wanting to awaken sleeping memories. But on this occasion I was delayed and had to spend longer than I would have liked in town. As I was finishing my business, I saw a carriage stop and a woman step out. I gasped. It was my sister. Instinctively I turned away so that she would not see me. I couldn't face her. I couldn't allow memories of my old life to revive. Most likely she would not have recognized me in my nun's garb, but it was an instinctive move to hide myself. In the few minutes that I had caught a glimpse of her, I could tell that prosperity had returned to our clan. She was dressed in beautiful garments and was surrounded by the wealth that I once had known. My heart was racing and continued to pound on the journey back to the monastery.

I went straight to the shrine room and let the tears flow. Tears for what, I didn't understand. I was content and joyful in my new life, far happier that I had ever been. Then why the tears? I felt his presence behind me, but I didn't look up. We sat there for some time in silence until I could regain my composure.

"I felt a ripple in the lake," he said simply. "So I came to calm again the waters."

"I don't know why I am crying," I replied, still not turning around to face him. "I saw my sister in town, and something stirred, I don't know what."

"It takes a long, long time for samsara to dissolve. It is not a matter of years, Mayu, but lifetimes. Do not expect all the layers of thoughts and emotions to dissolve so easily. There are layers upon layers that must be worked through. You have begun to penetrate and dissect what lies hidden. If you wish to greet your sister, after all these years, you may visit her. There is no harm in that."

I shook my head. "If I am thought to be dead, let it be that way." I wiped my tears and then turned to face him and asked, "If I don't wish for that life, then why the tears?" At the sight of his steady gaze, a calmness descended over me.

"To show you that you have not yet reached equanimity, although you may have thought you had. It is easy to find peace in the monastery, but then we must step outside, back into the world, to see what we really have attained. It was important for you to see this, Mayu. Wealth and pleasure still have their grip over you, but don't let this disturb you. Focus on your life now, in this moment, on what you need to do. Come, there is much work for us." And so I buried once more the feelings that had emerged.

Some weeks later, I was sitting in the garden in quiet meditation when I heard her voice from behind, shaking as she spoke my name. "Matsu, my sister, is it really you? Are you truly alive?" At those words she broke down and started to cry. I turned to find Mariko standing behind me. I didn't move. At the sight of me, joy came over her and she shed tears of happiness. "Can you ever forgive me for not coming to your aid?" she asked through her tears. "We all thought you dead, and I have berated myself these many years, blaming myself for what happened." I didn't know whether I was happy or sad to see her. I didn't know whether to embrace her or to remain seated. I didn't know what I felt. "We have tried to find the children, but they seemed to have disappeared. Now I know. I am so grateful to Sensei. I am so grateful that my sister is alive."

"How did you find me?" I asked, still stunned.

"Sensei came and told me that you have been here all these years. He told me how he helped you and the children escape the fire. Why did you not come to me after the war?"

I didn't know what to say. I didn't want to go back into the past and berate her for abandoning me in my time of greatest need. "I didn't know whether you would accept me after all that happened," I finally replied.

"Now that I have found you, everything will be fine. You and the children will come home with me and we will take care of everything."

"No, Mariko, I can't leave here," I replied with a faint smile. Standing up I gave her a long and warm embrace. "I mean, I don't want to leave. I have a new life here and I am very happy. I can't go back."

"We will talk about it later," she said. "Now, I want to look at you." She laughed between her tears. "Your new hairstyle becomes you."

I smiled, by now very used to my appearance without hair. We chatted for some time. I was mostly quiet but she went on and on about the family and all of our acquaintances. I listened patiently, as if hearing a story of a world far away. When it was time for her to leave, she asked if she could come visit me again soon. I nodded, not knowing quite how I felt about being discovered.

That evening, Sensei came to see me, with an apologetic look on his face. "Forgive me for calling Mariko here without your consent," he said quietly, in a tone that displayed some remorse. "I exceeded my bounds."

I didn't respond. He added. "I feel it is time for you to come out of the shadows. You are very much alive, and perhaps it would be good for society to know the life you have chosen."

I couldn't be angry with him. "I suppose it is for the better," I replied.

"Even the Goddess Amaterasu had to come out of hiding," he smiled. "You cannot go about your life fearing that one day you will be discovered. The war is long over, and there has been a general amnesty. It is time to make peace with the past."

"I have," I replied firmly.

Mariko continued to press me to leave the monastery, but eventually she came to accept my decision. I was grateful that she took charge of my two younger children, seeing to their marriages and that they were settled in a way that was befitting their station in life. My older son chose to continue his study under Sensei and took full ordination as a monk.

In my work with Sensei, often there would be no words between us. He was a quiet presence for me, and as my life became more interior, words often seemed superfluous. When I ran into inner struggles, a few words from him would clear my mind. I was very much aware of what he gave me, but at times I wondered what it was that he gained from me. Why did he want me near?

On occasion I would look up from my work and find him gazing at me with such tenderness, but it was so subtle that I would later wonder if I imagined it. But no, the special care he took of me was real, and to think of it would warm my heart and make me smile inwardly. He had become very dear to me. I came to assume that I held a similar place in his heart, but I couldn't be sure because no such words ever passed between us. There were other times when months would go by and we would hardly find a few minutes to be in each other's company. Those were difficult times for me, but I never spoke of it. I waited, knowing that the time would come when he would call for my assistance on some matter.

At one time I thought to ask whether my attachment to him was an obstacle to my spiritual progress, but I didn't raise the question. I suppose I didn't want to hear the answer. Then one day out of the blue he said to me, "The mind should be clear, Mayu, like a lake with no ripples, as still as a mirror. That will come with practice. It can't be forced, and until that time, there is no harm in feeling the emotions that you do. In time, there will be no preferences, but it will happen naturally. Do not be concerned."

I nodded. "Have you reached that place where there are no preferences?" I ventured to ask.

He shook his head with a smile. "No, Mayu. I am still waiting for that day to arrive. I am a very ordinary man, with ordinary feelings, but I will remain constant until I awaken to that state of clear mind."

"You are hardly ordinary," I smiled. "But it gives me comfort to know that we are not so different."

"Not different at all. Some time ago I realized that it is not really a matter of striving. If we keep up with the study, chanting, and meditation, one day everything extraneous will fall away, unveiling the Buddha Nature that has always been there. Without effort, we will enter that state. I have full confidence in that."

"All my searching after beauty those many years before I came here, were they then of no avail, did it mean nothing?"

He smiled. "Surely it is that search that led you here. The transient beauty of this world is but a faint mirror of our true nature. It is *that* you were seeking. Beauty is there to lure us to the reality beyond this physical world."

"You mean those years prepared me for the life I now have?"

"No doubt. The lover of beauty eventually is led to the path that takes us beyond beauty."

One day Sensei took ill. The weeks passed and he grew no better. We were all quite worried, but he began to prepare us for his departure. I was at his bedside caring for him. I hadn't left his side in days and would rest only for a few hours in the night in the room next to his. All my other duties were put aside. I began to give up hope of his recovery. For the first time in many years I felt sadness and anxiety. The thought of him departing this world was almost unbearable, but his face was serene. He shared none of the concern that I felt.

"Why be sad, Mayu? A clear mind knows no preference—neither a preference for life nor for death. You know this."

"But I have not reached that state," I replied sadly. "You have meant everything to me all these years. I cannot imagine being without you." I had never expressed these thoughts to him, but the words came quite naturally now.

He looked at me thoughtfully and then said, "So have you found the answer to your question?"

"My question? What question is that?" I asked.

"You have forgotten what you asked me long ago, when you first came here." A baffled look crossed my face. "When you first came, you asked me why I had sought you out on the bridge that day and why I had taken such care for your safety."

I smiled at him without responding. I did not look away as I used to when I sought to hide my emotions. I gazed deep into his eyes, those eyes that always had such a calming effect on me. There was no suffering, no sign of sadness. In all these years I had hardly seen him ruffled by anything.

For a moment our eyes locked. We had the most intimate relationship I had ever known, and yet we had never once been intimate in the physical sense. Never had he touched me, kissed me, or said anything that would lead to physical contact. No words of emotional endearment had ever crossed his lips. This was a different kind of intimacy. We shared few words and yet he knew my thoughts and feelings, as I had come to know his. It was a relationship that granted peace and comfort and security. It was one of trust, deep respect, and honesty. Never would he betray his vows and never would I ask him to. This was the unspoken trust between us. Yet, this did not prevent love from taking root, a love that needed no words. It never needed to be acknowledged or affirmed. It had developed so naturally over the years and was so present in its radiance that I assumed love was the natural state of being. In the brief exchange now between us, as he lay dying, something was transmitted and I knew that death would bring no diminishment to our relationship.

I didn't find any words to respond, so he continued. "Then you know there is no ending. Our relationship did not begin on the bridge that day and will not end here. You must know that now."

"Yes," I replied softly. "I know that, but it does not make the parting easier." My eyes began to tear at the thought. He took my hand, something he had not done before. I lifted his hand to my moist checks and held it there. Never had I expected when I came to the monastery that I would find love, and of such a deep nature. Could I allow myself to express it now? I began to speak but he put his hand to my lips. "Shh . . . Do not give words to that which is beyond language. Words cannot do it justice."

I continued to gaze into his eyes. They were steady and caring. Even as his body endured pain, he was able to relieve my anguish. "How grateful I am," I said, "for that day when you found me."

"It was a promise that I made to you long ago, long before this life began, to find you and bring you again onto the path. It is a path we have walked together, now and before. I, too, am grateful that in this life that promise could be fulfilled."

I did not leave his side that night. I stayed until he released his last breath and his light could merge into the greater light that animates all that is. In the months after, as I went through his writings, I came upon the poems he once read at the arts festivals, poems that I took no notice of at the time. They were not of the highest quality, but they touched me deeply. One was called "Mayu" and it was of the lady who was lovely like a lotus flower, the lady who presided over the arts, who inspired the painters and brought the ink of the poets to life, the lady who had entered his heart and given breath to beauty, who had given him eyes to see and ears to hear, the lady who was life itself. One poem after another was to this lady.

Now I knew what I had been to him—an ideal of love, an ideal that encouraged him silently on his spiritual journey, one that drew him deeper into the spiritual life. It was not me, but the ideal that he sought, the Goddess Amaterasu, the One who illumines, who brings clarity to the mind. For some karmic reason I could be the one who brought him to that ideal. All of those years, working beside him in the monastery, I had never understood the role I served for him, why he drew me close.

I shed no tears as I read through the poems. Had he loved me for so long and never spoken a word of love to me? What type of love was this? It was not one of words but of deeds. In those days following his death, I relived the many times that he had come to care for me, from that first day on the bridge to his rescuing me from the fire, his care for me at the monastery, and his subsequent attention to every detail of my children's lives. I had had a loveless marriage, but through Sensei had come to know the deepest kind of love, an unselfish love that doesn't seek its own pleasure but is beyond pleasure, beyond any demand or expectation, beyond separation and death.

"Sensei," I whispered, "ours is an eternal friendship and I know that we will meet again. Perhaps next time, it is I who will find you."

Some years later I was sitting in the garden enjoying the quiet of the soft summer air. The sun was at its peak, and I was warmed by the beams she shed. I looked up at the sun, and despite the brightness my eyes rested there. It was then that I saw her, the most beautiful woman emerging from the fiery ball that our physical eyes perceive as the sun. She was a form of light—the energy, the intelligence, the Goddess who animates the sun. My years of meditation had settled my mind and had cleared disturbances, so that finally I could see her as she was. Stunned by her appearance, I whispered, "So you are real after all." She smiled at me. I had entered the state of no mind, and it was in that state that I saw her, and it was in that moment that she took me. She had come to take me over, to help me leave my physical form and return to the world of light.

Chapter 23

I was in Kyoto, sitting quietly in one of the old temples, after having fully recovered the memories of my life in Japan. The award ceremony had filled me with great emotion, beyond what I could express to anyone. I was reliving the scenes of my life in Kyoto from many centuries ago, again and again and again, and yet I had to function fully in the present at press conferences and interviews with journalists.

The peace prize I received seemed as much for the work of Matsu as for Dena: Matsu, who long ago worked for peace among the clans and sought to elevate society through the arts to a place of beauty and harmony. I recognized that those impulses were still within me. I had been born in this life into a family for whom art was their religion; they worshipped beauty rather than any divinity. When I began working with my father for the Japanese spiritual organization that had founded a museum, I immediately resonated with their belief that beauty was a doorway to the divine—objects of great beauty elevate our consciousness so that we can experience the divine reality. Beauty was not an end in itself, but an expression of the divine and a call from beyond the physical world. Were these elements of my current life echoes from the life of Matsu, and had she been continuing a search that had begun in Persia?

Minoo had been touched by beauty, but was unable to pursue it as a simple village woman. Her love of beauty was to find fulfillment in the life of Matsu. It was as my Baba had said: the Lord fulfills our desires in time, when the conditions are ripe. All desires must be fulfilled or neutralized. That is universal law. I received as Matsu all the beautiful clothes I desired as the poor village girl in Persia. Matsu eventually left behind the world of beauty, or rather it was torn away from her. Was that because the samsara had dissolved, or did the seeds of desire go dormant to awaken again at a later time? Did Matsu really make peace with her new lot in life and really not long for the things she had lost? These were questions that now occupied my mind. Both my Baba and Sensei had tried to transmit to me the knowledge that love is the ultimate goal, the source of all happiness. This was a message that was given to me again and again, life after life. There always was a messenger to transmit this truth. How long would it take me to truly absorb it?

I was struck by the themes that connected the Rani Gita, the poor village girl Minoo, and then the upper-class woman Matsu. My happiest times had been with my Baba in our little hut and with Sensei in the austere monastery. It was the light of spiritual friendship and guidance that had bestowed this happiness, not any material wealth. Wealth offers a false happiness, but this only becomes clear when you look back over the long spiritual journey. Even objects of beauty do not grant the joy that spiritual companionship provides. Matsu found contentment in the monastery that she could not find in the world, despite her great treasures of art.

During the many years that I traveled to Japan, I had not understood my connection to the country. I remembered a fire, being overcome with fear and sadness, and an escape into the forest. I did know that I had a deep spiritual connection to the land and culture, but it didn't come together for me until these memories returned. Now I finally understood why Japan had always held such a dear place in my heart. My frequent trips to Japan had become a necessity for me. Fortunately there were plenty of opportunities as I worked with a number of Japanese religious communities over the years, and they provided much support for my interfaith work.

My trips to Japan were always for some spiritual project, but I always included a free day so I could wander the streets of Kyoto alone, visiting temples and monasteries, buying painted scrolls, pottery, and old textiles, and mentally traveling back to an earlier time. My house in New York filled up with beautiful items from Japan, so in a way I was regaining what Matsu had lost in the fire. I created in my own home a world of beauty. After the Japanese memories returned, I realized that perhaps the seeds of desire from that life had not been fully satisfied. Beauty still had its hold on me.

In the course of my spiritual journey from one life to the next, Japan had been not only a doorway to the arts and to beauty, but also to a special quality of love that emerges from true companionship and the cultivation of a regular meditation practice. In my previous birth in Persia, I learned service and devotion, and began to understand the formless divinity. Through my life in Japan, my experience broadened and I came to know another type of love, the one I had been yearning to know. In old Japan, I encountered the female divinity in the form of the Sun Goddess, the Divine Feminine, which was to become such a central part of the work of GPIW.

The return of my memories of Japan showed me what I had instinctively always known: I had lived as a Buddhist nun. During my work at GPIW, I had grown close to a number of Buddhist teachers; at the request of one of these teachers, I had participated in a few Buddhist meditation retreats. Since I began meditating at the age of 20, I had viewed the world through the lens of Hinduism, but as I delved into the Buddhist world, an internal Buddhist-Hindu dialogue about the nature of Ultimate Reality started to engage my mind. I sought to reconcile these two traditions, believing intuitively that there was no true distinction, only differences in language and emphasis.

Much of the conflict over the past centuries has been driven by the need of one group—one nation, one religion, one ethnic group—to dominate others. The belief that one religion has an exclusive hold on truth is evidence of this need to dominate, to feel superior. That paradigm is shifting as humankind evolves, perhaps for its own survival, to a new understanding. Increasingly, spiritual teachers are acknowledging openly that while their religion may be their path to truth, other religions are equally valid as avenues to the Ultimate Reality, whatever we may call that Absolute. Many years of interfaith activity helped me to evolve this understanding. As religious leaders were coming into close contact with leaders from other faiths, deep bonds of friendship were forming, and this was creating a transformation in understanding and perception. At the same time, extremism was spreading, as if to slow down the movement toward greater unity.

The purpose of interfaith engagement is not simply to learn to tolerate others or merely to coexist. That may have been an objective decades ago, but today far more is needed. Interfaith work enables people to appreciate and value traditions other than their own, to see their unique beauty and contribution. Religious diversity, like biodiversity and cultural diversity, is a treasure; without it, humankind would be that much poorer. To cultivate a greater understanding and appreciation of spiritual diversity, it is important to bring the Dharma traditions to the fore. The world is getting smaller, every religion is spreading around the globe, and a new understanding must emerge—an understanding of religious equality. Perhaps this is the last equality battle to be fought. Tolerance is not enough. Acceptance of the other is not enough. The religions that claim exclusive hold on truth must evolve to see the truth in all. This is the challenge of our time.

This theme of bringing the Dharma traditions to the fore was becoming more prominent in the work of GPIW, and as there were so few in the interfaith world to take up the charge, I made it one of our main commitments. My life was moving quickly and I had little time to dwell on the memories of Japan; we hardly had time to catch our breath between projects. We continued organizing projects annually in both Japan and India. For several years we had been organizing peace dialogues between Sufis and yogis in Kashmir, bringing yogis from other parts of India to meet with the Sufis in Srinagar, the capital of the Indian state of Jammu and Kashmir. Later we began working with a network of young peace activists there.

India was soon to call me back into the past. On my initial trip to Kashmir I had my first encounter with Lord Shiva, the transformative aspect of the divine energy in Hinduism. My own spiritual lineage was in the Vaishnaiva line—devotion to the aspect of the divine manifesting as Vishnu, the preservation force of the universe, best known to the world through the incarnations of Sri Rama and Sri Krishna. I had little personal acquaintance with the manifestation of Shiva. This all changed when I arrived in Kashmir, where I was to encounter for the first time Kashmiri Shaivism, an ancient and profound tradition that upon closer reflection seemed no different than what I learned from my teacher Yogananda. The peaks of Kashmir are still bathed in the presence of Lord Shiva, and one cannot help but experience this powerful energy. I was astounded to discover my love for this aspect of the Divine, which was to deepen over time.

In Srinagar, I visited the ashram of Swami Lakshmanjoo, the last of the great Kashmiri Shaivite masters, who passed away in the early 1990s. When riots forced the Hindus to flee Kashmir in 1989, he was one of the few who did not leave; he had numerous Muslim students and was considered a beloved saint. Kashmir was once a place of great confluence—home to Sufis, yogis, and Buddhist masters. Sadly, much has changed as radical Islam has taken root and a separation of the religious communities has forced people apart. Kashmir, a sacred region that was once a meeting place for the great religious streams, was losing to the fanaticism that was overtaking much of the religious world. I developed a strong commitment to Kashmir and to re-establishing the diversity that had once enriched the region, bringing back the love for Lord Shiva.

Ironically, it was in the spring of 2012 in Sweden that my memories of Kashmir returned. A few months earlier I had been invited to speak at an ashram in the Bahamas that was run by Israeli swamis. It was a beautiful place and I greatly enjoyed my time there. A few days before I was to leave, I was standing in line for the evening meal when I noticed a beautiful-looking man behind me. I greeted him and soon discovered he was a Sufi singer from Tehran, Iran. His music was set to the Sufi poetry of Rumi and Hafiz, as well as the poems of his own Sufi teacher, who had passed away some years ago.

I thought it amusing that he would be at an Israeli-run Hindu ashram, considering the great tension between Iran and Israel, and so hastened to inform him of such. "Do you realize that this ashram is run by Israelis?" I asked. The swamis seated at our table were all speaking Hebrew and he seemed perfectly at ease with the situation. In fact, he appeared to be on very friendly terms with them.

He nodded. "Of course. I have been coming every year for the last six years to give concerts here."

I was intrigued. We hear so much in the media about the hostility between these two countries, yet he seemed not to care about possible repercussions back home. I was set on getting to know him better. There were only two days left of my visit, and we spent much of that time together. I didn't expect to see him again or to hear from him, but a short while after returning to New York, I received a phone call from Tehran and he invited me to a performance he was giving in Sweden. I did something I had never done before—impulsively I accepted the invitation and in a matter of days was on a flight from New York to Sweden, driven by an instinctive knowing that I was being called somewhere. I thought I was being called to romance, but in fact I was being called to a memory of love.

As I sat in the concert hall, I sank into deep meditation, not moving for the full two hours of the concert. Soon after the music began, I felt myself rise from my body and expand into the universe, feeling and hearing the pulse of the stars and planets, the energy that gives manifestation to all. I became aware of cosmic sounds that were sustaining the universe, a most beautiful melody. His music was a bridge and a reflection of a deeper song. I was both present at the concert, listening to the skillful arrangement of sounds and, at the same time, I was embracing the universe, feeling like I was in every corner of space. Intermission came. I heard everyone get up for the break, but I could not move. I was completely absorbed and, when the music began again, my absorption continued. It was only with great difficulty that I brought myself back to my physical surroundings when the concert ended.

In the years following my divorce, I had spent much time with musicians, dating a number of them. Although that was long ago and I had closed that chapter of my life, music continued to hold a special appeal for me, especially spiritual music. However, I had not known this immersion in the cosmos through music before. This was a new and most unexpected experience. I left the concert hall in somewhat of a daze, unable to bring myself back to the everyday world. I felt myself floating somewhere between the present and the past, aware of shadows emerging but unable to pinpoint a time or place.

My Sufi friend greeted me after the concert and we went out in search of dinner. He never ate before performing and so was quite hungry. Although an inner silence still pervaded my being, I forced myself to engage in conversation and, by the time he dropped me off at my hotel, I had fully recovered.

That evening as I sat in meditation in my hotel room, I was sucked back into the past, pulled once more through the vortex of time. During the little time left of my visit, meditating in my hotel room, on the airplane back to New York, and in the days that followed, memory upon memory engulfed me. I was back again in India.

PART VII

17TH CENTURY INDIA

Death is certain for one who has been born,
and rebirth is inevitable for one who has died.
Therefore, you should not lament over the inevitable.
                                              —Bhagavad Gita 2:27

Since you came to birth in this world at this time,
in this place, and with this particular destiny,
it was this indeed that you wanted
and required for your own ultimate illumination.
That was a great big wonderful thing that
you thereupon brought to pass:
not the "you" of course,
that you now suppose yourself to be,
but the "you" that was already there before you were born.
You are not now to lose your nerve!
Go on through with it and play your own game all the way!
                                              —Joseph Campbell,
                                              Myths to Live By

Chapter 24

I was born as Mira into a Hindu Brahmin family in the sacred city of Kashi, also known as Varanasi. My father was a pious devotee of Lord Rama, and we observed all the required rituals. My mother was a quiet woman, respectful of her husband and faithful in her duties. Duty was a concept instilled in me from early childhood. My father had great respect for my mother and treated her as if she were Mother Sita herself; she, in turn, exhibited a near perfect balance of serving her husband and never losing the sense of her own innate dignity. My father had a rather progressive view of the world, and so my mother had more freedom of movement than most women of the time. This was something my father sought for me as well when it came time for marriage.

We lived not far from the holy river, and a ritual I remember from early childhood is my mother's daily walk to the Ganga to perform the evening *arti* just before sunset. I would often accompany her with some of the other children. We children tried to outpace the Ganga as she meandered along the riverbed. Except during monsoon time, she lapped gently through the plains, and it was easy for us to keep up with her. But sometimes she would outsmart us and suddenly increase her speed. We would then have to run along the river's edge, often tumbling down in the process. It was a game we played and she was our playmate, very much a living presence to us.

I viewed our rituals as more cultural habits than religious ones, and took little note of religion in my childhood. My father would regularly have priests come to perform pujas before the statues of Lord Rama and Mother Sita that dominated our small home temple. I did what was expected of me, but little more as my interests lay elsewhere.

The most important festival of the year for us was Diwali, the time celebrating the return of Lord Rama to Ayodhya after his long exile and the war to rescue Mother Sita from the demon king Ravana. Many people gathered at our home, illumined with hundreds of earthen lights turning it into a heaven realm. Mother dressed in her finest silk saris. Indeed this was the time the deities came alive for us. I loved this day, not so much for the religious aspect as for the music and chanting that continued for hours and hours without ceasing, bringing the celestial realms closer for that brief time.

When I approached womanhood, a marriage was arranged with the son of a prominent Brahmin family, also from Varanasi. My father confided to me that one of the reasons he had agreed to the marriage was because I would be able to have the same freedom of movement my mother enjoyed. I understood the importance of this and so was greatly pleased with the arrangement. I was still quite young when I went to live at the family home of my husband, a large complex close to the banks of the River Ganga.

Like my mother, I was a dutiful Hindu wife, keeping all the ceremonies and rituals. My husband's family was Shaivite, worshippers of Lord Shiva, so I made the transition from the perfunctory worship of the beautiful form of Lord Rama to the formless *Linga*, representing the pillar of light out of which Lord Shiva first emerged at the beginning of time. The temple at my husband's home had a large Shiva Linga, an oval stone structure seated on a circular base that symbolized the union of Shiva and Shakti, the masculine and feminine aspects of creation coming together as one. The worship of the Linga was new to me, and I experienced a strange inner tug, a conflict that I could not identify or articulate. As I grew older I began to understand this inner confusion as a questioning of the true nature of the divine. What should one worship: a formless God or a God in form? Which was the truth? I didn't know. Sometimes I would wrestle with this question, but my true interest was not in religious matters as such, but rather the arts, so for quite some time I buried this inner questing.

At that time in Varanasi there was a great flourishing of culture. My father was a patron of the arts, particularly music. When I was a child, we would have many concerts at our home and I found myself greatly drawn to the musicians. Great musicians came from all over and played many different instruments and styles, but they had one thing in common: the ability to invoke another world, to lift people's mind to unusual heights. I grew up surrounded by music and became accustomed to this experience. My father allowed me to sit in on the concerts even at a young age, and I watched as the music carried people off into their own worlds. I, too, began to feel these effects.

It was natural after I got married to continue this family tradition of organizing musical performances at our home. My husband did not object, although he didn't share my passion for music. Bindhu was a very sweet and kindly man, generous and attentive to me. There was little passion between us but a great sense of duty bound us together. He was involved in the affairs of the city, which kept him preoccupied, so he was happy that I had interests of my own.

I began to seek out the best musicians in Kashi, and then the surrounding towns. All sorts of musicians played at our home and these concerts became known throughout the region. Many eminent people attended, complimenting me on my choice of musicians. I didn't limit the concerts to only local and classical music. I was constantly on the lookout for new styles and musicians who were visiting from foreign lands.

I had been married for quite some years, with four young children, when one day I heard news of an accomplished musician who was visiting Varanasi. I sent a note with one of our household servants inviting him to perform at our home. The servant came back with a polite refusal. I couldn't believe it. This had never happened before. Most musicians viewed it as an honor to perform at one of our concerts.

Then I thought that perhaps he was expecting a personal invitation from me. He was from another culture and perhaps that was the custom there. He was staying with a family that was known to me, so I went there personally to make the request. When I entered the room, he did not get up to greet me, but rather continued his absorption in playing a classical Persian stringed instrument. I was taken aback by what appeared to be a coolness of manner, but sat quietly listening and waiting. His music was entrancing. He was clearly a master. His fingers sped up and down the strings with such speed, displaying techniques I had not heard before. His playing was superior to anything I had known. I closed my eyes and drifted off to the notes. How exquisite, I thought.

When he finished, I opened my eyes. He looked my way and nodded in recognition of my presence. "How beautiful," I said, introducing myself. I then asked him to give a concert at my home. He courteously declined, saying that he was in Varanasi on personal matters and was not giving concerts at this time. I was stunned to be twice refused. I thought surely he would accept my personal invitation. After a few minutes of polite exchange, I took my leave, giving him my name and address in case he reconsidered. He nodded, but not in a convincing manner.

I couldn't get his music out of my mind. The weeks passed. I sent a note inviting him to attend the concert of a well-known musician at my home, but again he declined. I was baffled. This third rejection made me more determined. I went again to meet him, but was told he was engaged and could not receive me. I began to ask around about his character. Nobody knew much about him. He had not circulated much in Varanasi society and kept mostly to himself.

It all would have ended there had I not met him by chance some weeks later at the home of an acquaintance. I caught sight of him as soon as I entered the room, without an instrument this time, and immediately all my hurt came to the fore. I sat at a distance and began conversing with my friend, but all the while my mind was on him. Out of the corner of my eye, I saw him take note of me from across the room. He finally approached and apologized for not being able to accept any of my invitations. I didn't respond. Ignoring my silence, he continued in a surprisingly warm manner; I again thought to convince him to put on a concert. "I do wish you would reconsider my invitation," I requested in a beseeching voice. "It would be a shame for the people of Varanasi not to hear you perform during your stay. From the little I have heard of your music, I know how well you will be received here."

He gazed at me for quite some time without responding. There was a strange look on his face and it drew me in. I felt my checks begin to flush so I turned my eyes away, confused by this strange attraction I felt. When I turned my eyes back to him, I saw that I had sparked his interest. Finally, he said with a slight smile, "You are persistent. I respect that and so, for you, I will accept."

I didn't know whether to be happy or sorry. Something had arisen in me in those few minutes that gave me cause for concern, but I tried not to show it. With a steady voice, trying not to betray any emotion, I said, "We will fix the concert then for the next full moon. Please come to my home tomorrow so you can see the room where you will perform. Many prominent musicians from this city have performed there."

"I know," he replied slowly. "I know of your concerts. It will be an honor to perform at your home." I felt a subtle tremor pass through my body as he spoke these words.

The next day he paid a visit and saw that the setting was quite appropriate. "It is a beautiful room," he said as I showed him where we always held the concerts. He had his instrument with him; he took it out of its case and began to play. "The sound is quite good," he said with some surprise. He then continued with what appeared to be a difficult technique, his fingers flashing to and fro across the strings like a bellowing wind. The soft but steady sound of his voice entered, harmonizing with the cry of the strings like consorts in a mesmerizing dance. His voice wove in and out among the notes as if seeking to merge with them, and then finally they did become one, as if the universe had gathered all of its energies into the long sought state of union. The sound of the merged voice and instruments rose in a crescendo and then slowly descended into silence.

I was quite shaken by the power of the music and couldn't speak for some time. He also remained still, absorbed in the music. Finally I remarked in a somewhat shaky voice, "I didn't know that you could sing as well. What a striking voice you have."

He put down his instrument and nodded. "I don't often sing in public. I play many instruments and am better known for that. It is a shame that I don't have more of them with me. But as I told you when we first met, this is a personal journey for me, not a professional one, and I had no intention of performing here in Varanasi. It is only because of your insistence..." His voice dropped away and, once again, I felt my face flush.

"Please continue," I urged him. "I love to hear you play." I closed my eyes, hoping not to display any of the confusion that had once more come over me. He took up his instrument, but this time did not add the sound of his voice. I could hardly bring myself back to the world when he finally put his instrument down. Even the silence could not absorb the resounding echo of his music. It continued on and on long after his fingers ceased, or so it seemed to me.

As he took his leave I said, "I really must thank you for this special honor, Ostadd."

"Please call me Atash," he said.

"Then you must call me Mira," I replied.

It was two weeks until the performance. I could hardly wait, such was my impatience. More people than usual came, as it was rare to have a musician from so far away. As soon as he began to play, a hush fell over the room. There was an intensity about him when he was performing, as if nothing but the music existed. The audience fixed its attention on him. He was deeply engrossed, as was I. I could feel the vibrations emanating from his instrument. When his voice began to accompany the sound of the strings and interplay with the notes, I closed my eyes and allowed the music to lift me outside of myself, to where the planetary bodies spun in harmony with one another, emitting an audible hum like a background choir to our earthly sounds. I could not tell whether the sounds I was hearing were coming from his music or the universe, such was the merging of all sounds into one; I could not tell whether the music was coming from the external world or from some internal source. It was as if he was mirroring what existed on a much grander scale, bringing to human ears melodies hidden in every crevice of creation. It was a totally novel experience for me to realize that it is not we who create the melodies; they are already encoded in the elements of the universe. We are merely transcribers, giving voice to what is there—the song of creation. Every movement emits a sound, every turn of the spheres, but our ears are not attuned to hear them. A special gift is needed to catch the frequencies not heard by the human ear, and he had this gift.

What joy emerged from the assembly of notes, one leading to another, modulating up and down the stairway of the universe! They carried a divine inscription, a message of a love so great the heart of one person could not contain it. One had to merge into the All in order to be able to contain that love. This was the awareness that took hold of me as I listened to the music, oblivious of all around me. The holy sound, the sound of Om, the original vibration that brought the manifest world into being, came alive for me that night. No longer was that sound simply a concept, something I had been taught. It became a reality. It was not a single sound, but one of many levels and depths that could be heard, and into which one could merge. It was the expression of love, the voice of the divine consciousness calling out to us to return. I understood this for the first time, and I had something of a religious conversion that night.

When the music ended, it took me some time to return to the world and to physical awareness. I was unable to speak, so entranced was I by the cosmic sounds. People approached to tell me what an extraordinary performance it had been. I simply nodded in agreement. The guests would not let him go. Many told me it was the best performance I had organized at my home. I was in such an elevated state that I could barely respond to their enthusiastic applause. That night I could not sleep. I went outside to peer at the stars, listening for the music that accompanies the flickering of their light. But without his music, my ears were deaf.

I went to see him the next day to thank him, and, before I could stop myself, I was sharing with him what I had experienced. "I never knew that there is music in the motion of the universe," I said, still feeling the glow. "Somehow your playing made that evident to me. For the first time I heard music emanating from every point in space. It was as if the Divine Being called to us. Shiva, Vishnu, Brahma—I didn't know what to call that Divine Being, but for the first time in my life I felt its presence. It was a deeply religious experience for me, and I have never been a religious person. I don't know how else to describe it, and I don't know what it means for me." It wasn't until later that I wondered how I could share such an intimate personal experience without questioning what he would think of me. Confiding in him came so naturally.

He looked at me with surprise and thoughtfully said, "You experienced exactly what I do when I perform. It is odd. I have shared this with nobody and no one has ever come to me saying what you have said. It is truly remarkable that you have picked up on this. When I perform, it is not me who is creating the music, despite what the audience thinks. I am merely a receptacle for music that already exists. I try to express outwardly what I hear inside so that others may experience it, but I hear the music whether I am playing or not. It is all around me, beautiful and haunting. I am driven to make audible what I hear inside, although what I can express is but a pale reflection of what I hear."

As he spoke I could hear a hidden pain in his voice. "How extraordinary," I said quietly. "I have always loved music but have never understood this. I never thought the music comes from elsewhere, that it has a divine source."

"Or perhaps it is that divine spark in us that awakens the memory of the original sounds, the vibrations that accompanied creation and that keep creation going," he replied thoughtfully. "Often at night, Mira, when I shut my eyes and sit alone, I lose myself in those sounds, the eternal music behind all that we see and hear."

Never had I felt so close to anyone, or shared something as intimate as this. He was a Muslim and I a Hindu, yet we were speaking the same language as we shared a very personal spiritual experience. I became flustered and thought that I should leave, but I couldn't. I couldn't bear the thought that this would be the end.

We sat for a while in silence and then I asked, "Are you . . . Are you leaving Kashi any time soon?"

"My personal affairs here are nearly done, but I will stay a bit longer."

"You have not told me whether you have a family at home," I inquired meekly.

He nodded, "A wife and son."

"If you don't mind, I would like to come listen to you play as much as possible before you leave."

He nodded his consent. Then with a smile he added, "Every afternoon you will find me here seeking to capture the cosmic song."

"I will be back tomorrow then."

The next day and the day after found me seated quietly listening to his music. On my third visit, he was out in the garden playing his instrument. I entered the open space and sat at a little distance from him listening to the notes with closed eyes. After a while I heard the music stop, but kept my eyes closed as I was feeling a great wave of joy. When I opened my eyes, I noticed that day had slipped into evening; the sun's light was barely visible. He was seated next to me, watching me intently. I looked into his face and smiled, no longer embarrassed by the closeness I felt with him. We didn't speak for some time. A comfortable silence surrounded us. Finally I said, "I suppose I should be going." He didn't answer. I didn't want to leave the spot and so I made no motion to move.

And then, very naturally, his lips found mine. I put my arms around him. The intimacy felt so right. His lips slide down my neck and onto my breasts. His hands were moving along my body, unwrapping my sari. Freed of the layers of silk, my naked body moved beneath him. His lips were running down my stomach and thighs and then his mouth was on mine again. We could not contain ourselves. All of my cells yearned for this merger.

For a long time we lay with limbs entangled, vined together. I could not bring myself to withdraw my body. Darkness swirled around us, and finally when I made a slight move to pull away, he began again, caressing and opening my body until the pain of separation was so intense that I was begging him to enter me once more. We went on thus for some time until finally I pulled myself away and began to dress.

"I must get home," I said in a daze.

"You will come again?" he pleaded.

"Yes," I nodded, "as soon as I can get away."

I didn't come to see him the next day as I was overcome by pangs of guilt. My sense of duty to Bindhu was very strong, but my love for Atash pulled at me with equal strength. It was more than a physical love. It was the spiritual intimacy that drew me in a way I couldn't resist. The relationship had opened a whole new world, and I had to follow wherever it would take me.

After a few days I returned.

"I wasn't sure you would come back," he said quietly, with a look of pain.

"I tried not to," I responded with equal pain.

He extended his stay by weeks and then months. I found myself living in a timeless realm, not wanting to look ahead into the future. I was living a dream, not realizing that it all must end one day. Our intimacy was not like anything I had experienced with my husband. The feelings evoked went far beyond sensual pleasure. It was as if our souls had merged; I couldn't tell where I ended and he began. If he were joyful on a particular day, I would feel it as well. If he struggled with the music, I would feel that frustration, too. I stopped thinking of us as two separate people. I did not know that such a union was possible in the physical world. It was this union that gave me life, and I could not imagine that it would be taken away. I deceived myself into thinking things were as they should be, and that there was no deception, no conflict between my family life and my time with him. There did not seem to be any contradiction, so natural did it all feel.

My husband seemed not to notice my mental absence. He was busy with his affairs and, in any case, was not a man of much passion. I made sure that I attended to all my duties and my children were looked after so there was nothing left undone. I could not confide in anyone, so I was left to my own devices to manage my dual life. In my happiness, I did not allow myself to consider what the effects of this situation might ultimately be.

Atash rarely spoke of his wife and son at home. Rather, he spoke more often of his Sufi teacher, every now and then weaving a story about him into our conversation. After a while, I began to yearn for such a teacher to come into my life. "I wish I could know your Master," I said one day after he had finished telling one of his tales.

He was quiet and then he said, "You can, Mira, if you come home with me."

Suddenly our conversation turned serious. "You can't mean that," I tried to smile.

"I do mean it, very much."

"You know that is impossible," I replied sadly.

"People do it, Mira, when they find a love like ours."

"I have a family, children." By now tears threatened to flood my eyes.

"As do I," he answered quietly.

"I was hoping you would stay here."

"And live like this?" he asked. "We cannot continue to live a lie. Either we declare our love or we end it."

"You cannot mean that."

"I do," he said solemnly. "It is not in either of our natures to live like this."

"It is true." I acknowledged inwardly the guilt that I had tried so hard to bury beneath the pile of my emotions. "But I also cannot imagine losing you." I let the tears flow, and that was our first goodbye.

He was gone only a few days when I received word that he had returned. He didn't get far on his journey home before heading back to Varanasi. Things resumed as they had been, with frequent visits, little conversation, and much lovemaking. Several weeks later, another conversation followed. We tried to separate again but failed once more, so I allowed myself to believe that his departure would not take place. Inwardly I had a foreboding of what was to come, but I denied it and pretended we would go on like this forever.

Then one day he was gone. No goodbye, only a note. I read the note over and over but could not believe that it was final. For sure he would return as he had in the past. I waited and waited, but this time he did not return. I was torn by the agony of separation and felt his pain as well as mine. All the beauty and joy of union had suddenly been ripped away from me. As the days passed my longing increased.

I spent the days in seclusion, weeping uncontrollably. Everyone in the household took me for being ill. Days became weeks and then months; my suffering grew worse until it overwhelmed me and I could not stand it any longer. It was as if part of my body had been torn away and the throbbing of that wound went on and on day and night. I could not envision life without him. I was filled with such deep pain and unbearable emptiness. My loss was not only the pain of physical separation but also that I had lost my most intimate friend, the one who understood and loved my spirit, with whom I shared my unspoken thoughts. And I had lost the music that had given me access to the divine realm. The stars no longer sang to me. I had become deaf once more. How could I live without his music, without him?

Desperate, I found myself praying for the first time in my life. Sitting before the Shiva Linga, I spoke to the Lord, "Just as Mother Parvati is your other half, he is my other half. How can I live apart from him?" I sobbed as quietly as I could.

One day Bindhu found me there in a sorry state. He was at a loss as to the cause of my grief, but he had come to attribute it to a miscarriage I had had a few months earlier. Naturally he had assumed the child to be his, although I knew otherwise. I had been both relieved and aggrieved when I lost the baby, my last link with Atash. Finding me dissolved in tears before the Linga, he tried to comfort me. "Don't mourn the child, Mira, there will be others."

My husband tried in every way to cheer me up, bringing me beautiful silks and jewels, but I looked at him with empty sunken eyes, seeing only a dark frightening abyss ahead. I barely ate. To my husband's distress, I was rapidly losing weight. He brought one physician after another, who tried all manner of potions and remedies, but nothing worked. I, too, was eager for a cure. But as the months dragged on, I was no nearer to peace or relief from my agony. I began to think that I was no longer fit for this world.

One day my husband called a priest to do a special *yajna* or fire ceremony to cure me of my illness. Bindhu solemnly called me to the temple. Obediently I seated myself before the fire pit while the priest performed the rituals, reciting the Vedic mantras as he put ghee, grains, and herbs into the fire. As the chanting began, I stared at the dancing flames. Agni, the deity of fire, was the messenger who carried prayers to the appropriate deities. Would he help me now? Would he carry my prayers to Lord Shiva, or Lord Vishnu, or was I beyond all aid? Doubts assailed me. I had prayed and prayed to Lord Shiva, but to no avail. Perhaps it was Lord Rama that I should have prayed to, who had guarded my family for all those years. Perhaps I was in this state because I had abandoned our family deity.

By now I wanted most of all to put Atash out of my mind, but I couldn't. He was in every cell of my being and to eradicate him I would have to eradicate myself. There was no help from any of the gods, not Lord Shiva nor Lord Rama. They had abandoned me. I was so confused and felt so far from anything I could call the truth, so distant from any understanding, that I could not bear it. Tears burst from my eyes and I ran from the temple. The priest called after me in a harsh tone, but I could not turn back. Bindhu's pitiful pleas became a background hum, pushing me further and further away. I locked myself in the bedroom and became deaf to Bindhu's pleadings. For hours I lay awake that night, tormented by my inability to regain my life.

I felt as if I was falling into a deep abyss.

It was a humid summer night, and the household was asleep, I got up and, as if in a dream, my feet led me down to one of the bathing ghats at the Ganga. The place was deserted except for a few sadhus sleeping by the side of the river. Mother Ganga had soothed me in my childhood, perhaps now she would do so again. The river was swollen with monsoon rains, racing with more speed than usual along the plains. Every day the rains pounded the earth, but this day no rain had fallen. Throughout the late afternoon and evening, the sky had been threatening but the rains had not come. Now in the deep darkness of this starless night, the sky cracked open with a loud roar and a flash of lightning. As I stood there staring into Ganga's swirling green-brown eyes, the fury of the rains came rushing over me. All I could hear was the gulping of the river as she eagerly drank the falling water. As if pulled by an invisible force, I entered the Ganga. I stood there numb to the pulsating rain, the waters swirling around my thighs, my head spinning.

"Mother," I cried softly, "is there no relief for me? Will I never know peace again?" I stood in the rushing waters praying for some solace, but then I thought I heard her call my name. I allowed myself to be pulled in deeper, until my waist was submerged. Her energy was overwhelming. She was tugging at me, luring me into her welcoming arms. At first I resisted, but as she began to engulf me I found myself letting go. Before I knew it, she had embraced my chest. Perhaps this is the way to peace.

"Mira, Mira." I heard my name wafting over the rising water. Softly she was calling me.

"Take me, Mother. In you I will find comfort," I cried, my tears now mingling with the rushing rains. Her cool water came over me, carrying me away, and I surrendered to her lifting waves.

Chapter 25

" **A** re you ready to hit the town," the cheerful voice of my Sufi musician friend came over the hotel phone, calling me back to the present. It was morning, the day after the concert and I had been deep in meditation, experiencing the trauma of that life in India, feeling myself submerged and carried away by the Ganga. Could I have taken my life? It did not seem possible that I would ever do this, but the visions were as clear as could be, and I was troubled by what I saw. I had heard the swishing of her waters around me, and I had felt myself engulfed by her waves, being carried away.

When I didn't respond, he asked again if he could pick me up; we could see something of the Swedish city where we were staying. I agreed, but my mind was far away.

There was an attraction between us and I had come to Sweden to explore the possibility of a relationship. The memories revived in meditation, however, had turned this possibility in a new direction. I was now more interested in finding out what happened so many centuries ago than in beginning something new, although I had to admit to the feelings that were percolating through my being. On the one hand, there was a closeness between us that needed no time to develop. From the day we had met standing in the dinner line at the ashram, there had been an immediate connection. We both knew it. On the other hand, I had become cautious about relationships. I had had relationships with a number of musicians after my divorce. Years ago I had turned away from the music world, and more recently from relationships as well. I had reached a time in life when I wanted to devote myself to spiritual practice and to my work. So I wondered why this man had come into my life now. I reasoned that it was because of my peace work. Iran, the U.S.—there was peace work to do. Perhaps this was the underlying reason for our meeting.

But after the memories evoked in meditation, I couldn't help but wonder if he was the musician that I fell in love with so long ago, or was he just a catalyst to awaken those memories? How could I know? Did it even matter? Whatever karma there was would be fulfilled. By now I had learned that the main point of these memories was to neutralize any desires or yearning that remained so they could be cleared from the subconscious mind.

We spent a few hours walking through the city. He talked extensively about his Sufi master, who had left Iran during the Islamic Revolution of 1979 and lived in England. Some Sufi paths are more linked to Islam than others. His lineage was universal and so was not strictly within the Islamic religious fold, although most of the followers were Iranian and born Muslim. I was intrigued by much of what his teacher taught.

We had dinner together and then it was time to say goodbye. I was to depart the next day for New York. "I wish you could stay on," he said, standing in the lobby of my hotel. "It is my birthday the day after tomorrow, and I would love for you to be here for that."

I smiled. "I have to get home." We were both quiet, hesitant to part ways. I had come all this way to Sweden to see him, but we now had to say goodbye. I was going back to New York and he to Tehran, without knowing when or if we would meet again. Suddenly a thought came to me.

"We are organizing a spiritual gathering in Greece next month, a reflection on their economic crisis. Come to that and we will have a concert there." The words were out of my mouth before I could really think it through. Greece was in the throes of a financial crisis and we were bringing spiritual leaders there from throughout Europe to reflect on the spiritual significance of the crisis. Why not have music as well? His music was beautiful and he carried the Sufi energy, which we very much wanted in our mix of traditions.

"I would love to," he responded right away. And so I gave myself another chance to see what would unfold.

That night I tried to get back into the past, but it was no use. I could see nothing more than my surrendering to the waves of the Ganga. "Perhaps that was the end," I thought. But no, there must be something more. On the plane home, further visions began to come forward, and then back in New York the rest of the story revealed itself.

* * *

The birds were chirping their early morning song, greeting each other in the awakening dawn. I lay there listening, with closed eyes. It was a familiar sound. Was I dead or alive? I could not tell. I remembered being carried away by the Ganga, sinking into her swirling waters. For sure, I had died. I lay still for a while and then opened my eyes. The tip of the sun was staring back at me, peering over the horizon. It was the same sun that I knew. I shut my eyes. My head was throbbing. Had I not died after all? Where was I?

"My child, you are yet alive." A gentle voice greeted me.

I opened my eyes again and caught sight of an elderly sadhu kneeling over me. He must have seen the confusion on my face.

"You have a big bruise on your head. You must have hit a rock as you got swept away. I found you and brought you here."

I was lying on the banks of the river. Then I realized what had happened. I hadn't died, but I couldn't come back to life. I must go to Mother Ganga again. I struggled to sit up, but my head ached so. My thoughts were on the river. I could hear her gushing sounds. She was swimming swiftly and could take me again. I must go to her, I must.

His gentle voice turned stern. He shook his head slowly and said, "Ganga will not take you. I have commanded her so."

Then the tears started to rain, first in droplets then in streams. "I cannot live," I murmured in a breaking voice. "You don't understand."

"My child, my child," he called softly, wiping my face with his thin shawl and then draping his shawl over my wet and shivering shoulders. "It is you who do not understand. It was the music of creation that you heard in his songs. Do not be deceived. It was none other than the Lord calling you. No mere mortal could penetrate your heart so. Through every atom in the universe, he is calling you. Do not be fooled."

My tears slowed their pace and I stared at the sadhu, whose white beard flowed down to touch his chest, his thin frosty hair tied in a knot on top of his head. His eyes were gentle yet penetrating. How did he know what was in my heart? How did he know about the music that had touched my being so deeply?"

"My child, you will recover. Your heart will heal. You must give it time. You can and will live. And your love will only grow stronger, you will see. It will expand and you will be able to shower it on all, not only on one."

I looked at him in confusion, still thinking he did not understand my situation.

He helped me to sit up. "Come with me now. We must tend to the wound on your head."

I touched the side of my head and felt blood oozing from a rather large wound.

"You need time to heal. I will arrange for you to be taken care of by a community of women before you go back to your family. I will send word to your husband of your condition. Do not worry. It will all be taken care of. When you are able to return to your home, you must give yourself to the Lord, heart and soul. Only then will you heal. In him you will find your true Beloved."

I shook my heard. "I can never go back to my family." The thought of going back to my old life seemed far worse than death to me.

The sadhu simply smiled and said, "Come now," as he helped me to my feet. "We must get that wound cleaned and you must rest. A feverish state will soon come over you. For days your emotions will burn through you and then you will begin to feel better. Come, let us go."

I began to shiver as he spoke and my head started to spin. Clinging to his arm, I grew faint and could hardly take a step. The trees, the river, the sky, all began to whirl around me and I felt my body falling, as if sinking through space, falling, falling, into the darkness that surrounded me.

He must have carried me to the women sadhus who were living not far away. I don't know how else I would have gotten there. When I came to, I was in a small room and an elderly woman was leaning over me, tending to my wound. A few other women were present, all peering over me. I could see they were all widows, as their heads were shaven and they were dressed in white.

The elderly woman helped me into dry clothes and bandaged my head. She was barely finished when I felt myself drifting off to sleep. I had not even the strength to inquire where I was or who they were. I let go and slept.

I was in and out of sleep for several days, wandering between feverish dreams and semi-waking states, eating nothing, calling out for my loved one. Finally I came back to the world. When I awoke, I found myself lying on some bedding in a small but clean room. An elderly woman with a kind and lovely face sat by my side.

"Feeling better?" She smiled when she saw my eyes open.

I didn't know where I was. I had little memory of what had taken place, but the image of the sadhu stayed with me. I touched my head and felt the large bandage. It still hurt.

"You received a bad bruise. We have been dressing it while you slept. In a few days the bandage will come off. You must eat now," she said. "You have eaten nothing for days. You are very weak. Here is some tea." I gladly took the tea and realized how hungry I was. As she prepared the food, I asked her how I got there. "It was Swamiji who brought you," she said simply. "You got caught in a rain storm and fell into the Ganga. He found you and brought you here. He has put you in our care."

"So he is real? I didn't imagine him?"

"Swamiji is very real," she replied with a chuckle.

"Where is he now?" I asked. "I would like to see him."

She smiled as she handed me some food on a platter. "One never knows where he is. He will show up one day and then be gone. But I am sure he will be back to see you. He has shown great care for your welfare."

I tried to remember his words. Over the next few days much of what he told me came back to me. He had said it was the music of creation that I heard. It was the Lord calling me. I knew it to be true, but it was through Atash's music that I first heard the divine call. Surely that must mean something. And why this unbearable pain of separation? How I wanted to free myself from that love, to end the pain, to come back to life! The sadhu's words continued to ring in my mind, but more than his words it was his gaze, his penetrating gaze, that left such a deep imprint. It was as if he knew my life, my thoughts, as if this meeting was not our first. In what I could recall of our brief exchange, I remembered something about his eyes, so caring as if I was his very own child. In that brief transaction he expressed such love that I could not understand it. I did not know what to think. It was as if he knew me.

It took me many weeks to recover my strength fully. I spoke little after my fever subsided. I simply sat in the corner of the room in silence as the women tended to my needs. The elderly woman who cared for me was simply called Mataji, or Mother. She seemed to be in charge of the community. I could see that she was beginning to worry about my state of mind. One day I had an urge to go back down to the Ganga. Nobody was around, so I slipped out on my own and wandered down to the riverbank. I seated myself on the bank of the river and poured out my heart to her.

"If I am to live, then I beg you to take this love from me," I pleaded with the Ganga. "I cannot stand it anymore. I beg you, empty my heart of this love. Only then can I come back to life. Wash it away as you wash away all our misdeeds. This is my offering to you, oh Ganga Ma. I give you this love that Atash awakened in me." As I spoke to her, my heart began to crack, and the tears welled up. An internal storm would have burst forth had I not heard the soothing voice of the sadhu, seemingly speaking from behind me.

"Such impatience," he said gently. "Give her time to heal you. Did I not tell you that you would return to life?" I did not turn my head, but kept my eyes fixed on her dark waters, muddied by the incessant rains. "She will fulfill your wishes, no doubt," he continued, "but do you really want to empty your heart of love, my child? Is that the solution you seek?"

Slowly I turned my head, but the sadhu was not there. I was alone with Mother Ganga. I rose and slowly walked back to where I was staying. On my way I saw Mataji hurrying toward me. Anxious and out of breath, she took me in her arms and hugged me, "I was afraid for you, my dear. How could I have faced Swamiji if something had happened?"

I smiled at her. "No, Mataji, I did not give myself to Ganga Ma again. I have returned." Then I asked, "Have you seen Swamiji? Is he here?" She shook her head. "But he must be here. He has come."

"No, he has not been here since he brought you to us. He has not returned." Then she said with a smile, "But do not worry. I am sure he will be back to see you." I stared at her in confusion.

"But he spoke to me just now, as I was sitting by the Ganga. I heard his voice as clearly as I hear your voice now. Surely he has come. He was there." I looked back toward the Ganga to see if I might catch sight of his figure.

She smiled again. "No, he has not been here. Perhaps he was speaking from inside of you. Swamiji can communicate across time and space. No matter where he is, he will know your thoughts."

The days passed, but I had no notion of time and didn't count as the weeks crept by, flowing one into another. Slowly memories of the past became just that—memories—and I had no thought of the future. Living only in the present moment, I began to heal. In time I regained stability of mind and began to offer my assistance to the women. They performed many social services for people in need and I joined them in their care of the local community. This was comforting. When I saw the everyday struggles of the women and children who came to them, I forgot my own pain. It didn't go away, but bit by bit it got tucked into some corner of my mind, becoming a dull ache that every now and then would awaken with force and then subside.

One day I found that a Muslim child, whose mother had died and whose father had fallen ill, had been brought to the ashram by a neighbor. She were poorly dressed and badly nourished. Mataji was busy and was not told of their arrival, and they were turned away. I was present when this happened and was deeply moved by the young girl's plight. I tried to intervene and speak with the ashram woman who had refused them.

"There are many children in our own community in need," she said in way of apology. "There are Muslim charities who can help the child. I have instructed the woman where to go for assistance."

I could not get the incident out of my mind and finally went to speak with Mataji about it. She must have seen that the young girl had awakened something in me.

"It is strange. I don't understand what I am feeling, but the thought of that little girl not having enough food, or her going to bed hungry . . . I can't sit by and do nothing."

"I would not have turned her away, but I hesitate to contradict our sister. She was in charge while I was busy with other matters."

"But it is not right to turn away a hungry child," I insisted.

She was quiet for a few minutes, then said with a glimmer in her eye, "You are coming back to life, Mira. I will send one of the women with you to go fetch the child. You may bring her back and care for her until her father recovers."

I hadn't left the ashram grounds in several months, so it was with some trepidation that I was to step back into the world. It was my first time entering a home in one of the poorer Muslim neighborhoods. There was an ongoing undercurrent of tension in our city and our communities did not mix. It was not only the Muslim/Hindu divide, but also an economic one. The home of the child was very poor and the scene shocked me. I explained to the bedridden father that we would look after his daughter until he recovered. I also said we would send someone to look after him. The woman accompanying me was quiet as I made these commitments. I don't know what came over me that day; I had no authority in the ashram and was a guest there myself. When I returned with the young girl, Mataji approved and sent someone to their home with food and medicines for the father.

Since arriving at the ashram in my sickly state, I had taken great comfort in the presence of Mataji, but after this incident I saw her in a different light. I saw her true stature and developed great admiration for her and the work of the women.

"I am glad you took the initiative to bring back that young girl," said Mataji one day, as she watched me preparing food for her. "I must help the others see that we must expand our services to include all communities."

"I was afraid that I may have overstepped my bounds," I replied to her with a faint smile. "After all, I am only a guest here."

"A most welcome guest," she responded lovingly. "It is up to those of us who have chosen to serve God to make no distinctions between people and communities. We are one human family," she said. "One day the world will realize this."

"I get much satisfaction caring for the child," I added hesitantly.

"I am glad to hear this, Mira."

Perhaps she knew that by caring for her, a longing for my own children would arise. In my distraught mental state, my children had receded, along with my husband, to a far corner of my mind. But as I fed, dressed, and put to bed the young daughter of an ailing Muslim father, the desire to hold and care for my own returned to me. Despite the emergence of this desire, I dared not ask Mataji when I was to return home, and she didn't bring up the subject.

The moon waxed and waned, and time continued its endless journey. One day as I was having tea with Mataji, she told me that my husband had been coming every week since my accident to check on me. He was quite distraught by what had happened and very much concerned for my recovery. "I have told him that he cannot see you until you have recovered. This has not been easy for him," she said quietly.

A slight shiver entered my body when I heard this. She inquired, "Don't you want to go home, Mira? Don't you miss your children? Your husband said they are missing you terribly. Every week he asks when you will return."

"I do miss my children, more and more. Seeing the young Muslim girl who lost her mother has made me realize what my own children must be going through without me." I paused, not sure how to express the tangle of emotions that still gripped me whenever I thought of my husband. "I . . . I know I should want to go home, but somehow I can't. I can't face him." I looked into her eyes, hoping that she would understand without my needing to explain. I had never spoken of the events that led me down to the river that stormy night. She looked at me with great kindness and replied, "I told him that you need a bit more time. But perhaps soon, Mira. You must begin to think of it and prepare yourself."

"You have been so kind to me. I don't know what would have happened to me without you," I said with deep feeling. "I wish that I could stay here with you. I could find solace in this life of service." A strong sense of guilt was ever present, no matter how much I tried to push it away. At the very mention of my husband, I was overwhelmed by this guilt and I didn't know how I would ever face him again.

"You have duties, and it will do you no good to abandon those put in your care," she replied gently. Noticing my distress, she said, "It will be Swamiji who finally will decide when you are to return."

"Swamiji," I repeated quietly. "Will he come again then?"

She nodded. "When he feels you are ready."

A few weeks later I had finished my chores and had walked down to sit by the Ganga, reflecting on what it would be like to return to my family. A sadness had come over me at the realization that I soon had to leave the community of women, but after my discussion with Mataji, I had begun to accept that this was a necessary course of events. I had to return. After a while I looked up and saw the sadhu silently gazing at me from a short distance away. I jumped up to greet him, surprised and most pleased. As I bowed to touch his feet, he laid a hand gently on my head in way of blessing and said, "I am glad to see that you are looking much better."

"Yes," I replied, overjoyed to see him. "I should thank you for saving my life. Surely I would have drowned had it not been for you."

"It was not your time," he said simply. Then after a pause he added, "You are almost ready to go home. Your duties await you."

"Duties," I repeated softly looking away. It seemed a long time since I had thought of my marital duties. "How long has it been since that night. I have lost track of all time."

"Nearly six months. You have needed this time, but your family cannot wait much longer."

"So I must go home then?" I said in a tone of resignation.

"Yes, it is by fulfilling your duties, your dharma, that you will find peace." He spoke with great firmness.

I gazed into the Ganga. The rains had longed passed and her waters were quiet now. "I would rather stay here with these women. They are very kind and I can be of service here. I want to serve. It gives me a sense of satisfaction, of purpose."

"Why do you think that you can only serve here?" He asked with a smile. "You know that you must go back to your family. They are patiently waiting for you. You can serve there as well. You must learn to be at peace wherever you are, my child."

The thought of returning filled me with anxiety. I had no knowledge of what my husband thought or knew of my situation. And what of my children? What had they been told?

The sadhu read my mind. "Your husband knows that you were ill and that you wandered out one night to pray by the Ganga, and in the night storm you fell into the river and were badly hurt. He knows that these women have been caring for you, and he has been very generous in his donations to them. They have been in touch with him regularly, and he is eagerly waiting for your return." Then he added quietly, "Have no fear. He need not ever know of your private matters. What is in your heart, my child, is between you and the Lord. It will do no harm if your husband believes you were mentally imbalanced. After all, that is what all desire is—a mental imbalance."

We were quiet for a few minutes. Then he continued, "In the distant past you have worshipped the Lord in his form of Sri Krishna. You have also worshipped the formless. Both are true. Put aside all doubt. The Lord cannot be confined to either form or the formless. He comes to his devotee in whatever way is most pleasing, in whatever way he can reach his devotee."

I listened attentively. Until that moment I did not even realize the degree to which this spiritual matter had puzzled me, but it all seemed to make sense now. Of course the Lord is both form and formless. How obvious it seemed. My confusion of many years fled in that moment.

"In this life, you will find solace in the Mother. The same Mother you found in the Ganga will be with you everywhere. Speak to her, pray to her, be absorbed in her, and you will find the joy you are seeking. That same Mother is in you, my child, you need only awaken her. You must find her strength inside yourself."

He fell silent. I closed my eyes to take in his words. When I opened them he handed me a small statue. It was Mother Durga, one of the forms of Mother Parvati, consort of Lord Shiva. I took the statue and stared at it. I had no knowledge of how to worship her.

"She will be your guide," he said. "By the next new moon, your husband will come for you and he will say nothing of your travails. You need not speak of them. He will be happy to have you back. He is a good man. Try to give to him the love that has been awakened in you, the love that he deserves."

I continued to stare at the statue he had given me, Durga on her tiger with many weapons in her hands. "How do I worship her?"

"She will guide you."

After a few minutes I asked, "Will I see you again?"

He did not answer right away, but then he replied, "Ganga will always be here for you. She is far more than just a stream of water, as you will discover. The world may see only that, but she is a living deity. She holds healing powers beyond what people know. Speak to her as a friend. Share with her what is in your heart. You will see what wisdom she imparts."

"But will I meet you again?" I insisted. "I don't know where to look for you if I should have some trouble."

"My child, do not bother to search for me. I will keep watch over you and in the right time, I will come."

He saw that I was still troubled. "A question lurks in your mind, child. Ask it."

"I don't know whether I can trust my prayers. I prayed so hard to Lord Shiva in my distress, and he gave no response. He did not take away the pain."

"Look again into your heart, child. Does any pain lurk there? I think not. Indeed, the Lord has taken it away. He has surely responded to your prayer."

It was true. I felt nothing, no pain, no remorse; even my guilt was beginning to recede. For the first time since my ordeal, I felt free of emotional turmoil.

He smiled. "The Lord's response is not always immediate or

recognizable, but the response is there without fail, once we learn the lessons we need to learn. Just as one must listen carefully to hear the cosmic song, so must one be ever attentive to see the divine response to our prayers." Reaching down, he took Ganga water in his cupped hand and sprinkled a few drops on my head. As he did, he uttered a mantra. I closed my eyes to absorb the blessings. After his chanting ceased, I stood for several minutes in silence, feeling a warm glow. He had settled my heart, which no longer quivered in pain. My agony had subsided. Yes, I could come back to life. I could go home. When I opened my eyes, he was gone. The figure of the orange-robed sadhu had retreated into the horizon.

At the next new moon, my husband came to take me home. I was as ready as I would ever be. He was caring and showed great concern for my well-being. We never spoke about the accident. He never asked me any questions. And so I began the long journey back to life. I set the small stature of Mother Durga that the sadhu had given me by the side of the Shiva Linga in our family temple and made it a place for daily prayers. For the most part it was more a formality to keep alive the memory of the sadhu than an outgrowth of any relationship with Mother Durga. I stared at the statue and spoke to her, but she was not alive for me.

It was difficult to return to my family routine. I tended to my children and fulfilled my family obligations, but with the lessening of my pain, there came a closing of my heart. I could feel little. My mental stability had returned, but I was lonely and lost. I tried to make regular visits to the Ganga. The bathing ghats were always full of people, and there was much commotion and noise, but when I sat there, we would be alone, She and I. Only She knew my secret and knew of the sadhu who had befriended me. When I sat by her side, the world disappeared and I would speak with her as to a mother or a friend. She was my confident.

One evening after I had been home for several months, my husband approached me, seeking intimacy. I turned away, unable to receive him. I felt his pain but could not overcome my resistance.

"Don't you want more children, Mira? It would help bring joy back into our lives."

I felt myself recoil. "No, Bindhu, I don't want any more children. After that last miscarriage . . ."

A troubled look crossed his face. "Is our marital life then over?"

"Give me time."

"How much time do you need, Mira? I have tried to be patient. You were gone from us for what seemed an eternity. Now that you are back, you still have not returned to me. Will you ever return? I pray for that day," he said, in a voice that betrayed great sadness. Rising from the bed, he went to sleep in another room.

I could not get to sleep that night and, when I finally did, I had a frightening dream. I saw Mother Durga in her most fearful form. Her black wrathful eyes stared at me from all directions. Her many arms held the most threatening weapons and they all seemed pointed toward me. Around her was fire, a wildfire spreading everywhere. I felt as if the fire was about to consume me when I awoke with a racing heart. I was overcome with fear. As soon as the morning rays appeared, I made my way to Mataji, who I hadn't seen since I left her ashram many months earlier. I was shaking. Was this retribution for my betrayal of my husband and for my rejection of him now? Would the Mother refuse me after all?

"Mira!" exclaimed Mataji when she saw me. "What has happened?" She saw the fearful look on my face.

I told her of my dream.

"What a blessing that the Mother has come to you," she said quietly. "How many yearn for a sight of her and are never granted the vision."

"I think she has come to destroy me," I replied in a trembling voice. "It is punishment for my deeds."

"No, no. You have it wrong," she answered fervently. "The Mother only comes to strengthen, not to destroy, never to destroy her devotee. She will stamp on your weaknesses but only to lift you higher. She is to be praised for that. She only destroys the impediments. Her weapons are for that purpose only. She was giving you a great blessing, showing you that She is transforming your nature. That was the fire, Mira. It is a purifying fire, not a destructive one. You must do daily pujas to Durga, and she will consume your fears."

I was quiet for a few minutes and then replied, "Every morning I sit before the statue as Swamiji has instructed me, but I feel nothing. I don't feel love for her as I should."

"Pray for that love to enter your heart. Pray with all your might, Mira, that you can transform your love into love for her."

I was quiet. I wanted to seek her counsel about my married life, but dared not ask.

"Speak to me. What is in your heart, Mira? Only then can I give you guidance."

"I find no joy in the things that used to please me before the accident. I only want to serve as you do. I want to live as you do. In my heart I want to be here with you, serving beside you, but I know I must be with my family. Swamiji told me as much," I sighed.

"You are under an illusion, dear," she said. "We are widows. Our circumstances have placed us here, and we are serving as best we can. You are not a widow. You have a husband still, and your service to him should be no different than your service to that poor Muslim child of whom you grew so fond. They are both part of the same Lord. You must let love enter your heart again, dear, but a different kind of love, one directed to God, and to Mother Durga. Look into my eyes, Mira," she commanded.

As I gazed into her gentle eyes, my fear departed.

"Whatever transpired between you and your husband is in the past. You have begun a new life. Take him into your heart. Tend to him as you tended to that poor child. Do not deprive him of your love. By loving him, you are loving Durga Ma. We serve her best in the place where she has put us, and now, in this life, your service must be to your family."

Her words had their desired effect, and slowly my life began to improve. Kindness, if not love, toward my husband returned, and he was grateful for whatever care I could give him. Bindhu hoped to encourage me to return to my musical interests and to begin organizing concerts again, but that world was over for me. I could not go back. "Our concerts are sorely missed," he insisted one evening, hoping to renew my interest. "Everyone has been asking."

I shook my head. He also saw that I had lost interest in my beautiful silk saris and elaborate ornaments that he took such pride in acquiring for me. I preferred now a simpler dress. "I was happy when I was serving with Mataji," I told him. "I found peace there, and I would like to continue helping at the ashram."

He nodded approval. "Yes, they do very good work and are filling a social need. I am proud for you to assist them. We can help them financially and, if you desire, then help them through service."

I smiled. He had always been a generous man.

And so I was able to return to Mataji and to continue assisting the women. The effort to alleviate the suffering of so many in our society assumed a place of great importance in my life, overshadowing my own challenges. I began to wonder how I had been so blind to the life struggles of people, so absorbed in my own world that I had taken no notice of what was happening in the community around me. This service gave me peace of mind and helped to restore the sweetness that once existed between my husband and me.

One evening we were sitting in the courtyard after our meal. It was a very hot and humid evening, very much like the one that saw me run into the arms of Mother Ganga, several years earlier. Bindhu looked at me and said, "Mira, have I told you that you are even more beautiful in your simple sari than you were in your finest silks."

I smiled. "Only a husband of many years could say that, Bindhu."

"You are happy now, my dear?" There was concern in his voice.

"I am content," I replied simply. A look of intense pain came over him. "What is wrong?" I asked.

"When I remember that I nearly lost you . . ."

I went over to him and put my hands around his face, touching his forehead with my lips. I was now performing all my duties as a wife, but my heart had never fully revived. I could not say that I felt love any more. I was very appreciative of his kindness, and a contentment had settled in, but my heart was still closed down and there was nothing I could do to open it again.

"It is the Mother who took me, and the Mother who brought me back," I said slowly. "My life is in her hands."

Some weeks later I was sitting by the Ganga, wondering why I still felt such a numbness, an emptiness in my heart, when suddenly I remembered the words I had spoken to her after my accident. I had asked her to take my love and to free me. She had taken it, and now I was empty. I felt no love in my heart. This emptiness was almost worse than the pain. I was going through the motions of life mechanically, but I felt no joy. I placed my feet into her waters and then waded in up to my waist. I felt her pulling me once again and all the memories of that night came back to me. My feet weakened as her tides pressed against me and her waves rose up against my chest. Would I surrender to her again? It would be so easy.

"No," I cried out suddenly. "I want to live. I want to feel again. Fill my heart with love, Ganga Ma. Let me feel love again." As I spoke these words, I felt a strength rise through my spine. Struggling against the tides, I made my way back to the shore. As I looked out at the Ganga, I saw Swamiji's face before me, smiling. It was not his physical form but a vision, a face of light. Nonetheless he was there, smiling at my determination and, at that moment, his blessings were as real, as tangible, as if his hand were upon my head.

"I know you are with me, Swamiji," I whispered. "I know you are never away. It is you who are bringing me back to life and filling my heart with love again."

Once back in the house I went straight to the temple and sat for a long time in front of the statue of Mother Durga. I remembered then the love that I felt permeating the universe the night of Atash's concert. That love was so palpable, so tangible, so real. Swamiji had told me that it was not Atash but the Lord calling to me. In my deepest core, I knew this to be true, but how to unlock that love, to feel it again? I had had a taste, a momentary experience. I now needed to find it without an external aid.

"Help me to love you," I repeated silently again and again. This was to become my prayer in the weeks, months, and years ahead.

Chapter 26

The years passed, and a quiet joy came back into my life. I found happiness in the little pleasures of family life—the joy of seeing the children grow, the comfort of Bindhu's steady presence. I made peace with my life as it was. I did not forget Atash, but when I thought of him it was with a gentle sense of love, not the raging passion that I once had felt. Since that day by the Ganga when Swamiji brought love back into my life, I began to see things differently. I saw how serving at Mataji's ashram was changing my nature. I would often find Mataji gazing at me; then she would say how she enjoyed watching Durga Ma's transforming hand, molding my character, turning me into a devotee.

"I am hardly a devotee yet," I said with a smile. "But I am learning and trying to be one." The truth was that Durga was becoming more of a presence in my life. When facing difficulties, I would find myself turning to her as I spoke to Ganga Ma, as I would to a friend, a confident. Sometimes I felt a response, but then I would reason perhaps it was only my imagination.

Communal tensions were growing in our city, but I continued to work with Muslim families, providing the same service that I did for the Hindu families, and in this Mataji encouraged me. I paid little attention to political affairs even though I was aware of the growing political problems. We were under Muslim rule but had been enjoying a peaceful spell, with many Hindus placed in high government positions. Suddenly this all changed. My husband was much distressed and one day announced it was no longer safe for me to enter the Muslim communities. I resisted at first, but after several Hindu families were attacked I understood that the wall of separation was sadly a necessity.

One evening he announced that it was best for us to leave Kashi for a while, until things settled down. He also thought a change of scenery would do us good. Our youngest child had recently married. This was the stage in life when Hindu couples began to think of pilgrimages to the holy Himalayan shrines. We were free to set out on a journey of our own.

"Where will we go?" I asked with great concern. Tensions were growing well beyond the borders of Varanasi.

"The Himalayas," he replied. The summer heat was upon us and Bindhu had always wanted to travel through the Himalayas. His responsibilities and care for the children had prevented us from much travel. "We will close up the house for a while. Ganapati can look after it while we are gone."

"But for how long . . ."

"I don't know, Mira. Perhaps in a year or two the situation will change."

And so we set out on a journey, traveling north through villages and towns, mountain passes and valleys. We both loved the quiet and peaceful life in the tiny Himalayan villages, where we could enjoy the simple pleasures of the abundant flowers and animal life. A year passed and then another. Every few months we would move on. Finally we came to the kingdom of Kashmir, a place that I had always envisioned as an earthly paradise and where Bindhu had long wanted to visit. We were in the throes of the hot pre-monsoon months and had no desire to return to the plains just yet. We decided to stay there for a while. A lovely small cottage was arranged for our stay. The gardens were exquisite with flowers of every color. A forest of pine trees grew beyond the gardens, perfumed with the pure and fragrant Himalayan air. Everything about Kashmir was exhilarating.

One day Bindhu had gone out on Dahl Lake while I stayed back to enjoy the garden. Since arriving I had had the urge to walk into the forest behind the house, but there had been no occasion to spend time alone. Now, free for a few hours, I could wander and fully take in the beauty of the pine trees. I was able to discern a narrow path and so began my walk. The forest was quiet. Every now and then I would stop to gaze up at the sun, which could barely be seen although its light shimmered through the pines, and to breathe deeply the fragrant air, which brought an inner tranquility. I had not walked far into the forest when I came to a small rather broken-down hut. The door was bolted shut, but I decided to knock to see whether anyone was inside. There was no answer. I sat on a nearby stone for a while and then returned to our house.

I loved Kashmir not only for the magnificent scenery but also for the mix of cultures. Muslims, Hindus, and Buddhists all lived together in apparent harmony, unlike what I experienced at home, and there was a distinct pride in the people, perhaps pride in their ability to rise above distinctions and find a common bond. There was something special about Kashmiri culture. It was different from anything I had seen, and I loved the colorful array of people and dress.

We spent a quiet summer wandering through the neighboring mountains, visiting sacred sites, and meeting interesting people. Whenever I could find some time alone, I would walk into the forest and visit the bolted hut. I felt mysteriously drawn to the place. I would always knock in the hope of finding somebody home, but there was never a response.

A man that my husband befriended in town told us that a long time ago a woman used to live in that forest hut, but people stayed away because there were reports of strange happenings. This sparked my interest even more, but made Bindhu advise me against wandering into the forest alone. These walks had come to mean too much to me and I could not refrain, but I agreed to go no further than the hut.

On one of my walks into the forest, I came to the hut and found the door slightly ajar. I knocked and, when there was no response, I pushed the door open and peered inside. The hut was composed of a single room, with only a small opening for a window. It was quiet and dark inside. As I entered and my eyes became accustomed to the dark, I saw a woman in the corner seated in meditation. Startled, I drew back. I didn't know whether to leave or to stay, so I simply stood by the door for a few minutes.

I couldn't see her features very well, but she seemed somewhat older than me. She was dressed in Kashmiri clothes and had a shawl wrapped around her head. She didn't move or speak. Finally I decided to leave, but as I stepped toward the door I heard her voice. I turned to find her eyes half open, as if she were slowly returning to the outer world.

"You may stay," she said, in a dialect that by now had become familiar. Hesitantly I approached her. She motioned for me to be seated, so I took one of the cushions in the room and moved it close to her so I could see her better. There was not much in the room, only a carpet and a scattering of cushions on the floor. I now noticed the statue of Durga in the corner and a rather large Shiva Linga, which was covered by many fresh flowers, the obvious result of a recent puja, or ceremony. I stared at these, surprised to find Durga Ma there.

Out of the corner of my eye I caught the woman's half smile, but her eyes remained only partially open.

"I see you know Durga Ma," she said slowly.

"Not really," I replied. "Yes, I do," I corrected myself.

I could see her more clearly now and could tell that she was older than I had at first thought. Strands of grey hair peeked out from her head covering. Her face bore the lines of weather, wind swept from the cold mountain air. I started to introduce myself.

"My husband and I are visiting, staying at a place just at the edge of the forest. We come from Kashi but have been here for some months now," I said. "I have walked by this place many times, but the door has always been locked. I was surprised to find it open today. I didn't mean to disturb you."

She didn't respond.

As I sat there, a yearning entered my heart. A yearning for what, I wasn't sure, but it was a newborn desire that seemed to burst forth. I gathered the courage to continue. "Since I came to Kashmir, I have felt a presence and I want to understand it. There is something special about these mountains, something that I . . ." I turned to face the Linga. "I was brought up with devotion to Lord Ram. It was easy for me to feel devotion to Rama and Krishna. I married into a Shaivite family and the Linga sits in my home, but I don't understand Lord Shiva. His presence is here in Kashmir. I can feel it, but I don't understand who he is, Shiva, the destroyer."

My confusion brought a half smile to her face and her eyes began to open fully. "The One the world calls the destroyer, yogis call the liberator," she said slowly, a warm light entering her eyes.

"Liberator?" I had not heard that word before to describe Him.

She was quiet for quite some time, then she said, "He liberates us from all that is false, from the false notion that we are confined to a body, from the false notion that the material universe is separate from him." I looked at her quizzically, hoping that she would explain further. "There is none other than the One, whatever form he takes, and in the ultimate sense he resides without form. Shiva, in his manifold aspects, liberates us from the illusion of separation, that we are separate from him. In truth we are ever abiding in him, the glorious One, the great Liberator, awakening us to our original nature, the undivided source of all. He is the aspiration of the yogis. Shakti enables that liberation. She shakes us free. Shiva and Shakti are One, but they become two in order to perform the work of transformation, of liberation." With those words, her eyes closed again and she fell silent. I waited for her to reappear, but when she didn't, I also closed my eyes and tried to absorb what she had said. Much time passed before she opened her eyes again.

"It takes man many lives and much suffering to even begin to wish to free himself from material bondage." She spoke as if in a trance. "You have had many blessings, not only in this life. Don't waste those blessings. It is no mere coincidence that has brought you here. In your heart is a hidden pain carried over from a previous birth, and even now its shadow remains, but that pain will be the cause of your awakening. The Mother will free you. She is aware of every thought, every feeling that arises. She sees into your deepest part and knows even what you do not know about yourself. Do not doubt her."

I was surprised to hear her words. It had been a long time since I felt pain over the events that had transpired earlier in my life. But as she spoke I became aware of very subtle feelings—a longing, a pain that was not associated with Atash, a pain from an unknown cause. It was submerged and barely discernable to my normal waking mind. The thought came to me that this pain had taken the form of suffering over separation from Atash, but that it was older than that, of an earlier origin, one that was beyond my ability to identify. What was this pain?

She seemed to know my train of thoughts. "All suffering stems from the original separation from the divine," she said. "Let me clarify: the appearance of separation, because, indeed, there is no real separation. It only seems to be so. Lord Shiva, or Durga Ma, liberates us from this false notion that causes so much suffering. Suffering takes many forms and seems to have many causes, but this is its origin." Suddenly she grew solemn and became silent again. The expression on her face changed as if she were seeing some tragic event, and my body jerked as if I was absorbing her premonition. Fear entered me. Then she spoke.

"The Mother will guide you. The path to freedom is fraught with many hurdles that must be overcome. There is no easy way to untangle the knots that bind us, knots of our own creation. In each life we take but a few steps forward, but most people slip back into unconsciousness, enduring the endless rounds of rebirth and suffering, racing after little bits of happiness when there is so much more to be had. You will not slip back as so many others do. You will move swiftly now, for the Mother has claimed you as her own."

I wondered what her premonition might be and I wondered what she meant by "swiftly." I knew that I was far from any thought of "liberation." Desire for it had begun to stir, but the achievement of it, well, that was of a wholly different order, far beyond what I could hope for in this life.

Her demeanor changed. She fully opened her eyes, coming back to the human world. "Human love is gifted for a deeper purpose," she continued. "It is to awaken the yearning for the ultimate union. It was not meant to be an end in itself. That only leads to suffering because it is transient. Seek that which is ever-abiding, beyond the changing face of time. Love is the very fabric of creation. You have seen this. Love is here right now. It is our very nature." As she spoke her eyes glowed like sparks of coal lighting up the dark. She continued her discourse. "Union with your own true nature, the one undivided Self, is the purpose of life. It is the union of Shiva and Shakti, the return to unity. That is the true love story of creation, the only goal of life."

Much time had passed since I had arrived at the hut, and whatever rays of sunlight had managed to creep in through the small window were now gone. The room had become quite dark. She rose to gather some brambles and wood to light a fire so that we could see each other more clearly. When the fire was burning, I could see that the distant look in her eyes had been replaced by warmth and kindness, which made me feel comfortable enough to speak openly. "I did have a sorrow in my life," I said, "but that was long ago. Durga Ma came to me in a dream around that time, but she came in a frightful form. That was the only time I had any experience of her."

"That is her blessed form," she corrected me. "Even the devotee is not aware of how she is working in our soul, freeing us from past ties and from sorrows to come. We cannot judge her actions, but you must know there is only one purpose to her work: to liberate you. There is no other goal."

We fell into silence again. I changed the subject and ventured to ask, "How is it that you came to the forest to live?"

She smiled and replied, "I lived here for many years with my teacher and from her I learned many things."

"A woman teacher?" I asked in surprise. She nodded. "I would love to meet your teacher."

"She is here and not here. Her body has passed away, or so I assume. She wandered off into the peaks many years ago and never returned. Sometimes I think she has been absorbed into Durga Ma." As she spoke, a faraway look came into her eyes as her gaze turned to the statue of Durga.

"And you continue to live here alone? Are you not afraid?"

She laughed a loud and hearty laugh. "You saw her form! Who can touch me with Durga Ma as my shield? When I am here, I keep up the pujas as directed by my teacher, but I also have become a wanderer. I go off into the mountains for weeks on end in pursuit of her. Along the way, there are holy people to visit."

"Sadhus?" I asked.

She nodded. "There are a few women hermits in these parts. I stay with them. My teacher was such a one. For many years she did ascetic practices."

I was amazed by what I was hearing. Mataji was the closest to a woman saint that I knew, but her focus was social service rather than ascetic practices. I didn't think it possible for a woman to live such a secluded and austere life. I looked at the slight woman before me. Who would think her a hermit? She was dressed neatly, her hair combed back in a tight braid beneath her shawl. The images of hermits that I had were of unkempt and unruly figures. How I admired her and envied her freedom—freedom from all responsibility—and her courage to travel the forests alone.

She laughed again, as if reading my thoughts.

"I envy you," I said, "being able to devote yourself fully to these pursuits. I wish I had your strength and determination. As much as I try to devote myself to meditation, I find myself distracted. I try to feel love for Durga Ma, but I cannot say that I truly do. I wish that I could feel as you do, that I could know her." Even though Durga had become a presence in my life, she was a still distant friend, one whom I approached with diffidence, rather than love.

"This love must be cultivated. It does not come in one lifetime. It takes repeated effort over many lifetimes." She got up to stoke the embers of the failing fire. "I wish I had some food to offer you but as you can see the house is rather bare."

"You have fed me plenty," I replied, "and you have stirred in me a desire for the great Mother, a desire that has been there, but which . . . well, which I suppose has not been strong enough. I think I still have fear of her wrathful form."

She took my hands in hers and smiled as she looked again into my eyes. There was such tenderness in her face. "Be rid of your fear forever. Nothing in this universe can harm you." Then she added, "One day you will come to know more intimately the ways of the Mother."

We sat together for some time in silence, then I said, "Many years ago, I nearly died. A sadhu saved me and gave me a small statue of Mother Durga. I sit with her in silence in the mornings, but I never learned how to do any proper pujas. Can you teach me?" I asked.

She didn't respond at first, but then said, "It is your love that the Mother seeks. Rituals are only useful if they open the heart to that love."

"But perhaps the pujas will awaken that love," I responded in a quiet voice.

She got up to put more wood on the fire. When the flames began to rise, she mumbled some words with closed eyes. Slowly her voice quieted and she fell into silence again. Suddenly I became aware of the time. I didn't know how long I had been there, but it seemed like much time has passed. I became fidgety but she didn't move. I wondered whether to stay or quietly get up and take my leave.

Something called me to close my eyes. As I sat there, for the first time my racing mind came to a halt and my thoughts fled. I fell into total stillness, resting in a waveless sea, with no movement at all. There were no more questions, nothing more to ask, nothing I needed to know. In this stillness I found myself calling out to the Mother, silently expressing my desire to know her. Again and again I called out to her until my calls became a mantra, repeating itself without any will of mine. This time she appeared, not with her weapons and fire but in the beauty of a lotus flower, which began to open, revealing universe upon universe, an unending stream of life unfolding like an infinite array of petals. There was no end to her magnificence. How could I feel fear before this wondrous vision? She was joy itself, all beauty and love. I was overwhelmed by the happiness that filled me, a joy that I could barely contain.

I do not know how long we sat, but I was brought back to the world by a gentle tap on my chest. My eyes opened and I saw the woman beside me sitting undisturbed with closed eyes. Her body emitted a soft glow, which seemed to light up the room, replacing the fading embers of the fire.

If it was not she who had tapped me, then who was it? In the Mother's kindness, she had come again to me, showing me her most bountiful form, but did I deserve it? I had closed my heart to her. I began to sob quietly, but these were not tears of sorrow. I didn't know why I was crying; it was the soft flow of love returning, the awakening presence of the Mother.

When she heard me, the woman opened her eyes. As she placed her hands over mine, my tears subsided. "The Mother is entering your heart," she said softly. "Let her flow through you. That is all you need to do." I looked into her face. My eyes were glowing with joy, grateful for the blessing she had bestowed on me. We sat there for some time longer, bathed in the Mother's presence.

Finally she said, "It is late. I will see you to the edge of the forest." I didn't speak, but rose and followed her as she walked outside into the fragrant night air. I breathed in deeply. I felt as if I had been reborn. When the edge of the forest was in sight, she said, "I will leave you here. It is safe for you to travel the rest of the way on your own."

I wanted to thank her, but couldn't find the words. A deep silence had come over me and my lips would not move. She smiled and nodded as she read my heart. All I could do was to touch my head to her feet in gratitude.

"Durga Ma has already responded," she said. With those words she turned and walked back into the forest. I realized then that I didn't even know her name. Who was this woman hermit who had brought me to the feet of the great Mother?

Bindhu was greatly worried when I didn't return after dark. He was on the verge of going to seek help from the villagers when he saw me returning. He began to upbraid me but when he saw the joy on my face, he relaxed, glad to have me home safely. I didn't speak a word of what happened, but several days later I began to ask everyone I came in touch with who the woman was.

"Nobody has lived in that hut for years," came the answer. "The old woman who used to live there died long ago.

"There was a woman hermit there, Bindhu," I insisted when he looked at me doubtfully. I met her. We spoke. We sat by the fire together and meditated. That is why I was so late. She had great knowledge. I must find her again." We inquired and inquired, but nobody could provide any clues. I took Bindhu to the hut several times, but it was always bolted shut.

"I am not imagining her," I said to him in despair. "Even if nobody else has seen her, I saw her."

"I believe you, Mira, but she is gone. Whoever you met is no longer there. Forget her. Perhaps it was a chance encounter. She may have been passing by, but she is gone now."

I could not forget the woman hermit, whose name I did not know. The few hours that I had spent with her changed my life. The Mother no longer was a stranger to me, a concept, an idea. She had become a reality that night, and that memory would stay locked in my subconscious mind for a long time to come. I had seen her. She had shown me universes, a vision I could not forget. As I reflected on my experience, I realized for the first time the truth of Swamiji's words when he rescued me from the Ganga. It was the divine that had called me through Atash's music, not the music itself. That love was a doorway, and in my ignorance I had failed to push open the door, failed to see who was truly calling me. It had taken me this long to understand the purpose of the experience gifted to me so long ago; it was the woman hermit who removed the obstacles that had hindered my mind.

We stayed in Kashmir until the first snows fell. I had wanted to see the mountains crowned with their white glory. It was already getting too cold for us to stay on, and so I took my last walk into the forest before we were to descend to the plains. I never saw the woman hermit again, but every time I passed the hut I sat for a few minutes beside the door and sent my love to the statue of Mother Durga that sat inside. It was with great reluctance that I said goodbye to that small hut. I prayed that my time in Kashmir would ever live in my memory, that I would not forget the beautiful forest, the peaks, the air, and most of all the woman hermit who had led me to the feet of the Mother.

I think our journey to Kashmir was only for the purpose of my meeting this forest dweller, the nameless woman who had a lasting impact on my life. I didn't know fear after this, and any residual guilt over my affair completely washed away. I was inspired to learn of the existence of women recluses and, long after my return to Varanasi, I would think of her and gain strength. Something had transpired between us in that brief interaction that changed me.

After the trip to Kashmir, I was able to carry out my household duties with newborn joy. Although I never mentioned my inner experience to Bindhu, our travels had bonded us in a way I never expected. We were happy together. But as is the human condition, there were also times of forgetfulness when I would take myself down to the river and complain to the Ganga about this or that. After all of these years she had become a friend. Most often she was a patient friend, listening without responding, but on occasion I would hear her guidance, a voice inside telling me not to dwell on a particular matter, and most of all not to feel sorry for myself.

The years passed. I grew older. My children had children of their own. Bindhu and I had become a great support for each other in our elder years and I was grateful for his presence. On occasion I would think how wise the sadhu had been to insist that I return to my family. Had it not been for his wise counsel, I don't know what would have become of me.

I was sitting by the Ganga in the early morning hours, when suddenly I heard a gentle voice from behind. "My child," he said simply.

I turned around and saw him, the same sadhu who had rescued me decades earlier. Although I had aged, he had not changed at all. My surprise must have shown on my face, because he smiled broadly. Overwhelmed with joy, I bowed and touched his feet with my forehead. I kept my head there, taking in the grace of his feet, until he gently lifted me.

"I see you have followed my advice and made friends with Mother Ganga. Has she not guided you well?"

"Yes. You were right. She imparts much wisdom. I don't know how I would have managed all these years without her. You were right about so many things," I replied quietly as I looked at him tenderly.

"Few know what a good friend she can be." He was quiet for a few moments and then said, "I see that you have advanced in your devotion. You have come to know the Mother. I am pleased."

I was happy to hear those words. Never had I expected to hear him praise my efforts and affirm the course my life had taken.

"I have watched you from afar, and I know the early struggles of your heart. That has long since passed. You are seeking the higher union now."

"Yes," I said with conviction. "Durga Ma has shown me that."

"You must keep expanding your love, my child."

We were quiet for a few minutes, then I asked, "Swamiji, my deeds of long ago, have I made amends for what I did?"

He didn't answer right away but then replied, "it is a not simply a matter of making amends. The laws of the universe bring us the fruits of our action, but in the right time and the right place. It is not to punish us, only to teach us. Had you given your life to the Ganga, had you not returned to your family, there would have been a great price to pay. That is why I had to intervene." He was quiet for a few minutes. "Your work with Mataji and your meeting with the Mother have brought you many blessings, blessings that you will realize in time."

Such love was emanating from him that it brought tears to my eyes. "Such love," I whispered inwardly. I wondered where it came from, his love for me. But he would not let me dwell on this question. As this thought entered my mind, the image of the woman hermit in Kashmir came before my mind. I saw her gentle smile and her glowing eyes. "The woman hermit in Kashmir, who was she?" I asked.

"What do you need to know, child? Is it not enough that she opened your heart to the Mother?"

"Yes, she opened my heart to Durga Ma, and for that I am eternally gratefully. I realized in that small mountain hut that the Mother has forgiven me."

He chuckled. "Forgiven? There is nothing to forgive. The Mother doesn't judge her children. She simply waits for them to awaken and return. You deemed yourself unworthy of the Mother's love and so you closed your heart, but you have given up this false notion of unworthiness. You were misguided, but have set yourself aright. This is all that matters."

I pondered his words. Deep inside I knew that I would meet Atash again, in some future life, but I didn't wish to undergo such suffering, so when I do meet him, I thought, let it be for a higher purpose. I do not wish to cause that pain to myself, to him or to any others, I silently affirmed.

"The laws of karma must be fulfilled," he said as if in response to my thoughts, "but they can also be amended by those who know how to do so. Cling to the Mother. That is all you need to know," he said. "That is the way to freedom, to liberation, and there is no other goal worth seeking. Remember this."

The thought entered my mind that I might not see him again. I gazed at him, wanting in some way to express the tremendous love that had arisen in my heart for him and to implant the memory of him in my mind. Unable to express myself, I simply fell to my knees and rested my forehead on his feet, letting them stay there for longer than normal. When he gently lifted me, I cried softly, "Swamiji . . ."

He smiled. "We will meet again at some future time. Do not limit yourself to this life only." There were no words to express my gratitude. He raised his hand in blessing and then I watched him as he walked away. I could not turn away my eyes until his form had disappeared. How much my brief interactions with him had given me. It seemed a lifetime of teaching had been transmitted in his few words.

Some weeks later, I was sitting with my husband after the evening meal. I had never shared with him my meeting with Swamiji, or much about my devotional life. I had not felt that he would understand. But for some reason I felt the need to ask him about that night so long ago.

"Do you remember when I took sick and nearly drowned? I asked him.

"How could I forget that time when I almost lost you?" His voice still echoed with sadness when we spoke of this time. He looked at me with great tenderness.

"You never asked me about that night . . . when I fell into the river."

"There was no need," he said. "A sadhu came here and explained it all to me."

"He did!" I exclaimed in amazement. "What did he tell you?"

"That you had a terrible fever and were having nightmares; that you went to the river to offer prayers, got dizzy, lost your balance in the storm, and fell into the rushing water."

"You never wondered how the sadhu found you, how he knew who you were?"

"I assumed you told him to come to me when he rescued you."

I shook my head. "That sadhu knew my thoughts without me speaking them. I had not the state of mind to tell him anything."

"How strange," said my husband. "Anyhow, I am eternally grateful that he found you and brought you back."

That was so like Bindhu, not to inquire further. He didn't need to know anything more. I don't know why I brought up the subject that night, except to see perhaps whether he had any lingering doubts. Swamiji was right about this as well. There had been no need to pain him with my own troubled emotions.

Suddenly I was feeling very weary. "I will go rest now," I said.

My husband took my hand and said with such trust, "All that ever mattered to me was that you came home." I smiled at him, grateful for his unwavering devotion to me. It was almost childlike in its purity.

Swamiji had been wise to send me home. It was far better that I hadn't left my husband. It would have broken his heart. Yes, it was good I had listened to him. I lay down on my bed. I was so very tired. I closed my eyes. I had only one regret: if I had come to know Durga Ma earlier, I could have served her better. I could have been more useful to her. If only I had known . . . if only I had found her at a younger age . . . I could have gone much deeper in meditation, if I had known, if I had been shown a way . . ."

My mind began to drift. I felt the sweet waters of the Ganga swirling around my feet. Ganga Ma, you have been a dear friend to me. Her waters began to whirl faster and faster until I saw a form emerge. No longer was she the rushing green waters that for so long had comforted me. For the first time I saw her true form—her beautiful maiden figure, her long flowing hair and smiling face. She was beyond description, my Ganga Devi. She was real after all. She was not merely rushing water; she had a form that could be seen. As she rose from the waters, she seemed to be telling me something. I couldn't quite hear or understand, until I heard the voice of Swamiji.

"You may take her now," he said. "It is her time."

I was ready. There was nothing left undone. And there was no fear. I had lost all fear in Kashmir. I was calm and peaceful, filled with a joy I had thought would forever evade me. All would be taken care of. Whatever karma needed to be fulfilled would find fulfillment in the right time. I could let go and finally enter Ganga's waters. I could surrender myself to her beckoning form.

Chapter 27

M y relationship with my Iranian friend continued to develop. After joining us in Greece, I invited him to join a gathering we were organizing in Bhutan on the theme of New Models of Development, based on the Bhutanese Gross National Happiness Index. He performed a concert there, joined by a Buddhist nun from Nepal who was also a renowned singer. Their voices merged as they sang together the name of Allah and mantras—*Om Mani Padme Hum* and *Om Namah Shivaya*—bringing into one stream the great traditions of Sufism, Buddhism, and Hinduism. Next I invited him to give a concert at a gathering in Boulder, Colorado. By this time, I had come to realize that our proper relationship in this life was as dear friends. If there had been any karma between us had been initiated long ago, it was now neutralized.

Some five years before the memories of my life in Kashi returned, my work at GPIW took me to Kashmir. After the summit we had organized in Jaipur, India, in 2008 on the Divine Feminine, a Kashmiri Hindu woman who had participated in the Summit invited me to visit Srinagar, the capital of Kashmir, a state in the north of India. I fell in love with the region and began to read up on its recent history.

Before British colonization, many separate kingdoms composed Hindu India, tied together by a common culture and religion. Despite being under Muslim rule since the Mughal invasions many centuries earlier, the Hindu culture and way of life had remained strong. After independence from Britain and the subsequent partition into India and Pakistan in 1947, Pakistan invaded Kashmir, which had not yet decided whether or not to join the newly born state of India. The Maharaja of Kashmir sought the protection of India; in doing so, he chose for Kashmir to become part of India, but in the end it was divided—part of Kashmir resides with India and part with Pakistan. This is still a matter of dispute between the two nations and several wars have been fought over it during the last few decades. The India part of Kashmir has become more restive in recent decades as militants infiltrated the area from across the Pakistan border.

The woman who invited me to Kashmir had been organizing peace dialogues in the state with young people. Her family had fled during the communal riots of 1989, when most of the Hindu families had been forced from their homes. I traveled to Kashmir knowing little of its history and was surprised to find the degree to which the separatist movement affected the culture there. With most of the Hindus gone, there was little evidence of Hindu culture, except for a few ancient Hindu shrines, mostly unvisited and guarded by the Indian military. I discovered that even the Sufis were under threat by radical elements. I felt a great sadness there, and nothing came of this visit.

Kashmir stayed on my mind. I started to follow news of the region. After the Hindus fled, an influx of money from the Gulf countries helped to radicalize the prevailing Sufi culture, turning it toward Salafism, an extreme form of Islam emanating from Saudi Arabia. It seemed that history was repeating itself. What I had experienced centuries earlier as the young Rani in northern India during the Muslim invasion was still happening.

After this visit, I began studying Kashmiri Shaivism and once again came into a relationship with Lord Shiva. This new spiritual energy brought me deeper understanding of some of the more esoteric yogic practices associated with the worship of Shiva, a process that is still unfolding for me. These teachings, reserved for the adept, lead to the ultimate union of Shakti, the female creative force, with Shiva, the unmanifest primordial consciousness. This yearning for union—or more accurately re-union—is the impulse behind all human love, central to the human experience. I suspect it was that day in the forests of Kashmir many centuries ago when this knowledge was first implanted in my mind. Why had it taken so long to re-emerge? If we could only see the many thoughts and desires that lurk half buried in the subconscious mind waiting to be fulfilled. The working out of karma is one of life's great mysteries: we must continue to undergo a seemingly unending array of experiences until we can come to know the true purpose of human life, only to regain what once we had lost.

Some years later I was invited back to Kashmir and decided to bring a group of Hindu spiritual teachers for a Sufi-Yogi Dialogue. The atmosphere in Srinagar was very tense, made more so by the fact that I was traveling with Hindu swamis into an area threatened by growing Islamic militancy. The local Sufis were very welcoming of the initiative, but they too were hesitant to be seen in any public way. Despite all this, the dialogue went well and we returned the following year for a dialogue between Hindus and Buddhists on the theme of "the Nature of Ultimate Reality."

We also began working with a network of young people in Kashmir, who are the ones most vulnerable to the fundamentalism that continues to spread across the region. With high unemployment and little vision for the future, Kashmir is a region in great need of attention. It is a place of tremendous spiritual riches, where Buddhists, yogis, and Sufis once came together in profound exchange. Ironically, the region's most beloved saint is a woman, Lalleshwari, known as Lal Ded, an ecstatic yogini who wandered naked through the mountains teaching a universal love and wisdom to Muslim and Hindu followers alike.

The spiritual damage imposed on Kashmir is matched by an ecological destruction that is the result of an outdated model of development. Overcrowding in the city, traffic and pollution, deforestation, and damage to the great Dahl Lake and its ecological system are breaking the spirit of what was once considered the paradise of the world. That paradise can be restored. The spirit of Kashmir can rise again, but for this to happen Hindus, Muslims, and Buddhists must come together in a newfound unity. The people of Kashmir must reject regressive foreign forces and move beyond the confines of religious separation, finding greater value in a shared spiritual narrative. The teachings of Lal Ded must reign once again. The yogis and Sufis must be called back to their mountain abode.

The awakening of my memories of this life in India brought me deeper into reflection on the workings of karma. I wondered at the course of my journey from the Rani in India, to the Sufi in Persia, to the Buddhist nun in Japan, to the devotee of Durga in India. There seemed to be strong links between these four lives. Matsu and Mira were linked by a common love for the arts and then a retreat into a more reclusive lifestyle. Was it the subconscious memory of the Buddhist monastery in Japan that made Mataji's ashram so appealing to Mira, which made her yearn for that type of reclusive life? And there was a link between Mira and Minoo—the attitude of service that my Sufi father had instilled in me was to reappear in the life of Mira. It was through service that she found healing. Her attraction to the Sufi musician and to working with Muslim children, were these inspired by subconscious memories of Persia, of the musician rejected by my Sufi father?

Those lives clearly influenced my present life as Dena. I was born into a family that worshipped the arts as their religion. For many years after my divorce, I dated only musicians. Was that inspired by subconscious memories from the life of Mira? And my interfaith work, seeking to bring together Hindus, Buddhists, Muslims, Jews. The more I saw, the more complex it became, a growing web of interconnections. I was beginning to understand something of the workings of karma, but I was also beginning to see how many times we go through the same experience, in slightly different scenarios. Is it so difficult for us to learn our lessons that we must keep repeating them? There must be a way to speed up the process, I thought. That is the role of *sadhana*, spiritual practice, to awaken us so that we do not continue to repeat the narratives.

From Varanasi, the journey of my lives took me to Africa, and I was born as Thema. It was in the life of Thema that I truly came to know the Goddess Durga, called by another name. It was none other than Durga that I saw when Didi transformed herself into the Great Mother. From Africa, I journeyed to America, where I began my search again for the teachings of India.

What did all these lives amount to? The one constant was that in every life there was always a guide, a holy person to point the way. That was the one comfort I could find in every life—a guide pointing in the direction of the divine. When I put them together, the message was always the same. There was the sadhu who came to Rani Gita, my Sufi father Baba, the Sensei in Japan, the sadhu who saved Mira, and the woman hermit in Kashmir, Didi in Africa, Mr. Emerson and the swami who appeared in dream to Elisabeth, and then my dear guru Yogananda who came to rescue Sonya and who has led me in this life as Dena. As I dwelt on the meaning of all of this, my gratitude to my guru deepened, and I wondered why these many blessings, why was I so looked after. Clearly my relationship with him had an earlier history. Germany was not my first sighting of my guru.

Soon memories were to awaken from 1,000 years ago, to a time when I lived in close association with my guru. These memories came back to me when I was taking a break from work and visiting a family friend in

London. She invited me to join her on a trip to the coast of England, to Dover, where she said there were many antique shops. I love antiquing as much as she does and so off we drove. Before we began our shopping expedition, we stopped by the cliffs overlooking the sea. As we were sitting there, my consciousness became interiorized. I closed my eyes and sank into a deep meditative state. A scene arose before my closed eyes: a plentitude of Old World ships sailing across the channel. I was on one of the ships, on my way to join my husband in the newly conquered land of England. I knew intuitively, as well as by the dress of those on the ships, that it was during the time of William the Conqueror. Many of Yogananda's close disciples knew that he had been William in one of his incarnations. My eyes flew open; the ships were still there, making their way across the channel. It didn't matter whether I closed my eyes or opened them, the scene before me was the same.

"Come, we must hurry before the shops close," urged my friend, tapping me on the shoulder and bringing me back to the present world. I didn't move. She urged me again. I got up and slowly followed her through the narrow streets into one antique shop after another. I barely looked at the items spread before me. Normally, the teapots, bits of lace and old fabrics, and other odd objects would have captured my attention, but my mind was elsewhere this day. It was in the third or fourth antique shop that my eyes fell on something of interest. In the corner of one of the shelves was a small ivory figure of Lord Krishna playing his flute. I thought it odd that in this tiny store in a small corner of England I would find him there, the One whom my guru so loved. I purchased this Krishna and took it as a sign that what I had seen was true. I keep that statue of Krishna by my bedside to this day.

Once back in London, I was able to withdraw into meditation and observe the scenes that unfolded before my eyes. It was like watching a movie, with myself as the main character.

William conquered England in 1066 and brought his most loyal nobles from Normandy to help administer the land. My husband was such a one. I was pregnant with my tenth child when I went to live in the newly constructed castle that had been built for us. It had been a very difficult pregnancy and I didn't know if the child or I would survive.

After we were established William came to see us. I normally stayed much in the background, but he called me to him this day. "This daughter will be your last child," he said. "She will be a very special child. She will be sickly, but she will survive. Keep her in your care and guard her well, as she will bring many blessings to this land."

My hands were on my protruding womb as he spoke these words. I was glad to hear there would be no more pregnancies. I didn't think I could survive any more, and I was even more grateful when he confirmed that the child would survive. Indeed, the child was sickly when she was born and ill for much of her first two years. At one time I didn't think she would live, but I remembered William's words. He came to visit us around the time when she was two and very ill with fever. He asked to be alone with her. When he emerged from the room, he said. "She will stay. She has promised me that."

When she grew older, she preferred to play alone rather than to be with the other children. She was always wandering off seeking solitude. One day I asked her, "Don't you want to play with the others, my dear?"

She shook her head and with a broad smile whispered, "I will tell you a secret, mama, but you must promise not to tell the others." I nodded. "It is only when I am alone that the angels come to play with me."

"Angels?" I asked in alarm.

She nodded. "They are so beautiful. I wish you could see them, mama."

This ability of hers became more apparent as she grew older and my husband began to think she was mentally unfit. He worried that we would never be able to find a husband for her. My daughter was a beautiful girl, with the sweetest, gentlest disposition. "Any noble man would be fortunate to marry her," I insisted. But that was not to be her fate.

As she approached marriage age and heard her future being discussed, she protested. "But I am already married, mama."

I looked at her in confusion. "What are you saying, my dear?"

"Look." She held out her hand. Her wedding ring finger was wrapped in a string of small flowers.

"Who gave that to you?" I asked in alarm. She was hardly out of my sight and I knew no man had visited her.

She laughed her sweet, gentle laugh. "It was Lord Jesus himself who gave this to me."

"Truly, my dear, tell me who gave this to you."

"It was none other than he," she insisted.

My husband grew furious when he heard these word, accusing me of encouraging her fantasies. He knew our daughter had a strong religious bent, but this was exceeding all bounds. "Have you not taught her it is a sin to lie," he scolded me.

When we were alone, I asked her, "Was it really the Lord who gave you this ring?"

She nodded. "I can never marry another."

My daughter began to wander off, singing sweet songs, evading the knights who watched over her, making her way to the village to dispense whatever food she could get from the castle kitchen.

One day William arrived and I unburdened my heart to him, telling him of my fears for my daughter. "I had foretold this when she was born," he said. "Leave her to her work. Do not interfere."

She no longer would live in the castle, so we built a small cottage on the property where she could come and go as she pleased, with knights posted nearby to ensure her safety. I would visit daily. When she was not at home, I would leave baskets of food by her door, with blankets and warm clothing and other items for her comfort. They would always be gone by the next day, so I assumed that she was making good use of the things I left for her. One day when I made my daily visit, I found her returning to the cottage. I was shocked by her appearance. In the time since I had seen her last, she had become quite thin. Her beautiful golden locks were knotted, no longer the beautiful mane of which I had been so proud. She was dressed in only a light cloak.

She must have seen the horror on my face because she was quick to assure me that she was fine.

"But the warm cloak I left. Why are you not wearing it?"

"Mama, there are those who have far greater need than I."

"And all the food . . ."

"How could I not share it, when my Lord has given me so much?"

I drew her frail figure to my chest and began to weep. "If only you knew how difficult it is for me to see you thus."

She comforted me and dried my eyes. "Mama, if only you knew how great is his glory and how much he has given me, you would not weep. You would rejoice that he has deemed your daughter worthy of such love." It was then that I learned of her austerities as she described her nights in prayer. "The nights turn into day and then night again, but I cannot pull myself away from the glories of that world, the world where the angels dwell," she told me. "What need have I for food, mama, when they are filling me so with their glory?"

I could not bear to see her deprivations. Hearing that William was again in England, I went off to see him. I described her situation, barely restraining my tears. He listened patiently and, when I was done, replied, "You see her simply as your child. I see her differently. She has come to bless the land, and that she is doing. You mustn't interfere with her work no matter how hard it is for you. She has all the protection she needs."

I began to protest that she would die if she had to endure these states much longer.

"Then let her die!" he exclaimed with a fierceness I had not seen in him before. "It is her choice, not yours. She is doing the bidding of a higher authority." I was shaken by his words and began to weep. Then in a gentler voice he said, "One day you will come to understand who she is, and one day you will reap the blessings from her life."

I couldn't comprehend his meaning, so I asked, "I beg you, will you come visit her? She will listen to you, I am sure of that. I have total faith that you can help her."

William came to see her and they spent some time alone. When he emerged from her small cottage, he was beaming. I pressed him to tell me what had transpired. "I have appointed many officials in the church and built monasteries to house many good men and women of faith, but she is of a different order. Look into her eyes. You will find no suffering there."

"Can you not help her then?"

He smiled. "Help her? Your daughter needs no assistance. You do not know the extent to which she is helping me as we establish this land. Your husband and the other nobles are helping to establish the social order, but what she is doing is far greater." I looked at him quizzically. "If you wish to serve me, you will serve her. Your only duty is to continue caring for her physical needs the best you can, as you have done these many years."

There is nothing I would not have done for William, our Sire, our

Lord. He was the one who had sustained us all these years, and we had far more than mere admiration for him. He was our all. But to sacrifice my daughter, that was almost more than I could bear. Yet it was he who had brought her back to life when my two-year-old daughter was at death's door. Did I not owe her life to him? Therefore, I was bound to obey him.

If I thought William would talk my daughter out of her austerities, I was wrong. Her fasting, her nights at prayer without sleep, increased. I saw her looking more and more gaunt, and I despaired. But the suffering was indeed mine, not hers. When I looked into her eyes, they were aglow with joy. She was ever radiant, describing to me some visit from the angels, some words of comfort from the Lord himself.

One day, my greatest fear came true. I entered her little abode to find her lying peacefully, with no breath in her body. I was beside myself with grief. If only I had been more insistent about looking after her. Then I heard her sweet voice. "Why weep, mama, when I am with him, my Lord. Finally he has come to take me. I have only gone home."

William came to see me soon after her passing and directed me to walk among the people and discover what had been her life. And so I did. In the villages I heard stories of my daughter's deeds, her distribution of food and clothes, her tender touch when there was illness and death in a family, her care for the young and the old. She was dearly beloved. It was only than that I captured a glimpse of who my daughter was.

How few women could do what she did, I mused one day as I sat in her cabin, reflecting on her life. I had made peace with her death and comforted myself in knowing that I had allowed her to have the life she wanted, as William had directed me to do. None of it would have been possible without his direction. I had come to see that she had been given a rare freedom, a freedom that I wished other women could know. Somewhere inside I understood what that freedom meant.

Some may view William as a ruthless conqueror. I know a different William, one of great foresight, who was infusing the land he ruled with a spiritual energy that would bring benefits for centuries to come. Who knows the forces that enabled Britain to rise to the position in the world that it held for so long? Those forces are hidden, not seen with the naked eye. William's work was far greater than conquering and administering a land. He was sowing seeds that would guide history long after he left the body.

As I ended my visit to London and returned to New York, I had a strange experience. I connected with that being who had been my daughter in old England. That being was now in a man's body, a yogi living in a far Himalayan abode, remembering me as I was recalling the memories of her. Perhaps, I thought, a male yogi had taken birth in a woman's body centuries ago to show the world that indeed a woman can achieve the highest spiritual states. Since this incident, I have not lost contact with that soul, and on every visit to the Himalayas I wonder if we will meet again. During times when the work has been difficult, when I have been caught in places of conflict where violence has occurred, I have felt the hidden blessings flowing from that Himalayan yogi. We may not meet in this life, but our connection is eternal and the love has not died. Indeed, as William said so long ago, I did not then know the blessings that would come to me from my care and love for that child. I now believe that the blessings from that life sustained me through the travails of many subsequent lives, and I believe it was my guru who placed me in that role so I could be the recipient of those blessings.

Such is the love and ever-watchful eye of the guru.

PART VIII

BETWEEN BIRTHS

The soul is neither born, nor does it ever die;
nor having once existed, does it ever cease to be.
The soul is without birth, eternal, immortal, and ageless.
It is not destroyed when the body is destroyed.

—Bhagavad Gita 2:20

And if I forget how many times
I have been here, and in how many shapes,
this forgetting is the necessary interval of
darkness between every pulsation of light.

—Alan W. Watts,

The Book: On the Taboo
Against Knowing Who You
Are

Chapter 28

I have written much about memories of my different stays on earth, but equally important are the times in between. Where do we go between births? One can look at this a different way and see birth as a death—a dying to the world of light, a suppression of those memories. In the same way that we forget our previous births on earth, we forget about that world of light each time we take on a new human body. Which is our true home? Which is the real going out: our visits to earth or our visits to the world of light? The answer to this question came to me some years ago as I relived the memories of my most recent death at Sonya's brother's home in Prague.

Swami Yogananda was calling me to follow; he had come to take me to America as he had promised. Yet the agony of seeing Yuri and the other Jews in such a deplorable state in the concentration camp held me back from entering the light; I could not turn away from their torment. To see a man of his character and intellect being reduced to this state, subjected to such indignity, no, I could not leave Yuri now that I had seen his fate. I would find a way to free him and the others. This determination rose within me. My heart cried out to him, but he seemed not to hear me. He seemed not to see me standing by his side, trying to reach him, trying to let him know that I was there beside him. Yuri, Yuri, I don't want to leave you like this!

As I struggled with these emotions, I began to see beautiful rays of light emerge and take form, beings who were silent witnesses to what was taking place. Then I heard again Swamiji's call. I had waited so long for Swamiji and finally he had come. I could not lose sight of him now. I turned to find him standing at a distance, drawing me like a magnet, calling me to follow. I couldn't see to where, but I trusted him. He had told me he was taking me to America. That was my greatest desire, to follow him there and to study with him. The thought entered my mind, "You can help from the other side as well." As this thought arose, the scene before me dissolved. Yuri and the other Jews were gone. Even my Swamiji was gone. I had to find him. In the background I vaguely heard my brother Andrei crying my name, and I saw my body lying there, still as a rock. Caught in the crosscurrents of emotions, all I wanted was to sleep. I was so tired, so very tired. Life had worn me out. I would follow Swamiji to America, but first I needed to rest, to get my energy back. With this thought in mind, I lost consciousness, and Sonya died.

I awoke in a beautiful room, one very familiar to me. It didn't take me more than a minute to realize where I was. I was *home*. I slipped out of bed and hurried outside into the radiant light, down the stone path I knew so well. My feet led me past meadows of flowers to the small cottage where he was waiting for me, all smiles: the golden one, my male companion, who was always waiting there for my return. I was overjoyed to see him and could not stop my eyes from roaming again and again over his form of light, his golden hair and beaming face.

We communicated through an exchange of thoughts about my dream of the life of Sonya. He knew all the details. He had watched my travails from this place, extending what solace he could, he said. He could see the shadows of that life still lurking around me, although it seemed now but a dream. The memories and emotions had not dissipated, and I still carried the burdens of the story I had lived. I had to free myself now that I was home and awake.

We went first to the abode of my father, to the sacred grove where he stayed in eternal meditation, surrounded by sages absorbed in bliss. I sat down before him. His eyes opened slightly to acknowledge my arrival and the hint of a smile crossed his face. I stayed there for some time with my companion. The measurement of time is so different in the astral planes. What may appear to be a day there would be a year on Earth, and yet from there we are unaware of how time is passing on the physical plane.

Memories from Sonya's life flashed through my mind, and the highlights came before me: my yearning to dance as a child, my attachment to my mother and our separation, the dreary days after the departure from Russia, the death of my sister, meeting Yuri, Arnaud the art professor, my meeting with Swamiji, Andrei coming to rescue me and his calling out to me as I lay dying, and then the war, the horrible scene I encountered as I departed my physical body. And where was my

Swamiji? He had come to take me and now he was gone. My eyes flew open as an emotional disturbance ruffled my being, like a gathering wind. I could not let go of my identification with the life of Sonya.

"He is yet on Earth," came the voice of my father from inside, referring to Swamiji. "He will come soon enough to take you. Now calm yourself. Let go of these dreams and come back to your true nature."

I glanced at my father. He sat unperturbed in meditation, as did all the others. In their unmoving state they were providing guidance to universes. Vast is this creation, with many worlds and many planes of life. The great Ones work on many levels, without moving, by attuning their consciousness to where the need is.

I tried unsuccessfully to harmonize myself with the high vibration of this sacred grove, but I had only recently arrived and still carried memories of Earth. Along with my memories I could see what was taking place there now, the horror of the war, the devastation to man and nature. I shut my eyes, but the images continued to move across the screen of my mind. Even here, in this beautiful abode, I could not shut out the sight of what was taking place on Earth, nor could I rise above it as the others had. It was as if my astral form was here in this beautiful world, but my mental frame was caught somewhere in between. My companion saw my plight. He took my hand and led me to where we could have a quiet exchange.

The universe is teeming with life, not only the physical worlds but the astral ones as well, and the even subtler causal worlds are inhabited by beings who no longer return to the Earth, having freed themselves from every Earthly desire and karmic tie. There are planes of great darkness and planes of great beauty and light, where beings remain absorbed in the bliss of the one all-pervading consciousness, sending vibrations of love throughout the manifest worlds. It is this love that sustains universes.

I had come home to a world I knew well—a world of elevated vibrations, where there was so much love and wholeness—yet I could not shut out the cries of Earth. I was happy to be home, overwhelmed with joy to see my companion and my father, but yet there was something I couldn't express, something lurking in my mental being.

My companion led me to the crystalline lake by our cottage. We sat there for a long time, watching the gently lapping waves of the deep blue-green water rise and fall. He knew that for me this was a place of healing, where memories would fade and sink into the subconscious mind. I loved this lake; its waters crystallized at the bottom and fed into the water bodies of Earth. Here was the source, the spiritual beginning. It was a place of renewal for me where I could re-energize my spirit and tap into the greater life force. We sat there for a long time. From that place I could travel to see others. I saw that Sonya's mother Marie had been reborn and was a child now on earth.

"You will meet her when you return," my companion silently informed me through an exchange of thoughts. The question of whether she would again be my mother entered my mind, and the immediate response was no. She would have another role to perform.

My sister Anna was still in the astral plane. I was able to find her and project the form of Sonya so that she would recognize me. In that world we are able to project any of our personalities we deem fit as we meet others we know from previous births. I saw that her karma, the onward movement of her soul, was calling her to descend again very soon.

I had many questions as yet unanswered. Sitting there, I recalled my previous stay in the astral world, memories that had been submerged during my recent life on earth. The last time we sat by these waters, I had reviewed my life as Elisabeth. Those memories left me when I was reborn as Sonya, but now my companion was helping to awaken them so I could understand the cause and effect that led to Sonya's life events. I remembered why I, as Elisabeth, had been born in the American south to find my African son who had been stolen from Thema and sold as a slave. My love drew me to where he had been taken. As I sat by the lake with my companion, I smiled as I remembered our last exchange when I had left the life of Elisabeth. I had asked him why I had not found my African son when I was reborn in America.

He smiled and nodded. "Don't you remember the abolitionist in the North, the freed African slave to whom you brought money so that other Africans could reach freedom? Unknowingly you were helping your African son achieve his mission in that life." When he communicated these thoughts through images, the memory of that man flashed through my mind. And I realized then why I had felt such a fondness for him.

Remembering how my companion had closed that circle for me, I now asked through unspoken words, "My feelings for the Russian prince led me to take birth in Russia, but I didn't find him this time." I was recalling why I had been born in Russia, drawn by the man who had helped me fund a school for girls in my life as Elisabeth.

"But you did find him, and you repaid that debt." I looked at him inquiringly. "You brought him the means to help other professors escape. The money from the family jewels helped him achieve one of his missions in life."

"Yuri?" I asked in disbelief. Why had I not recognized him? He nodded. "But the prince was such a noble man. Why did he have to suffer such a fate in the life of Yuri?"

"Did Yuri not have the same nobility of character? There is personal as well as collective karma. He had much guilt in his life as a prince and was deeply disturbed by the pogroms against the Jews. He struggled for some way to make amends, but could not in that life, so he sacrificed his own life as Yuri to help other Jews escape. In this way he chose to pay off much karmic debt."

"But why this terrible war?" I asked.

"When the negative forces of greed, arrogance, anger, and fear build up to such an extent, there is a release, which sometimes takes the form of war. In the past, the conflicts were contained, but man's utilization of technology is developing rapidly and war is becoming too dangerous. The pace of evolution must quicken so man will gain the wisdom needed to use this technology." He conveyed the image of the nuclear explosion, which was taking place on Earth.

"Japan," I murmured, recalling my life there. "Why Japan?"

"There are places that absorb collective karma. But you know the karma of all beings is intricately connected. It is all by choice; nothing is imposed. Individually and collectively we choose the lessons that will lead to growth, not consciously but at a deeper level."

We were communicating through a rapid exchange of images. As I saw the tragedy unfolding on Earth, I thought how little I could do. How little any one soul can do.

"You mustn't think that way. It is the combined efforts of many, many beings that brings forth evolution."

"But why could Swamiji not stop this war?"

"The collective human consciousness must be lifted to a higher level. That is a matter of evolution and takes time. There is a speeding up now of the process. Many are helping. To raise the collective, individuals, one by one, must evolve to a higher understanding. That is the work of Swamiji and many others."

I saw then how Yogananda was bringing meditation and the teachings from India to America, and that many people were following him. I remembered how as Elisabeth I had yearned for such teachings, and how that yearning had only grown in the heart of Sonya toward the end of her life.

"How much Sonya had wanted to go to America and be a part of his work," I reflected. "Ironically, it would have meant returning to the place from which she had recently come." I smiled. How strange was this play of karma.

"And so she will," he responded.

I looked inquiringly into his face. "I feel there was much completion in this life of Sonya."

"And more will come in the next round."

"The next round?" I was not prepared for that. I had only arrived, or so it seemed. I was not prepared to think about the next return to Earth, if there needed to be a next time.

"Do you not remember your urgent prayer at the end of Sonya's life, and the dreams you had as Elisabeth?" I was baffled for a moment. "And the promise Swamiji made to you?"

That I remembered. "He said he would take me to America." But that no longer seemed relevant. Now that I was home, I had no desire to depart again. With my companion and my father and the other blissful beings around me, what more did I need?

"Look further back, my dear. You have made commitments in your heart. Would you turn away from them now?"

The image of my saintly daughter came before me from my life in old Britain. I remembered her struggles and my desire to ensure that all women would have the freedom to pursue their spiritual life, and I remembered many centuries later my effort to bring education to the girls of the American south. The memory of Didi arose. In my life in Africa, none believed that a woman could have her capabilities and I felt a determination to prove the reality of her life. I had a deep commitment to the Divine Mother, to evoking her presence on Earth. These images flew across my mind, and then memories of Japan arose.

He caught these images and conveyed the thought, "Many resources will come from there for the work that you will do. You have not yet reaped all the benefit that you generated in that life." Images of my lives in India came before me as well. "That will be your place of refuge," he said. "From there you will receive all the spiritual resources you will need. Your heart is anchored there, I know." He smiled. "It was long before any of these lives that you and I were on Earth together. Do you remember?"

An image of a far distant past came before me, the time when he let me know that he would not be returning to Earth but that we would meet in between my times on Earth. I nodded, remembering that exchange. I said, "It is painful to forget so much. On Earth we have no memory at all. Everything is hidden. That is the hardest part."

"There will come a time when there is no more forgetting. All knowledge will be present when all parts of your being are awake. But as long as there is karma to fulfill, you must put away distractions and focus only on the opportunities that each life presents."

I looked out into the waters. The waves stilled and I could penetrate the depths. There seemed to be no bottom to this lake, no ending, because at a certain point it began to crystallize into physical atoms and materialize as physical water. Peering into it I began to see elements of my next life take form. I saw the family in which I would take birth. I saw my marriage and my sons. I smiled and was glad for this. Since my life in Africa I had not had children and I missed the feeling of motherly love. I would know it again. Then I saw my global work and was startled. This drew me out of my reverie. My lives had all been more contained. My nature had always been a more reticent and retiring one. I had never held a public role at all, and I did not feel prepared for this.

"The world is changing rapidly," he said in response to my reaction. "It is going through transition, moving into a higher age. Much work will be required to elevate the collective consciousness to suit this new era. Such is the work of Swamiji. He, as well as others, took birth for this purpose." He paused. "And for this, the memory of the Mother must awaken on Earth. You have been preparing for this."

"But I am not prepared!"

"Swamiji will guide you every step of the way. The blueprint is already being laid. Look inside."

I saw many things unfolding, the overview of my next return to earth. "So I will be with Swamiji, finally," I mused. A surge of love entered my being as I recalled the moment when he gazed at me in my life as Sonya. Yes, I would take birth for that purpose. He shook his head. "No?"

"Not this time."

"I don't understand."

"Do not think about it, my dear. It will all unfold as it should. What you see are the imprints taking form. Allow them to reveal themselves. Many decisions are yet to be made."

"So it must be. I will go when he calls." My mind fell silent, absorbed in the joy of being home, when suddenly the image of Mother came into my mind. "Mother," I whispered. "I have not yet seen you. I cannot leave before taking your blessing." Suddenly I felt an urge to be in her presence, to feel her gaze upon me.

My companion smiled. No thought emerged from him. His mind was as still as the lake, unruffled, not disturbed even by the slimmest wave, shining like a freshly polished jewel. I entered that clarity, a oneness where I could not distinguish between his being and mine. The consciousness of separation vanished and the joy that bubbled up was indescribable.

In that state I knew her. I was one with her. He and I and Mother. There was no division. I emerged from her being and saw her in one of her infinite forms. The light from her eyes washed over me and I bathed in her smile, filling myself with her expanse of love. Words cannot describe what that was. She was the One I had been unknowingly seeking through every birth on Earth. It was the memory of her that propelled me forward—the remembrance that she was not separate from me, that I was not separate from her, except when we needed to be. Such is the nature of the manifest mind. It creates appearances so the world can exist.

Time passed and gradually the pull of Earth began to weaken. I gave closure to the life of Sonya and submerged the last of her mental vibrations into the subconscious field that we carry from birth to birth. With each passing day, Earth became more and more like a distant dream. Was it real, I sometimes wondered? But every now and then images from what was taking place on Earth would reach me. I saw the end of the war and the devastation it left. I saw the rebuilding and a time of spiritual shift. I saw the work of my Swamiji growing, and somehow I knew the time was coming for my descent.

All that we hold beautiful on Earth is but a reflection of the beauty of that world, a world where color is more vibrant and alive, where one thinks things into being, where one has access to the pleasures of a higher nature. In the same way as this physical world needs tending, so too does that world. There are those who care for the different aspects of life—those who tend to the flowers and the fruits, and those who purify the land through their mental vibrations by remaining in the consciousness of One, knowing all as an emanation of the divine source. The most striking aspect of that world is the love that pervades all beings. No deceit, no hostility, no anger. There is full transparency because thoughts or emotions are not hidden. Some have given themselves to the cause of uplifting universes and helping all life awaken to its true nature. There is work to be done and they are there to do it.

I found my place again in the scheme of things, with most of my time spent in loving harmony with my companion, taking in the beauty of the scenes before me and replenishing my spirit. My work was of the dawn, helping to awaken life when the light returned. His work was very much directed toward maintaining the Earth, providing assistance to those who consciously or not tune into a higher plane. On Earth we do not realize how much assistance we receive, how many prayers are answered and blessings bestowed, how many conflicts are eased and natural disasters prevented. On Earth we are blind to what is given from these internal worlds. So many beings are assisting us. The world would not remain intact were this not so.

The day came when I heard Swamiji calling. At first I didn't pay it much mind, but sitting by the lake with my companion one day, the call came again more strongly. I stood up abruptly and glanced at him.

"It is time," he said.

"But I am not ready," I protested. "The time here has been too short."

"You will be back before you know it," he expressed through thought.

I must remember. I must remember, I thought to myself, gazing into the face of my beloved companion, trying to etch deeply into my consciousness his presence. "I must prepare . . ."

"My dear, it is time."

I looked around and took in the beauty of the scene around me.

Would I forget all of this? Would I lose yet again the memory of this world, my home, the realm of the Mother where her presence permeates everything. "I don't want to forget her this time," I murmured. "I don't want to forget."

"You know you are always protected," he said. "There has always been someone to bring you back."

I sighed, still gazing into the face of my beloved companion, he who was blessed to remain in that world and no longer return to Earth.

"I will be here supporting you," he said lovingly, "awaiting your return. Try to remember that. In reality, there is no separation. There is only the appearance of separation. You are not leaving our home. You will simply dream it is so." I kept gazing at him, not wanting to depart.

"I will forget again."

"To be fully present there, you must put to sleep the memories of here. That is the nature of things, the law of return. But this time, you will retain some memories."

Swamiji's voice called again and this time I responded. As I began to recede, the light of that world become fainter and fainter. My companion became a mere outline of light on the horizon as I began to withdraw. I gazed upon him still, trying to keep his presence with me. "This time you will remember, Usha. You will remember who you are." That was the last thought of his that I caught as the world of light slowly faded away.

I found myself in a dark place, descending, but then I stopped. I felt a presence approach me, one I recognized although I could not see the face. He was still on earth but was about to leave his body. I was departing, and he was soon to arrive. We met midway. I hesitated. If I did not stay, we would not meet this time.

Swamiji called again in a commanding tone. "Come now." His voice rang through my soul with an urgency. Still I hesitated, not knowing whether to go or stay. I was not ready yet. The time had been too short, and now this presence stood before me, someone I knew I had to meet. "I will find you," I cried out with certainty. "I will find you." Those were my last thoughts before I lost awareness of my surroundings and fell into a semi-sleep state. I was born nearly one year to the day before my guru left his body. Almost ten years had passed since the death of Sonya. As Dena, it took me many years to recover from the fact that I was not able to be with my guru physically in this life. To be with him was the reason,

I thought, that I had again taken birth.

It was through repeated pilgrimages to the upper regions of the sacred Himalayas—Gangotri, Badrinath, Kedernath—that the memories of my life between births began to return. This subtle world of light, which is more our home that this condensed world of atoms, slowly opened and I found myself living there while at the same time living here.

It was as I was meditating by the source of the Ganga in Gangotri that I remembered the lake that I loved so dearly, which I understood to be one of the spiritual sources of my beloved Ganga. I remembered that moment when I was descending into physical form, when I felt the presence of one I was to meet. I remembered calling out with great conviction, "I will find you." I recognized who that was, a very dear spiritual friend in this life who became an essential part of my interreligious work. We have a shared mission; I don't know if I would be able to do the work set before me without his partnership. When I look back at the circumstances that led me to the ashram in India where he lives, I realize that it was not my doing. How on earth would I have ever found him? There had been a guiding hand, always a guiding hand. Each one of us receives support and assistance to help us achieve our mission in life—the things we have come here to fulfill—but most often we are unaware of the enormous help we receive.

I know there are reasons for forgetting. If we were to remember everything, it would be hard to focus on the task at hand. With each life that I recalled, I spent months trapped back in that time period, experiencing all the emotions of that life. To what avail? The greatest gift that these memories have given me was overcoming the demarcation of time, helping me to understand that in reality time is a creation of the mind, as is so much else that we perceive to be "real." I have come to realize it is not the specifics of any life that matter; it is the realization of our eternal nature, the knowing that this play of karma is ongoing, at least until we learn to master the game, to remain *in* it but not *of* it.

Now, in a single day I may find myself momentarily transported to 16th century Japan, or to 17th century India, or remember something about my time in 19th century America. Parts of me still return to pre-World War II Europe, as another conversation, another interaction from that time is recalled. I cross time periods easily and have come to see that Dena is simply another one of the personalities that this eternal consciousness has assumed. In fact, sometimes I feel I am living all of these lives simultaneously, and the future as well. I have learned to be watchful that this crossing of time periods does not detract from my ability to be perfectly present, functioning in the moment as if no other moment exists, because indeed all these dreams are taking place in the eternal now.

When my memories of my astral home awakened, spatial demarcation also disappeared for me. Space became as much an illusion as time. I know myself to be living there, by the side of my beloved companion, at the same time that I am living in New York City. From there, we derive so much guidance and assistance. The beings who do not need to return to earth are as active on this plane as we are, trying to assist the earth and all its creatures, as well as the multiplicity of planets, to evolve, to reach their potential. We limit ourselves by believing in the confines of space and time. In truth there is no limitation, no condensing of our infinite nature. It is as if we put on glasses to limit ourselves to a particular point in time and space, but once the glasses are taken off, our true nature comes forth. If our consciousness is unbounded by time and space, we can be aware of many things happening in different time and spatial zones.

It is the samsaras from the past that bring about our rebirth: unfulfilled desires, even positive ones, commitments, attachments to people and things. One by one they can be neutralized so that we return not by karmic decree but for the purpose of uplifting the collective consciousness of the world. That is the goal to be sought. I no longer think of a time when I don't need to return to this world. Would I truly choose to remain in that world of beauty and light when there is so much need here?

As my consciousness awakened, the work of GPIW changed. We began our work by bringing spiritual resources to places of conflict, bringing people together in dialogue so they would gain some peace, some wider perspective despite their difficult lives. Then we began to focus on bringing to the fore the awareness and energy of the Divine Mother for the healing of the world. Our focus then expanded to include the shifts in consciousness needed to help evolve our world, especially the remembrance that all of nature is consciousness—sacred living forces rather than commodities to be bought and sold—and the remembrance that all religions stem from one truth and are equally able to reveal Ultimate Truth. It is time for the institutions that divide us to change or to drop away. New institutions will emerge that are based on the underlying unity of all spiritual paths, with none being greater than any other.

We each have a role to play is this awakening. I have come to realize the greatest contribution we can make is to live these truths, to manifest them in our daily lives, to live free of time and space, free of any limitations, to recognize who we truly are. As more of us awaken into this consciousness, the collective reality of earth will change. We will gain the wisdom, compassion, and discrimination to know how to use new technologies, not for the destruction or manipulation of life, but for its preservation and safekeeping.

My guru once said that as long as there is a single soul lost in the darkness he will keep returning to Earth to bring others to the shores of wakefulness. In this life as Dena, I have pledged myself to my guru and to assisting in his work to the best of my ability.

Afterword

A little while, a moment of rest upon the wind,
and another woman shall bear me.

—Kahlil Gibran, *The Prophet*

I remember so many births, so many deaths, so many loved ones—fathers, mothers, sisters and brothers, children, husbands, lovers, and teachers. I remember wealth and poverty. I remember jungles and cities and plantations, palaces and forest huts. I remember suffering and joy. They are all dreams. But through these dreams, I know that I am not the dreams, not the personalities, not the stories that unfold. I am the dreamer, projecting myself through time and space.

Must I continue to dream these stories? Must I continue to believe I am the one going through these experiences, that these stories are real? Must I continue to take on new faces, to come to know myself by new names, seek old friends in new forms? How long must I repeat thought patterns that were set long ago, that I have outgrown and seek to shed? How long will I be under the spell of cause and effect, reaping fruit from seeds I do not remember having sowed?

The choice is mine. It is a matter of simply awakening to who I am.

Who Am I?

I am the mother grieving over the daughter
>Who wasted away, faint but full of ecstasy.
I am the Hindu queen who hid her love for the Lord
>And watched in pain the destruction of temples.
I am the poor daughter of a Sufi saint who served him
>But felt unworthy as a woman.
I am a wife betrayed in Japan, devoted to beauty,
>Bereft of all, I sought refuge in the Buddha.
I am the Brahmin wife who betrayed and sought death in the Ganga
>But was given new life by the Mother.
I am the African girl who found the Mother in a jungle seer
>And lost her son to slavery.
I am the southern belle who longed for culture
>But found instead the teachings of the East.
I am the Russian exile, trapped in war-torn Europe,
>Rescued by the Guru she had long awaited.
I am the interfaith organizer who seeks to implement
>Her Guru's teachings and bring humanity together as One.
I am all of these and none of these.

I am the One who sends our projections, who dreams
>And then takes the dreams to be real.
I am the body of light seated by the source of river Ganga
>One ray of the radiant dawn.
I am Her dream, Her projection, Her child,
>And some day I will know that I am Her.

Acknowledgements

I want to express my gratitude for those who have helped bring this book to fruition:

Special appreciation for my father, David Finn, who for so many years encouraged me to write.

Kristina Mayo and Anne Glauber, the first readers of the book, who motivated me to keep moving forward with it.

My editor, Parvati Markus, for her many hours of pouring through the text and for helping to bring this vision to fruition.

The support and guidance of Sraddhalu Ranade, who strongly encouraged me to come forward and speak openly about my memories. Without his coaxing, these stories would have stayed locked in my own memory bank.

I also want to express my gratitude to the mentors and guides who have helped fund and develop the interfaith work that I have been involved in for so many years, especially Rev. Joan Brown Campbell and Sister Joan Chittister, who from the beginning believed in and supported my vision.

I am grateful for Venerable Master Sheng Yen and Swami Dayananda Saraswati in upholding the role of women spiritual leaders at a time when too few came forward in support of female leadership.

And I want to acknowledge the many spiritual teachers and friends who have been part of the GPIW family; they have contributed to the awakening of my memories, which have provided so much insight, understanding, and gratitude for all the help I have received in this long evolutionary journey of life after life.

About the Author

DENA MERRIAM

Since the 1990s Dena Merriam has worked to create a more inclusive and balanced interfaith movement, one that would give greater voice and leadership to women and well as the dharma based spiritual traditions, In 2000, she served as the Vice Chair of the Millennium World Peace Summit of Religious Leaders, which brought spiritual leaders to the United Nations headquarters in New York for the first time. Two years later she organized the Global Peace Initiative of Women Religious and Spiritual Leaders at the UN in Geneva. From that gatherings the Global Peace Initiative of Women (GPIW) was born. Since then Dena has traveled the world with a team of spiritual teachers, women and men, helping to foster dialogue in places of tension and conflict. In 2008, GPIW brought a group of spiritual teachers to the United Nations Climate Conference to lead a session on the spiritual dimensions of the climate crisis, continuing this effort each year at the annual UN climate conferences.

Although working actively for social change, Dena considers herself a contemplative.

For 45 years she has been a student of Paramahansa Yogananda and a practitioner of Kriya Yoga meditation. She holds a Master's Degree from Columbia University in sacred literature and over the years has served on numerous boards of religious and spiritual organizations. In 2014, she was awarded the Niwano Peace Prize for her interfaith peace efforts. Dena is the author of My Journey Through Time: A Spiritual Memoir of Life, Death and Rebirth, The Untold Story of Sita, When the Bright Moon Rises: Awakening Ancient Memories, Rukmini & the Turning of Time: The Dawn of an Era, and is currently working on a book entitled Dancing with Dakinis that takes place in 12th century Tibet. Dena is a frequent speaker on such themes as understanding karma and rebirth, learning from our past and how to set the blueprint for our future.

You can contact her at www.denamerriam.com